Collins
gem

SCRABBLE™

BRAND Crossword Game

HINTS & TIPS

Published by Collins
An imprint of HarperCollins
Publishers
Westerhill Road
Bishopbriggs
Glasgow G64 2QT
www.harpercollins.co.uk

First Edition 2014

10 9 8 7 6 5 4 3 2 1

© HarperCollins Publishers 2014

ISBN 978-0-00-753800-3

www.collinsdictionary.com
www.harpercollins.co.uk/scrabble

Typeset by Davidson Publishing
Solutions, Glasgow

Printed and bound in China by
South China Printing Co., Ltd

The contents of this publication
are believed correct at the time of
printing. Nevertheless the publisher
can accept no responsibility for
errors or omissions, changes in the
detail given or for any expense or loss
thereby caused.
HarperCollins does not warrant that
any website mentioned in this title
will be provided uninterrupted, that
any website will be error free, that
defects will be corrected, or that the
website or the server that makes it
available are free of viruses or bugs.
For full terms and conditions please
refer to the site terms provided on
the website.

A catalogue record for this book is
available from the British Library.

If you would like to comment on any
aspect of this book, please contact us
at the above address or online.
E-mail: puzzles@harpercollins.co.uk
 facebook.com/collinsdictionary
 @ collinsdict

Acknowledgements

We would like to thank those authors
and publishers who kindly gave
permission for copyright material
to be used in the Collins Corpus.
We would also like to thank Times
Newspapers Ltd for providing
valuable data.

Introduction

This handy pocket-sized Scrabble book is aimed at casual Scrabble enthusiasts or those who like to Scrabble dabble. It deals with each letter of the alphabet in turn, covering brief advantages and disadvantages of each letter, followed by a selection of useful and manageable wordlists of words beginning with that letter.

For the most part the wordlists are not intended to be thorough and complete because that would make them too unwieldy and cluttered with words which may not actually be that useful for Scrabble. They are designed to serve as an introduction to useful words that you might be unfamiliar with and to inspire you to increase your Scrabble vocabulary. For example, the three-letter words lists exclude very common words and those that cannot be formed from two-letter words (unless they are worth 8 points face-value or more). Any words that might be deemed offensive are also excluded. Having said that, because of their importance in the game, the lists of two-letter words are complete, as too are the lists showing how those two-letter words can be extended into three-letter words. There is also a complete dictionary of all the three-letter words and definitions at the end of the book for added interest.

THE BASICS

What is Scrabble?

Scrabble is a game for two to four players or, occasionally, teams. Each player draws seven tiles at the start of the game and takes it in turns to form words on the board. After the first word is played, every word formed must touch or intersect a word already on the board, incorporating the tile at the crossover point in the new word. When letters have been played, they are replaced at each turn by drawing tiles from a bag to make up a full rack of seven. High scores may be achieved by using the rarer, high-value letters, by forming words on premium squares on the board, and by playing all seven letters at once to achieve a 50-point bonus.

The Scrabble set

The full list of letters and their values in the Scrabble C set is as follows:

Letter (Vowel)	Number in set	Value
A	9	1
E	12	1
I	9	1
O	8	1
U	4	1
BLANK	2	0

Letter (Consonant)	Number in set	Value
B	2	3
C	2	3
D	4	2
F	2	4
G	3	2
H	2	4
J	1	8
K	1	5
L	4	1
M	2	3
N	6	1
P	2	3
Q	1	10
R	6	1
S	4	1
T	6	1
V	2	4
W	2	4
X	1	8
Y	2	4
Z	1	10

Origins

Scrabble was invented by an American: Alfred Butts. It was originally called Lexico when it was invented in the 1930s but became successful in its current form in the 1960s.

Gameplay tips

Use a dictionary when you play to check which words are eligible when challenged and to avoid any arguments. We suggest Collins Official Scrabble Dictionary, where you will find the meanings for all the words used in this book.

Shuffle the tiles on your rack: rearrange them, jiggle them around, and place them in alphabetical order. Also try to form prefixes or suffixes, verb inflections (-ED, -ING, etc) as this can help to form words in your mind.

Play longer words early on in a game if you can to get the board open to reach those elusive triple word squares. The more places there are to make plays the more you can make wise choices and avoid getting a clogged up board and be forced just to play one or two letters at a time.

The challenge rule: you may challenge a word your opponent plays. If your challenge is successful, i.e. the disputed word is not in the Official Scrabble Dictionary, or the dictionary you are using, your opponent takes back his or her tiles and loses their turn.

Note on diagrams: Diagrams in this section depicting word plays, for aesthetics, don't necessarily show words covering the centre square. In actual games the first move must cover the centre square.

Forming words

Scrabble words can be formed in several ways other than by simply playing a new word to intersect with a word already on the board through a common letter, or by adding letters to an existing word. The key to successful Scrabble is constant awareness of the various opportunities for forming words on the board.

When words are formed in ways other than simple intersection or expansion, more than one new word is created in the process, potentially giving a higher score. The main ways of doing this are 'hooking' and 'tagging'.

Double Word   Double Letter

Triple Word   Triple Letter

Hooking

This is the term for the act of 'hanging' one word on another – the word already on the board acts as a 'hook' on which the other word can be hung – changing the first word in the process. The player adds a letter to the beginning or end of a word already on the board in the process, transforming it into a longer word, as in the following example:

Player A has played COMET. Player B then plays HOUSE on the end of COMET, forming COMETH and HOUSE, and scoring 13 for COMETH plus 16 for HOUSE. COMET is an 'end-hook'; any word ending in H or S can be 'hung' on it.

S is a particularly useful letter when hooking, as most nouns have a plural formed by adding it to the end of the singular.

The following example shows how to add a 'front hook' to the word OX:

Here the player gets the 17 points for FOX as well as those for FICKLE. Thus hooking is generally a more profitable method of word formation than simply playing a word through, or adjacent to, one that is already on the board. In particular, hooking allows players the chance to benefit from high-scoring power tiles played by an opponent, as with the X in FOX in the above example. It is important to note that, when scoring double words like this, only the face value of tiles already played is counted and if the original word had been played on a premium square its bonus value would not count.

Blocking

Words that cannot form other words by having a letter added to their front or back are known as blockers, as they prevent other players from adding words by hooking.

Blockers are useful for preventing your opponent from capitalizing on words that you have played, and for blocking off sections of the board. If you are ahead on the scoreboard in the latter part of a game, you may wish to play tactically by concentrating on blockers, and thereby prevent your opponent from getting further opportunities to play high-scoring words.

Some examples of blocker words are as follows:

Tagging

Playing a word parallel to one already on the board, so that one or more tiles are in contact, is known as tagging. Tagging is more difficult than hooking because you need to form one additional word for each tile in contact with the word already on the board. These will usually be two-letter words, which is why these short words are so vital to the game. The more two-letter words you know, the greater your opportunities for fitting words onto the board through tagging – and of running up some impressive scores!

Player A has played:

Player B now 'tags' TROLL, also forming ET, AR and NO (all valid two-letter words). This play scores 10 for TROLL, 2 each for ET and AR, and 4 for NO, so a total of 18.

Short words are obviously very handy for tagging, as seen in the following example:

Power Tiles

It is important to use the 'power tiles' (J, Q, X and Z) wisely when they land on your rack. Learning some of the words that contain these letters will help you to employ the power tiles to maximum effect when they appear on your rack. Of special interest are words that use Q but not U, as these allow you to avoid the problem of needing to find a U to play your high-scoring Q tile. In the average two-player Scrabble game, you are likely to have two of the power tiles on your rack at some point during play and learning some words using these letters will help you to manoeuvre them onto premium squares for really high scores.

Two- and three-letter words

Two-letter words are essential for tagging: generally, you need one two-letter word for every point of contact. Three-letter words are also very useful in Scrabble, as a crowded board will often prevent you from playing longer words late in the game. Moreover, some very respectable scores can be generated by tagging with three-letter words – creating more two-letter words in the process. While many two- and three-letter words will be familiar, it's a good idea to learn the less common ones, as knowing whether a given combination of two or three letters is a valid word can be vital when you are trying to get a high-scoring set of tiles onto the board through tagging or hooking.

The Appendix lists all the two- and three-letter words that are valid for Scrabble.

Using the S and Blank tiles

S

The S tile is very useful as it can be placed at the
end of many words (nearly every noun and verb,
in fact) thus making it the ideal tile for end-hooking.
This quality also makes S very handy for bonus
words, as the odds of making a bonus word from
six tiles plus an S are greatly improved from making
a bonus from seven letters. However, a player can
often get a good score without trying for a bonus
by simply hooking an existing word, and scoring for
both. S is also well suited for use as a front hook,
particularly alongside words starting with H, L, P, T.
Also watch out for hooking an S onto a Q word.

Blank

A blank tile has no value but may be used in the
place of any letter, thus making it extremely useful,
especially when it comes to forming bonus words.
It is very important to use the blank tile wisely and
not to waste it on a low-scoring word. Look at the
letters on your rack and when considering the
blank tile, run through the alphabet in your mind
when thinking of the letter value to assign to it.
Remember, it is much easier to form a bonus word
from six letters plus one which you can choose
than by using seven letters over which you have
no control, so save the blank for a bonus word if
you can. Finally, never ever change a blank tile!

Bonus words

Always remember that no matter how many words you form, you are likely to achieve a higher score by playing all seven of your letters in one go, as this earns you a 50 point bonus. It takes a lot of power tiles or bonus squares to achieve 50 points, so playing a bonus word (bingo in the US) is the most reliable method of getting an impressive score.

A bonus play generally involves a word of seven or eight letters – either by tagging or hooking a complete seven-letter word onto a word already on the board, or by forming an eight-letter word intersecting an existing word by playing all seven tiles.

Scrabble Glossary

BLOCKER a word which cannot have a letter added to its beginning or end to form another valid word.

BONUS SQUARE (also called PREMIUM SQUARE) one of the squares on the board that provides extra points: double letter, double word, triple letter or triple word.

BONUS WORD a word that uses all seven of a player's tiles, earning a 50 point bonus.

FRONT-HOOK a word that can form another valid word by having a letter added to its front.

END-HOOK a word that can form another valid word by having a letter added to its end.

HEAVY WORDS (either VOWEL-HEAVY or CONSONANT-HEAVY) words which have many consonants or vowels.

HOOKING playing a word perpendicular to and in contact with another word, so that the first played word (the hook) has a letter added to it.

POWER TILES (J, Q, X or Z) the tiles that score eight (J and X) or ten (Q and Z) points.

RACK the small plastic shelf that holds a player's tiles; the combination of letters on the tiles currently held.

TAGGING playing a word parallel to, and in contact with, another word so that a valid word is formed at each point of contact.

TILE one of the small plaques bearing letters that are used to form words on the board.

Words Ineligible for Scrabble

There are several categories of ineligible words:
- Hyphenated words
- Multiple-word phrases
- Capitalized words
- Abbreviations
- Words over 15 letters in length

Essential info
Value: 1 point
Number in set: 9

A

A is a common tile and is very useful for forming
short words to squeeze into tight corners, as it can
be added easily to the majority of other tiles to
form two-letter words. A can even be added to
itself (to form AA, a Hawaiian word for rough
volcanic rock, 2 points). A is also very helpful for
short, high-scoring words such as AXE (10 points,
or 9 points with its US variant AX). Some more
unusual examples of three-letter words include
AAL (an Asian shrub, 3 points), APO (a type of
protein, 5 points) and the high-scoring ADZ (a tool
for cutting roof tiles, 13 points). A is one of the
letters of the RETAIN set and is therefore a good
letter to keep if trying to get a bonus word.

Two-letter words beginning with A

AA	AG	AM	AT
AB	AH	AN	AW
AD	AI	AR	AX
AE	AL	AS	AY

Some three-letter words beginning with A

AAH	AFF	ALA	ANA	ASP
AAL	AGA	ALB	ANE	ASS
ABA	AGO	ALF	ANI	ATT
ABB	AHA	ALP	ANN	AWA
ABO	AHI	ALT	APO	AWL
ABY	AIA	AMA	ARB	AWN
ACH	AIN	AMI	ARD	AYE
ADO	AIT	AMP	ARF	AYU
ADZ	AKA	AMU	ARY	AZO

Hooks

Hooking requires a player to look at words already on the board without being distracted by their pronunciation. This can lead to simple hooking solutions being overlooked. Fortunately, A is one of the easier tiles to play as a hook or a tag and it can be front-hooked to many words as their negating form (e.g. MORAL can be changed to AMORAL).

Some front-hooks
Two letters to three

A-AH	A-GO	A-LA	A-PO
A-AL	A-HA	A-MA	A-RE
A-AS	A-HI	A-MI	A-SH
A-BA	A-ID	A-MU	A-TE
A-BO	A-IN	A-NA	A-WE
A-BY	A-IS	A-NE	A-YE
A-CH	A-IT	A-NY	A-YU
A-DO	A-KA	A-PE	A-ZO

Three letters to four

A-BED	A-HOY	A-NAN	A-SEA
A-BET	A-IDE	A-NEW	A-SHY
A-BID	A-JAR	A-NIL	A-TAP
A-BUT	A-KIN	A-NON	A-TOP
A-BYE	A-LAP	A-NOW	A-VOW
A-DRY	A-LAY	A-PAY	A-WAY
A-FAR	A-LEE	A-POD	A-WED
A-GAS	A-LIT	A-RED	A-WEE
A-GIN	A-LOW	A-RID	A-WRY
A-HEM	A-MEN	A-ROW	A-YES
A-HIS	A-MID	A-RUM	

Four letters to five

A-BACK	A BUZZ	A-GAZE	A-ISLE
A-BAND	A-COLD	A-GENE	A-ITCH
A-BASE	A-CORN	A-GENT	A-KING
A-BASH	A-CUTE	A-GIST	A-LACK
A-BASK	A-DOWN	A-GLEE	A-LAND
A-BEAM	A-DOZE	A-GLOW	A-LANE
A-BEAR	A-DUST	A-GONE	A-LANT
A-BIDE	A-FEAR	A-GOOD	A-LATE
A-BLED	A-FIRE	A-GRIN	A-LEFT
A-BLOW	A-FOOT	A-HEAD	A-LIEN
A-BODE	A-FORE	A-HEAP	A-LIKE
A-BOIL	A-FOUL	A-HIGH	A-LINE
A-BORE	A-GAIN	A-HIND	A-LIST
A-BOUT	A-GAPE	A-HINT	A-LIVE
A-BRAY	A-GATE	A-HOLD	A-LOFT
A-BRIM	A-GAVE	A-HULL	A-LONE

3

A-LONG	A-NEAR	A-RISE	A-VALE
A-LOUD	A-NIGH	A-ROSE	A-VAST
A-LURE	A-NODE	A-SCOT	A-VINE
A-MAIN	A-PACE	A-SHED	A-VOID
A-MASS	A-PAGE	A-SIDE	A-WAIT
A-MATE	A-PAID	A-SKEW	A-WAKE
A-MAZE	A-PART	A-STIR	A-WARD
A-MEND	A-PEAK	A-STUN	A-WARE
A-MICE	A-PEEK	A-SWAY	A-WARN
A-MINE	A-PERT	A-SWIM	A-WASH
A-MISS	A-PING	A-TILT	A-WAVE
A-MOLE	A-PORT	A-TOLL	A-WING
A-MOVE	A-READ	A-TONE	A-WOKE
A-MUCK	A-REAL	A-TRIP	A-WORK
A-MUSE	A-REAR	A-VAIL	A-YELP

Five letters to six

A-BASED	A-BOUND	A-ETHER
A-BASER	A-BRAID	A-FIELD
A-BATED	A-BROAD	A-FLAME
A-BIDED	A-BURST	A-FLOAT
A-BIDER	A-BUSED	A-FRESH
A-BLATE	A-CATER	A-FRONT
A-BLAZE	A-CIDER	A-GAZED
A-BLING	A-CRAWL	A-GEIST
A-BLOOM	A-CROSS	A-GHAST
A-BLUSH	A-CUTER	A-GLARE
A-BOARD	A-DREAD	A-GLEAM
A-BODED	A-DRIFT	A-GOING
A-BORNE	A-DROIT	A-GREED

A-GUISE	A-SHORE	A-TWAIN
A-HORSE	A-SLAKE	A-TWEEL
A-LIGHT	A-SLANT	A-TWEEN
A-LINED	A-SLEEP	A-TWIXT
A-LINER	A-SLOPE	A-TYPIC
A-MATED	A-SLOSH	A-UNTIE
A-MAZED	A-SMEAR	A-VAUNT
A-MIDST	A-SPINE	A-VENGE
A-MORAL	A-SPIRE	A-VENUE
A-MOUNT	A-SPORT	A-VERSE
A-MOVED	A-SPOUT	A-VISED
A-MUSED	A-SQUAT	A-VITAL
A-MUSER	A-STARE	A-VOUCH
A-NEATH	A-START	A-VOWED
A-NIGHT	A-STERN	A VOWER
A-PIECE	A-STONE	A-WAKED
A-RAISE	A-STONY	A-WAKEN
A-REACH	A-STOOP	A-WATCH
A-RIDER	A-STRAY	A-WEARY
A-RIGHT	A-STRUT	A-WEIGH
A-RILED	A-SWARM	A-WHEEL
A-RISEN	A-SWING	A-WHILE
A-ROUND	A-SWIRL	A-WHIRL
A-ROUSE	A-SWOON	A-WOKEN
A-SCEND	A-TONAL	A-WRACK
A-SCENT	A-TONED	A-WRONG
A-SHAKE	A-TONER	A-ZONAL
A-SHAME	A-TONIC	
A-SHIER	A-TOPIC	
A-SHINE	A-TRIAL	

Six letters to seven

A-BANDED	A-LONELY	A-SPROUT
A-BASHED	A-MASSED	A-SQUINT
A-BASING	A-MAZING	A-STABLE
A-BATING	A-MENDED	A-STATIC
A-BETTED	A-MENDER	A-STONED
A-BETTER	A-MENTAL	A-STOUND
A-BIDING	A-MOTION	A-STRAND
A-BIOTIC	A-MOVING	A-STRICT
A-BODING	A-MUSING	A-STRIDE
A-BOUGHT	A-NEARED	A-SUDDEN
A-BRAYED	A-NOTHER	A-SUNDER
A-BRIDGE	A-PAYING	A-THIRST
A-BROACH	A-PLENTY	A-THRILL
A-BUBBLE	A-QUIVER	A-TINGLE
A-BUTTED	A-RAISED	A-TONING
A-BUTTER	A-REALLY	A-TROPHY
A-CLINIC	A-RIPPLE	A-VAILED
A-CORNED	A-RISING	A-VENGED
A-CUTELY	A-SCARED	A-VENGER
A-CUTEST	A-SCONCE	A-VERTED
A-CYCLIC	A-SCRIBE	A-VOIDED
A-DEEMED	A-SEPTIC	A-VOIDER
A-DUSTED	A-SHAMED	A-VOWING
A-FEARED	A-SHIEST	A-WAITED
A-GENTRY	A-SHIVER	A-WAITER
A-GROUND	A-SOCIAL	A-WAKING
A-LAYING	A-SPIRED	A-WARDED
A-LENGTH	A-SPRAWL	A-WARDER
A-LINING	A-SPREAD	A-WARNED

Seven letters to eight

A-BANDING
A-BASHING
A-BATABLE
A-BEARING
A-BEGGING
A-BETTING
A-BOUNDED
A-BRAIDED
A-BRAYING
A-BRIDGED
A-BROOKED
A-BUTTING
A-CENTRIC
A-CERATED
A-CHROMIC
A-COSMISM
A-COSMIST
A-DEEMING
A-DREADED
A-DUSTING
A-DYNAMIC
A-ESTHETE
A-ESTIVAL
A-ETHERIC
A-FEARING
A-FEBRILE
A-FLUTTER
A-GENESIS
A-GENETIC

A-GLIMMER
A-GLITTER
A-GNOSTIC
A-GRAPHIC
A-GREEING
A-GRISING
A-GUISING
A-KINESES
A-KINESIS
A-KINETIC
A-LEGGING
A-LIGHTED
A-LOGICAL
A-MASSING
A-MAZEDLY
A-MEIOSIS
A-MENAGED
A-MENDING
A-MIDMOST
A-MIDSHIP
A-MISSING
A-MITOSIS
A-MITOTIC
A-MORALLY
A-MORTISE
A-MOUNTED
A-NEARING
A-NEURISM
A-NODALLY

A-NOINTED
A-NOINTER
A-PIARIST
A-PLASTIC
A-PRACTIC
A-PYRETIC
A-PYREXIA
A-RAISING
A-REACHED
A-READING
A-RETTING
A-SCENDED
A-SCRIBED
A SEISMIC
A-SEPTATE
A-SHAMING
A-SHINESS
A-SLAKING
A-SOCIALS
A-SPARKLE
A-SPERSED
A-SPHERIC
A-SPIRANT
A-SPIRING
A-SPORTED
A-STARTED
A-STERNAL
A-STEROID
A-STONIED

A-STONING	A-TROPISM	A-VOUCHED
A-STONISH	A-TWITTER	A-VOUCHER
A-STUNNED	A-TYPICAL	A-WAITING
A-SYNERGY	A-VAILING	A-WAKENED
A-SYSTOLE	A-VAUNTED	A-WAKENER
A-TECHNIC	A-VENGING	A-WANTING
A-TONALLY	A-VENTURE	A-WARDING
A-TREMBLE	A-VERSION	A-WARNING
A-TROPHIC	A-VERTING	A-WEARIED
A-TROPINE	A-VOIDING	A-WEATHER

Handy Hint: The Challenge

Never be afraid to challenge a word which looks
unusual, misspelled or which you do not recognise.
Many a word has slipped through the net this way,
and you have nothing to lose by challenging your
opponent. DO NOT BE INTIMIDATED.
Gamesmanship occurs in Scrabble too and your
opponent may be hoping you will let their mistakes
or guesses go unnoticed or unchallenged.

Some end-hooks
Two letters to three

AB-A	BA-A	IT-A	PI-A
AG-A	BO-A	KO-A	PO-A
AH-A	CH-A	MA-A	SH-A
AI-A	ER-A	MO-A	TE-A
AL-A	ET-A	OB-A	UT-A
AM-A	FA-A	OD-A	YE-A
AN-A	GO-A	OR-A	ZO-A
AW-A	HO-A	PE-A	

Three letters to four

ALB-A	KAT-A	RAJ-A
ARE-A	KOR-A	RAT-A
BET-A	LAM-A	ROM-A
BON-A	LAV-A	ROT-A
COD-A	MAL-A	SAG-A
COL-A	MAM-A	SOD-A
DAD-A	MAY-A	SOM-A
DIV-A	MEG-A	SOY-A
DOP-A	MES-A	TOG-A
FET-A	MON-A	TOR-A
FIL-A	NAN-A	TUB-A
GAG-A	ORC-A	TUN-A
GAL-A	PAP-A	VEG-A
GAM-A	PIC-A	VIN-A
GIG-A	PIN-A	VIS-A
HAH-A	PIT-A	WET-A
IDE-A	PUP-A	

Four letters to five

BALS-A	HOND-A	PUCK-A
BURK-A	HYEN-A	PUNK-A
CHIN-A	KANG-A	RAGG-A
COCO-A	LAIK-A	RAIT-A
COMM-A	LOOF-A	RAST-A
COST-A	MANG-A	SALS-A
DELT-A	MANI-A	SUNN-A
DERM-A	MOCH-A	TAIG-A
DICT-A	MOOL-A	TIAR-A
DOON-A	MULL-A	TONK-A
DRAM-A	MURR-A	VEST-A
FAUN-A	PAND-A	VILL-A
FELL-A	PARK-A	VIOL-A
FETT-A	PASH-A	VOLT-A
FLOR-A	PAST-A	
GAMB-A	POLK-A	
GUAN-A	PRIM-A	

Five letters to six

CREST-A	NYMPH-A	SENOR-A
FASCI-A	ORBIT-A	SHISH-A
FAVEL-A	ORGAN-A	SPIRE-A
FIEST-A	PAGOD-A	STELL-A
GRAMP-A	PATIN-A	STERN-A
KORUN-A	PLASM-A	TALUK-A
LORIC-A	QUANT-A	TAPET-A
MAXIM-A	RHUMB-A	TARSI-A
MIASM-A	SATYR-A	TUNIC-A
MINIM-A	SCARP-A	VALET-A

10

Six letters to seven

ADDEND-A
ALUMIN-A
ANALOG-A
ANONYM-A
ARABIC-A
ASHRAM-A
BUZUKI-A
CANDID-A
CANTAL-A
CEMENT-A
CHIASM-A
CHIMER-A
CHOLER-A
CODEIN-A
CORTIN-A
CURIOS-A
CYATHI-A
DEJECT-A
DEODAR-A

DRACHM-A
EMBLEM-A
EXOTIC-A
FAVELL-A
FORMIC-A
GALLET-A
GALLIC-A
GUNNER-A
INFANT-A
INGEST-A
KHALIF-A
LAVOLT-A
LOCUST-A
MADRAS-A
MOMENT-A
PAISAN-A
PERSON-A
PLACIT-A
POTASS-A

PROPYL-A
QUININ-A
ROBUST-A
ROSACE-A
ROTUND-A
SCHISM-A
SECRET-A
SELECT-A
SEQUEL-A
SERING-A
SHEIKH-A
SIGNOR-A
SULTAN-A
TAMBUR-A
TARTAN-A
TAVERN-A
TEMPER-A

Seven letters to eight

ANGELIC-A	EPITHEM-A	QUILLAI-A
ANTEFIX-A	EXCERPT-A	RAKSHAS-A
ARBORET-A	FASCIST-A	SALICET-A
AUTOMAT-A	HEPATIC-A	SARMENT-A
BASILIC-A	JAVELIN-A	SCIATIC-A
BOTANIC-A	MANDIOC-A	SIGNORI-A
BRONCHI-A	MARCHES-A	STROBIL-A
BROUGHT-A	MARINER-A	SYNTAGM-A
CHAMPAC-A	MATADOR-A	TAMANDU-A
CHARISM-A	MELODIC-A	TAMBOUR-A
CISTERN-A	MOLLUSC-A	THERIAC-A
CONSULT-A	MONSTER-A	TORMENT-A
DEMENTI-A	NYMPHAE-A	TOURIST-A
DIASTEM-A	PERFECT-A	UNGUENT-A
DULCIAN-A	PIGNOLI-A	

A

Handy Hint: say AA

If you have too many vowels on your rack, some useful short words beginning with A and using no consonants are: AA, AE and AI (2 points each). It is also worthwhile remembering common words which feature many vowels such as ADIEU (6 points), EERIE (5 points) and COOKIE (12 points).

Blockers

It is useful to know which words are blockers and can't therefore be extended before or after. You may want to play a blocker that your opponent can't extend, or you may want to avoid playing a blocker because you want to keep the board open.

Three-letter blocker beginning with A
AUE

Some four-letter blockers beginning with A

ABLY	AHOY	ALSO	AROW
ACHY	AJAR	ANEW	ASEA
ADRY	AJFF	ANOW	AWRY
AESC	ALAE	APEX	AXAL
AGLY	ALEE	AREG	
AHEM	ALIT	AREW	

Some five-letter blockers beginning with A (except words ending in '-ED', '-J', '-S', '-X', '-Y' or '-Z')

AARGH	ABRIM	AFOUL
ABACK	ACERB	AGAIN
ABASH	ACHOO	AGAST
ABASK	ACRID	AGLEE
ABEAM	ADOZE	AGLOW
ABLOW	AFIRE	AGOOD
ABOIL	AFOOT	AHEAD
ABORE	AFORE	AHEAP

13

AHIGH	ALTHO	ASTIR
ALACK	AMAIN	ASWIM
ALGAE	AMINO	ATILT
ALGAL	APACE	AURAL
ALGID	APAGE	AVAST
ALIKE	APAID	AWASH
ALIVE	APART	AWAVE
ALOFT	APIAN	AWORK
ALONE	AREAR	AXIAL
ALOOF	AROSE	
ALOUD	ASKEW	

Some six-letter blockers beginning with A (except words ending in '-ED', '-J', '-S', '-X', '-Y' or '-Z')

ABLAZE	AFIELD	AKIMBO	APEMAN
ABLEST	AFLAME	ALBEIT	APEMEN
ABLOOM	AFLOAT	ALMOST	APIECE
ABLUSH	AFRAID	ALUMNI	APTEST
ABOARD	AFRESH	AMBUSH	APTING
ABORNE	AFRONT	AMEBIC	ARCANE
ABURST	AGHAST	AMIDST	ARDENT
ACETIC	AGILER	AMMINO	AREACH
ACHIER	AGLARE	AMORAL	ARISEN
ACIDER	AGLEAM	ANEATH	AROUND
ACIDIC	AIDMAN	ANEMIC	ASHAKE
ACRAWL	AIDMEN	ANOXIC	ASHINE
ACUTER	AIMFUL	ANYHOW	ASHORE
ADRIFT	AIRMAN	AORTAL	ASLANT
ADROIT	AIRMEN	AORTIC	ASLEEP

ASLOPE	ATOPIC	AWATCH	AWSOME
ASTERN	ATWIXT	AWEIGH	AXEMAN
ASTOOP	AUDIAL	AWEING	AXEMEN
ASTRUT	AVERSE	AWHILE	AXONIC
ASWARM	AVIDER	AWHIRL	AZONAL
ASWING	AVITAL	AWOKEN	
ASWIRL	AVOUCH	AWRACK	
ATONAL	AWARER	AWRONG	

Bonus Words

Bonus words on your rack can be hard to spot, especially for the less experienced player. One way to help find them is by using prefixes and suffixes.

Many longer words include a common prefix or suffix – remembering these and using them where you can is a good way to discover any longer words on your rack, including any potential bonus words. The key prefixes to remember beginning with A are AB-, AD-, AIR- and the key suffixes are -ABLE, -AGE, -ANCE, -ANCY and -ARCH.

Some words beginning with AB-

Seven-letter words

AB-ASHED
AB-ASHES
AB-DUCTS
AB-JOINT
AB-LATED
AB-LINGS
AB-LUTED
AB-OUGHT
AB-RAIDS

AB-REACT
AB-REAST
AB-RIDGE
AB-ROACH
AB-ROADS
AB-SEILS
AB-SENTS
AB-SOLVE
AB-SORBS

AB-STAIN
AB-SURDS
AB-THANE
AB-USAGE
AB-USERS
AB-USING
AB-UTTER

Eight-letter words

AB-ASHING
AB-DUCTED
AB-EARING
AB-EGGING
AB-ERRANT
AB-ESSIVE
AB-LEGATE
AB-NEGATE
AB-NORMAL

AB-ORALLY
AB-ORIGIN
AB-RAIDED
AB-RAYING
AB-RIDGED
AB-RIDGER
AB-ROOKED
AB-SEILED
AB-SENTED

AB-SOLUTE
AB-SOLVED
AB-SOLVER
AB-SOLVES
AB-SONANT
AB-SORBED
AB-STRICT
AB-USABLE

Some words beginning with AD-

Seven-letter words

AD-AGIOS
AD-APTED
AD-APTER
AD-AWING
AD-DICTS
AD-DRESS
AD-DUCES
AD-DUCTS
AD-HERES
AD-JOINS
AD-JOINT
AD-JUDGE
AD-JUROR

AD-JUSTS
AD-LANDS
AD-MIRED
AD-MIRES
AD-MIXED
AD-MIXES
AD-NOUNS
AD-OPTED
AD-OPTER
AD-PRESS
AD-READS
AD-RENAL
AD-SORBS

AD-VENTS
AD-VERBS
AD-VERSE
AD-VERTS
AD-VICES
AD-VISED
AD-VISES
AD-VISOR
AD-WARDS
AD-WARES
AD-WOMAN
AD-WOMEN

Eight-letter words

AD-APTING
AD-DEBTED
AD-DEEMED
AD-DICTED
AD-DOOMED
AD-DUCTED
AD-EQUATE
AD-ESSIVE
AD-JACENT
AD-JOINED

AD-JUDGED
AD-JUSTED
AD-JUSTER
AD-MASSES
AD-MIRING
AD-MIXING
AD-MONISH
AD-NATION
AD-OPTING
AD-OPTION

AD-SCRIPT
AD-SORBED
AD-UMBRAL
AD-UNCATE
AD-VERSER
AD-VERTED
AD-VISING
AD-WARDED

Some words beginning with AIR-

Seven-letter words

AIR-BAGS	AIR-HOLE	AIR-SHIP
AIR-BASE	AIR-LESS	AIR-SHOT
AIR-BOAT	AIR-LIFT	AIR-SHOW
AIR-CREW	AIR-LIKE	AIR-SICK
AIR-DATE	AIR-LINE	AIR-SIDE
AIR-DROP	AIR-LOCK	AIR-STOP
AIR-FARE	AIR-MAIL	AIR-TIME
AIR-FLOW	AIR-PARK	AIR-TING
AIR-FOIL	AIR-PLAY	AIR-WARD
AIR-GAPS	AIR-PORT	AIR-WAVE
AIR-GLOW	AIR-POST	AIR-WAYS
AIR-HEAD	AIR-SHED	AIR-WISE

Eight-letter words

AIR-BASES	AIR-DROME	AIR-PROOF
AIR-BOATS	AIR-DROPS	AIR-SCAPE
AIR-BORNE	AIR-FARES	AIR-SCREW
AIR-BOUND	AIR-FIELD	AIR-SHAFT
AIR-BRICK	AIR-FRAME	AIR-SPACE
AIR-BRUSH	AIR-GLOWS	AIR-SPEED
AIR-BURST	AIR-GRAPH	AIR-STRIP
AIR-BUSES	AIR-HOLES	AIR-THING
AIR-CHECK	AIR-LIFTS	AIR-TIGHT
AIR-COACH	AIR-LINER	AIR-WAVES
AIR-CRAFT	AIR-PLANE	AIR-WOMAN
AIR-DRAWN	AIR-POWER	AIR-WOMEN

Some words ending with -ABLE
Seven-letter words

ACT-ABLE
ADD-ABLE
AFF-ABLE
AMI-ABLE
BAT-ABLE
BUY-ABLE
CAP-ABLE
CIT-ABLE
COD-ABLE
CUR-ABLE
DAT-ABLE
DIS-ABLE
DRY-ABLE
DUP-ABLE
DUR-ABLE
DYE-ABLE
EAT-ABLE
EQU-ABLE
EYE-ABLE
FIX-ABLE
FLY-ABLE
FRI-ABLE
FRY-ABLE
GEL-ABLE
GET-ABLE
GIV-ABLE

HAT-ABLE
HEW-ABLE
HID-ABLE
HIR-ABLE
LIK-ABLE
LIN-ABLE
LIV-ABLE
LOS-ABLE
LOV-ABLE
MAK-ABLE
MIN-ABLE
MIR-ABLE
MIX-ABLE
MOV-ABLE
MUT-ABLE
NAM-ABLE
NOT-ABLE
OWN-ABLE
PAR-ABLE
PAY-ABLE
PLI-ABLE
POK-ABLE
POS-ABLE
POT-ABLE
RAT-ABLE
ROW-ABLE

SAL-ABLE
SAV-ABLE
SAY-ABLE
SEE-ABLE
SEW-ABLE
SIZ-ABLE
SKI-ABLE
SOW-ABLE
SUE-ABLE
TAK-ABLE
TAM-ABLE
TAX-ABLE
TEN-ABLE
TOT-ABLE
TOW-ABLE
TRI-ABLE
TUN-ABLE
TYP-ABLE
UNH-ABLE
USE-ABLE
VAT-ABLE
VOC-ABLE
VOL-ABLE
VOT-ABLE
WAD-ABLE
WAX-ABLE

Eight-letter words

ADOR-ABLE	EDUC-ABLE	KNOW-ABLE
AGIT-ABLE	ENVI-ABLE	LAUD-ABLE
AMEN-ABLE	ERAS-ABLE	LEAS-ABLE
AMIC-ABLE	EROD-ABLE	LEND-ABLE
ARGU-ABLE	EVAD-ABLE	LIKE-ABLE
ATON-ABLE	FACE-ABLE	LIVE-ABLE
BAIL-ABLE	FARM-ABLE	LOCK-ABLE
BANK-ABLE	FEED-ABLE	LOVE-ABLE
BEAR-ABLE	FILE-ABLE	MAIL-ABLE
BEAT-ABLE	FILM-ABLE	MEND-ABLE
BEND-ABLE	FOLD-ABLE	MISS-ABLE
BILL-ABLE	FUND-ABLE	MOVE-ABLE
BITE-ABLE	GAIN-ABLE	NAME-ABLE
BLAM-ABLE	GETT-ABLE	OPEN-ABLE
BRIB-ABLE	GIVE-ABLE	OPER-ABLE
CASH-ABLE	GRAD-ABLE	PALP-ABLE
CAUS-ABLE	GROW-ABLE	PASS-ABLE
CHEW-ABLE	GUID-ABLE	PICK-ABLE
CITE-ABLE	HEAR-ABLE	PITI-ABLE
CLOS-ABLE	HEAT-ABLE	PLAY-ABLE
COIN-ABLE	HOLD-ABLE	PORT-ABLE
COOK-ABLE	HUNT-ABLE	POSE-ABLE
COPY-ABLE	IMIT-ABLE	POUR-ABLE
CULP-ABLE	INVI-ABLE	PROB-ABLE
CUTT-ABLE	JOIN-ABLE	PROV-ABLE
DENI-ABLE	JUMP-ABLE	QUOT-ABLE
DRAW-ABLE	KICK-ABLE	RATE-ABLE
DRIV-ABLE	KILL-ABLE	READ-ABLE
EDIT-ABLE	KISS-ABLE	REAP-ABLE

RELI-ABLE	SING-ABLE	TRAD-ABLE
RENT-ABLE	SINK-ABLE	TURN-ABLE
REUS-ABLE	SIZE-ABLE	UNST-ABLE
RINS-ABLE	SMOK-ABLE	VALU-ABLE
RIPP-ABLE	SOCI-ABLE	VARI-ABLE
SACK-ABLE	SOLV-ABLE	VIEW-ABLE
SALE-ABLE	SORT-ABLE	VIOL-ABLE
SAVE-ABLE	SUIT-ABLE	VOID-ABLE
SEAL-ABLE	SURF-ABLE	VOTE-ABLE
SEIZ-ABLE	SWAY-ABLE	WALK-ABLE
SELL-ABLE	SYLL-ABLE	WASH-ABLE
SEND-ABLE	TAKE-ABLE	WEAR-ABLE
SERV-ABLE	TALK-ABLE	WINN-ABLE
SHAK-ABLE	TAME-ABLE	WORK-ABLE
SHAM-ABLE	TEAR-ABLE	WRIT-ABLE
SHOW-ABLE	TEAS-ABLE	

Some words ending with -AGE
Seven-letter words

ACRE-AGE	CARN-AGE	HAUL-AGE
ASSU-AGE	COIN-AGE	HERB-AGE
AVER-AGE	COLL-AGE	HOST-AGE
BAGG-AGE	CORS-AGE	LEAK-AGE
BAND-AGE	COTT-AGE	LINE-AGE
BARR-AGE	COUR-AGE	LINK-AGE
BEER-AGE	FLOW-AGE	LUGG-AGE
BREW-AGE	FOLI-AGE	MASS-AGE
BULK-AGE	FOOT-AGE	MESS-AGE
BUOY-AGE	FROM-AGE	MILE-AGE
CABB-AGE	GARB-AGE	MONT-AGE

ONST-AGE	RIBC-AGE	UMBR-AGE
OUTR-AGE	RIFF-AGE	UPST-AGE
OVER-AGE	RUMM-AGE	VANT-AGE
PACK-AGE	SALV-AGE	VILL-AGE
PASS-AGE	SAUS-AGE	VINT-AGE
PEER-AGE	SEEP-AGE	VOLT-AGE
PLUM-AGE	SIGN-AGE	WARP-AGE
POST-AGE	SOIL-AGE	WAST-AGE
POTT-AGE	STOR-AGE	WATT-AGE
PRES-AGE	TEEN-AGE	WEBP-AGE
RAMP-AGE	TONN-AGE	YARD-AGE

Eight-letter words

AMPER-AGE	GRAIN-AGE	SABOT-AGE
BARON-AGE	GROUP-AGE	SEWER-AGE
BEVER-AGE	HERIT-AGE	SHORT-AGE
BIRDC-AGE	HOMEP-AGE	SLIPP-AGE
BLOCK-AGE	LANGU-AGE	SPILL-AGE
BREAK-AGE	LEVER-AGE	SPOIL-AGE
CARRI-AGE	MARRI-AGE	STEER-AGE
CLEAR-AGE	METER-AGE	STOPP-AGE
COVER-AGE	MISUS-AGE	SUFFR-AGE
CREEP-AGE	MORTG-AGE	TRACK-AGE
CRIBB-AGE	OFFST-AGE	TUTEL-AGE
DRAIN-AGE	OVERP-AGE	TUTOR-AGE
DRESS-AGE	PILOT-AGE	UNDER-AGE
ENVIS-AGE	PLANT-AGE	VAUNT-AGE
FRONT-AGE	PUPIL-AGE	VERBI-AGE
FUSEL-AGE	ROUGH-AGE	VICAR-AGE

Some words ending with -ANCE

Seven-letter words

ADV-ANCE	DUR-ANCE	ROM-ANCE
AID-ANCE	ENH-ANCE	SON-ANCE
ASK-ANCE	FIN-ANCE	SUR-ANCE
BAL-ANCE	JOY-ANCE	VAC-ANCE
CRE-ANCE	PEN-ANCE	VAL-ANCE

Eight-letter words

ABEY-ANCE	ELEG-ANCE	PAST-ANCE
ABID-ANCE	ENTR-ANCE	PIQU-ANCE
ACUT-ANCE	EXIT-ANCE	PITT-ANCE
ADAM-ANCE	FEAS-ANCE	PORT-ANCE
AFFI-ANCE	GUID-ANCE	RADI-ANCE
ALLI-ANCE	INST-ANCE	RELI-ANCE
AMBI-ANCE	ISSU-ANCE	RESI-ANCE
AMOR-ANCE	ITER-ANCE	RIDD-ANCE
BECH-ANCE	LAIT-ANCE	SORT-ANCE
BRIS-ANCE	NOND-ANCE	TADV-ANCE
BUOY-ANCE	NUIS-ANCE	TEND-ANCE
CREP-ANCE	ORDN-ANCE	VALI-ANCE
DEFI-ANCE	OUTD-ANCE	VARI-ANCE
DEVI-ANCE	OUTR-ANCE	VIBR-ANCE
DIST-ANCE	PARL-ANCE	VOID-ANCE

Some words ending with -ANCY
Seven-letter words

ERR-ANCY	SON-ANCY	UNF-ANCY
INF-ANCY	TEN-ANCY	VAC-ANCY
PLI-ANCY	TRU-ANCY	

Eight-letter words

ABEY-ANCY	GEOM-ANCY	RADI-ANCY
ADAM-ANCY	IMIT-ANCY	RAMP-ANCY
BLAT-ANCY	INST-ANCY	REGN-ANCY
BUOY-ANCY	MORD-ANCY	UNCH-ANCY
CLAM-ANCY	MYOM-ANCY	VAGR-ANCY
DEVI-ANCY	PECC-ANCY	VALI-ANCY
DORM-ANCY	PERN-ANCY	VERD-ANCY
ELEG-ANCY	PIQU-ANCY	VIBR-ANCY

Some words ending with -ARCH
Seven-letter words

AUT-ARCH	MON-ARCH	TRI-ARCH
END-ARCH	NAV-ARCH	XER-ARCH
HEX-ARCH	NOM-ARCH	
MES-ARCH	TOP-ARCH	

Eight-letter words

ETHN-ARCH	OMNI-ARCH	POLY-ARCH
HEPT-ARCH	OUTM-ARCH	RESE-ARCH
HIER-ARCH	OVER-ARCH	TAXI-ARCH
HIPP-ARCH	PENT-ARCH	TETR-ARCH
OLIG-ARCH	PHYL-ARCH	UNST-ARCH

Unusual letter combinations

If you find you have a preponderance of vowels on your rack, a few words from World English can come in handy. Fortunately, there are many from which to choose.

Australian words

ADJIGO	yam plant
ALF	an uncultivated Australian
ARVO	afternoon
ASPRO	associate professor

Canadian words

AGLOO	breathing hole made in ice by a seal
AMAUT	hood on an Inuit woman's parka for carrying a child
ATIGI	Inuit parka

Hindi words

AKHARA	gymnasium
ALAP	vocal music without words
AMBARY	tropical plant
ANKUS	elephant goad
ANNA	old copper coin
ARTI	Hindu ritual
AYAH	maidservant or nursemaid

New Zealand words

New Zealand English features a great variety of words adopted from the Maori language. Many of these words use two (and sometimes three) As but are often also dependent on a consonant such as K or T.

ATUA	spirit or demon
HAKA	war dance
KAUPAPA	strategy, policy or cause
TAIAHA	ceremonial fighting staff
WAKA	Maori canoe

South African words

South African English is fed into by various different languages, including Afrikaans and Nguni languages such as Zulu and Xhosa. Afrikaans-derived words often feature a double A and Nguni words frequently contain two or three.

AMADODA	grown men
AMANDLA	political slogan calling for power to the Black population
BABALAS	drunk or hungover
KRAAL	stockaded village
PLAAS	farm

B 3

Essential info
Value: 3 points
Number in set: 2

B

B can form a two-letter word with every vowel except for U. If you have a letter B you can form various short everyday words, some of which can be high-scoring such as BOX (12 points), BAY (8 points), BOW (8 points), BUY (8 points) and BYE (also 8). Some more unusual three-letter words beginning with B are BEY (an official in the Ottoman Empire, 8 points) and BEZ (the second spike of a deer's antler, 14 points).

Two-letter words beginning with B

BA	BE	BI	BO	BY

Some three-letter words beginning with B

BAA	BEL	BOA	BOP
BAC	BEN	BOD	BOR
BAH	BEY	BOH	BOT
BAL	BEZ	BOI	BUR
BAM	BIO	BOK	
BAP	BIZ	BON	

Hooks

Hooking requires a subtle change in a player's thought process, in that they must look at words already on the board without becoming distracted by their pronunciation.

Some front-hooks
Two letters to three

B-AA	B-AT	B-IN	B-OO	B-UN
B-AD	B-AY	B-IO	B-OP	B-UR
B-AG	B-ED	B-IS	B-OR	B-US
B-AH	B-EE	B-IT	B-OS	B-UT
B-AL	B-EL	B-OB	B-OW	B-YE
B-AM	B-EN	B-OD	B-OX	
B-AN	B-ES	B-OH	B-OY	
B-AR	B-ET	B-OI	B-UG	
B-AS	B-ID	B-ON	B-UM	

Three letters to four

B-AFT	B-AUK	B-ILK
B-AIL	B-AYE	B-ILL
B-ALE	B-EAR	B-INK
B-ALL	B-EAT	B-IRK
B-AND	B-EAU	B-ISH
B-ANT	B-EGO	B-LAB
B-ARE	B-END	B-LAD
B-ARK	B-EST	B-LAG
B-ARM	B-HAT	B-LAW
B-ASH	B-HUT	B-LAY
B-ASK	B-ICE	B-LED

B-ATE	B-IDE	B-LET
B-LEY	B-OLD	B-RAY
B-LIP	B-ONE	B-RED
B-LOB	B-OOH	B-RIG
B-LOG	B-ORE	B-RIM
B-LOT	B-OUT	B-ROD
B-LOW	B-OWL	B-ROO
B-OAR	B-OXY	B-ROW
B-OAT	B-RAG	B-RUT
B-ODE	B-RAN	B-URN
B-OFF	B-RAT	B-YES
B-OIL	B-RAW	

Four letters to five

B-ALAS	B-IOTA	B-LENT
B-ALKY	B-LACK	B-LESS
B-ALLY	B-LADE	B-LEST
B-ALMS	B-LADY	B-LIMP
B-ARMY	R-LAME	B-LIMY
B-EACH	B-LAND	B-LINK
B-EARD	B-LANK	B-LIST
B-EAST	B-LARE	B-LITE
B-EAUX	B-LASH	B-LIVE
B-EGAD	B-LAST	B-LOCK
B-EVER	B-LATE	B-LOOM
B-HAJI	B-LAUD	B-LOOP
B HANG	B-LAWN	B-LORE
B-HOOT	B-LAZE	B-LUSH
B-IFFY	B-LEAK	B-OGLE
B-IGGS	B-LEND	B-OINK

29

B

B-ONCE	B-RASH	B-ROCK
B-ONUS	B-RAVE	B-ROOK
B-OOZE	B-RAZE	B-ROOM
B-ORAL	B-READ	B-ROSE
B-OWED	B-REAM	B-ROSY
B-OWER	B-REED	B-RUIN
B-OXEN	B-RENT	B-RULE
B-RACE	B-RICK	B-RUNG
B-RAID	B-RIDE	B-RUNT
B-RAIL	B-RING	B-RUSH
B-RAIN	B-RINK	B-RUSK
B-RAKE	B-RISE	B-RUST
B-RANK	B-RISK	B-USED
B-RANT	B-ROAD	

Five letters to six

B-ACHED	B-EARED	B-LEACH
B-ADDER	B-EATEN	B-LEAKY
B-ADMAN	B-EATER	B-LEARY
B-AILED	B-EGGED	B-LIGHT
B-ALLOT	B-ELATE	B-LIMEY
B-ALLOW	B-ENDED	B-LITHE
B-ANGER	B-ENDER	B-LOBBY
B-ANGLE	B-IONIC	B-LOTTO
B-ARROW	B-LAMER	B-LOUSE
B-ASHED	B-LANKY	B-LOUSY
B-ASKED	B-LATER	B-LOWED
B-ASSET	B-LAWED	B-LOWER
B-EAGLE	B-LAZED	

B-LUNGE	B-RACED	B-REACH
B-OAKED	B-RACER	B-READY
B-OATER	B-RAGGY	B-RIDGE
B-OFFED	B-RAINY	B-RIGHT
B-OILED	B-RAISE	B-RISKY
B-OILER	B-RAKED	B-ROACH
B-OLDEN	B-RANCH	B-ROGUF
B-OLDER	B-RANDY	B-ROOMY
B-ORATE	B-RATTY	B-ROUGH
B-ORDER	B-RAVED	B-ROWED
B-OTHER	B-RAVER	B-UDDER
B-OUGHT	B-RAWER	B-UNION
B-OUNCE	B-RAWLY	B-URNED
B-OVATE	B-RAYED	B-USHER
B-OWING	B-RAZED	B-UTTER
B-OWNED	B-RAZER	

Six letters to seven

B-ACHING	B-ELATED	B-LATTER
B-AILING	B-ENDING	B-LAUDED
B-ANGLED	B-INNING	B-LAZING
B-ASHING	B-LACKED	B-LEAKER
B-ASKING	B-LADDER	B-LENDER
B-ASSIST	B-LADING	B-LESSER
B-ATONED	B-LAGGED	B-LETTED
B-EAGLED	B-LANDER	B-LINGER
B-EATING	B-LASTED	B-LINKED
B-EERIER	B-LASTER	B-LINKER
B-EERILY	B-LATEST	B-LISTER
B-EGGING	B-LATHER	

B-LOBBED	B-OOZING	B-RAUNCH
B-LOCKED	B-ORATED	B-RAVING
B-LOCKER	B-OWNING	B-RAWEST
B-LOGGER	B-OXLIKE	B-RAYING
B-LOOMED	B-RABBLE	B-RAZING
B-LOOPED	B-RACING	B-REAMED
B-LOOPER	B-RACKET	B-RIDGED
B-LOUSED	B-RAGGED	B-RIDING
B-LOWING	B-RAIDED	B-RINGER
B-LOWSED	B-RAIDER	B-RISKED
B-LUBBER	B-RAILED	B-RISKER
B-LUNGED	B-RAINED	B-ROCKED
B-LUNGER	B-RAISED	B-ROCKET
B-LUSTER	B-RAKING	B-ROOKIE
B-OFFING	B-RAMBLE	B-ROOMED
B-OILING	B-RANKED	B-RUSHED
B-OINKED	B-RASHER	B-RUSHER
B-OLDEST	B-RASHLY	
B-OOZILY	B-RATTLE	

Seven letters to eight

B-AILMENT	B-ELATING	B-LENDING
B-ARTISAN	B-ENDWISE	B-LETTING
B-ASHLESS	B-ESPOUSE	B-LIGHTED
B-ATONING	B-LACKING	B-LIGHTER
B-EAGLING	B-LAGGING	B-LINKING
B-EARDING	B-LASTING	B-LITHELY
B-EARLIKE	B-LAUDING	B-LOGGING
B-EATABLE	B-LEACHED	B-LOOMING
B-EERIEST	B-LEACHER	B-LOOPING

B-LOUSIER	B-RAISING	B-RIDGING
B-LOUSILY	B-RAMBLED	B-RIGHTEN
B-LOWDOWN	B-RANCHED	B-RIGHTER
B-LUNGING	B-RANCHER	B-RIGHTLY
B-OLDNESS	B-RANDING	B-RIMLESS
B-ORATING	B-RANKING	B-RINGING
B-ORDERED	B-RASHEST	B-RISKING
B-ORDERER	B-RATPACK	B-ROACHED
B-RABBLER	B-RATTIER	B-ROADWAY
B-RAGGIER	B-RATTISH	B-ROGUISH
B-RAGGING	B-RATTLED	B-ROILING
B-RAIDING	B-REACHED	B-ROOMING
B-RAILING	B-REACHER	B-RUSHIER
B-RAINIER	B-REACHES	B-RUSHING
B-RAINILY	B-READING	B UTTERED
B-RAINING	B-REEDING	

Handy Hint

The more difficult or uncommon words you remember, the greater your chances of clearing your rack and achieving a high score. You could even be lucky enough to have two power tiles at your disposal to be able to play some rare high-scoring gems. Some excellent examples beginning with B are BANJAX (to ruin something, 22 points) and BEZIQUE (a card game, 27 points).

Some end-hooks

Two letters to three

AB-B	DI-B	JA-B	MI-B	RE-B
AL-B	DO-B	JO-B	MO-B	SI-B
AR-B	FA-B	KA-B	NA-B	SO-B
BI-B	GI-B	KO-B	NE-B	TA-B
BO-B	GO-B	LA-B	NO-B	UR-B
DA-B	GU-B	LI-B	NU-B	WE-B
DE-B	HO-B	LO-B	OR-B	YO-B

Three letters to four

BAR-B	COB-B	FOR-B	LAM-B
BIB-B	CUR-B	GAM-B	NIM-B
BOA-B	DIE-B	GAR-B	PRO-B
BUR-B	DOR-B	HER-B	TOM-B
CAR-B	FEE-B	JAM-B	WAR-B
CHI-B	FLU-B	JIB-B	

Four letters to five

ACER-B	DEMO-B	THRO-B
BLUR-B	PLUM-B	ZEBU-B
CUBE-B	SLUR-B	

Five letters to six

SCRAM-B	SUPER-B

Six letters to seven

POTHER-B	PROVER-B	REPLUM-B

Blockers

It is useful to know which words are blockers and can't therefore be extended before or after. You may want to play a blocker that your opponent can't extend, or you may want to avoid playing a blocker because you want to keep the board open.

Three-letter blocker beginning with B
BEZ

Some four-letter blockers beginning with B

BABY	BEVY	BUBO
BADE	BLEW	BURY
BEEN	BODY	BUSY

Some five-letter blockers beginning with B (except words ending in '-ED', '-J', '-S', '-X', '-Y' or '-Z')

BANAL	BELCH	BRUNG
BARER	BIRCH	BUILT
BATCH	BLASÉ	BURNT
BEGAN	BLOWN	BUTCH
BEGAT	BLUER	BUXOM
BEGOT	BOXEN	

Some six-letter blockers beginning with B (except words ending in '-ED', '-J', '-S', '-X', '-Y' or '-Z')

BADDER
BADMAN
BAGMAN
BALDER
BALING
BANISH
BAREST
BARFUL
BARING
BARISH
BARMAN
BASEST
BATMAN
BAYMAN
BEATEN
BECAME
BEFORE
BEGONE

BEHALF
BEHELD
BENIGN
BEREFT
BIFOLD
BIFORM
BIGGER
BINMAN
BITTEN
BLANCH
BLEACH
BLUEST
BLUIER
BLUISH
BOGMAN
BOLDER
BONIER
BONZER

BOOING
BOWMAN
BOXIER
BOYING
BOYISH
BREACH
BREECH
BRICHT
BROKEN
BROOCH
BRUNCH
BRUTAL
BUSIER
BUSMAN
BUYING
BYPAST

Bonus words

Bonus words on your rack can be hard to spot, especially for the less experienced player. One way to help find them is by using prefixes and suffixes.

Many larger words include a common prefix or suffix – remembering these and using them where you can is a good way to discover any longer words on your rack, including any potential bonus words. The key prefixes to remember beginning with B are BE- and BI- and the key suffixes are -BACK, -BALL, -BAND and -BIRD.

Some words beginning with BE-

Seven-letter words

BE-ACHED	BE-HAVER	BE-NEATH
BE-ARISH	BE-HEADS	BE-QUEST
BE-AVERS	BE-HINDS	BE-RATED
BE-CAUSE	BE-HOLDS	BE-REAVE
BE-COMES	BE-HOOFS	BE-SIDES
BE-DECKS	BE-JEWEL	BE-SIEGE
BE-DEVIL	BE-LATED	BE-SPOKE
BE-DRAIL	BE-LAYED	BE-STOWS
BE-DROLL	BE-LIEFS	BE-TIDES
BE-ECHES	BE-LONGS	BE-TRAYS
BE-FALLS	BE-LOVED	BE-TWEEN
BE-FOULS	BE-MOANS	BE-TWIXT
BE-GUILE	BE-MUSED	BE-WITCH

Eight-letter words

BE-ACHING	BE-GRUDGE	BE-MUSING
BE-ARABLE	BE-GUILED	BE-RATING
BE-BOPPED	BE-HAVING	BE-REAVED
BE-CALMED	BE-HAVIOR	BE-REAVER
BE-CHANCE	BE-HEADED	BE-SIEGED
BE-COMING	BE-HEADER	BE-SIEGER
BE-CURSED	BE-HOLDEN	BE-SMIRCH
BE-DAUBED	BE-HOLDER	BE-SPOKEN
BE-DAZZLE	BE-HOOVED	BE-STOWED
BE-DECKED	BE-HOVING	BE-STREWN
BE-FOULED	BE-KNIGHT	BE-SUITED
BE-FRIEND	BE-LAYING	BE-TIDING
BE-FUDDLE	BE-LIEVER	BE-TITLED
BE-GETTER	BE-LITTLE	BE-WARING
BE-GINNER	BE-LONGED	BE-WIGGED
BE-GOTTEN	BE-LONGER	BE-WILDER

Some words beginning with BI-
Seven-letter words

BI-AXIAL	BI-LEVEL	BI-SECTS
BI-BLESS	BI-MODAL	BI-SHOPS
BI-BLIST	BI-OLOGY	BI-TABLE
BI-CARBS	BI-OPTIC	BI-TINGS
BI-CYCLE	BI-PARTY	BI-TONAL
BI-DINGS	BI-PEDAL	BI-VALVE
BI-FOCAL	BI-PLANE	BI-VINYL
BI-KINGS	BI-POLAR	BI-ZONAL

Eight-letter words

BI-ANNUAL
BI-CHROME
BI-COLOUR
BI-CONVEX
BI-CUSPID
BI-CYCLED
BI-CYCLER
BI-CYCLIC

BI-FACIAL
BI-FORMED
BI-HOURLY
BI-LINEAR
BI-MANUAL
BI-METHYL
BI-PARTED
BI-PHASIC

BI-RADIAL
BI-STABLE
BI-TEWING
BI-TINGLY
BI-UNIQUE
BI-VALVED
BI-WEEKLY
BI-YEARLY

Some words ending with -BACK
Seven-letter words

BUY-BACK
CUT-BACK
DIE-BACK
FAT-BACK
FIN-BACK

FLY-BACK
LAY-BACK
OUT-BACK
PAY-BACK
RED-BACK

SET-BACK
SUN-BACK
TIE-BACK

Eight-letter words

BARE-BACK
BLOW-BACK
BLUE-BACK
CALL-BACK
CASH-BACK
CLAW-BACK
COME-BACK
DRAW-BACK
FALL-BACK
FAST-BACK

FEED-BACK
FLAT-BACK
FULL-BACK
GREY-BACK
HALF-BACK
HOLD-BACK
HUMP-BACK
KICK-BACK
LIFT-BACK
LOAN-BACK

PLAY-BACK
PULL-BACK
ROLL-BACK
SEAT-BACK
SNAP-BACK
TAIL-BACK
TALK-BACK
TURN-BACK
WING-BACK

Some words ending with -BALL
Seven-letter words

EYE-BALL	LOW-BALL	ODD-BALL
GUM-BALL	NET-BALL	PIN-BALL

Eight-letter words

BASE-BALL	FOOT-BALL	MEAT-BALL
BLUE-BALL	GOOF-BALL	MOTH-BALL
CORN-BALL	HAIR-BALL	PUFF-BALL
FAST-BALL	HAND-BALL	SNOW-BALL
FIRE-BALL	HARD-BALL	SOFT-BALL
FISH-BALL	HIGH-BALL	SPIT-BALL
FOOS-BALL	KICK-BALL	

Some words ending with -BAND
Seven-letter words

ARM-BAND	HAT-BAND	HUS-BAND
DIS-BAND		

Eight-letter words

BACK-BAND	HEAD-BAND	SARA-BAND
BASE-BAND	NECK-BAND	SIDE-BAND
BROW-BAND	NOSE-BAND	WAVE-BAND
HAIR-BAND	RAIN-BAND	WIDE-BAND

B

Some words ending with -BIRD

Seven-letter words

ANT-BIRD	COW-BIRD	OIL-BIRD
AXE-BIRD	FAT-BIRD	RED-BIRD
BOO-BIRD	JAY-BIRD	SEA-BIRD
CAT-BIRD	MAY-BIRD	SUN-BIRD

Eight-letter words

BELL-BIRD	KING-BIRD	REED-BIRD
BLUE-BIRD	LADY-BIRD	RICE-BIRD
CAGE-BIRD	LOVE-BIRD	SNOW-BIRD
FERN-BIRD	LYRE-BIRD	SONG-BIRD
FIRE-BIRD	OVEN-BIRD	SURF-BIRD
GAOL-BIRD	PUFF-BIRD	WHIP-BIRD
HANG-BIRD	RAIL-BIRD	YARD-BIRD
JAIL-BIRD	RAIN-BIRD	

Handy Hint: Blank Tiles

A blank tile is, by its nature, incredibly versatile as
it can be substituted for any other letter. Although
it scores no points in itself, the blank tile can make
forming bonus words that much easier and players
should never, ever change a blank tile should they
be lucky enough to find one on their rack.

Unusual letter combinations

If you have an unusual combination of letters on your rack, or want to impress your opponent with an unusual word, a few words from World English can come in handy.

Australian words

BARRO	embarrassing
BAUERA	small evergreen shrub
BEAUT	outstanding person or thing
BELAH	casuarina tree
BERKO	berserk
BIFFO	fighting or aggressive behaviour
BILBY	burrowing marsupial
BIZZO	empty and irrelevant talk
BOAB	baobab tree
BODGIE	unruly or uncouth man
BOGAN	youth who dresses and behaves rebelliously
BOOBOOK	small spotted brown owl
BOOFY	strong but stupid
BORA	native Australian coming-of-age ceremony
BORAK	rubbish or nonsense
BRASCO	lavatory
BROLGA	large grey crane with a trumpeting call
BRUMBY	wild horse
BUNYA	tall dome-shaped coniferous tree
BUNYIP	legendary monster

Canadian words

BABICHE	thongs or lacings of rawhide
BARACHOIS	shallow lagoon formed by a sand bar
BATEAU	light flat-bottomed boat
BEIGNET	deep-fried pastry
BREWIS	bread soaked in broth, gravy, etc
BUTTE	isolated steep-sided flat-topped hill

Hindi words

BABU	Mr
BAEL	spiny tree
BAHADUR	title for distinguished Indian during the Raj
BANDH	general strike
BANYAN	tree whose branches grow down into the soil
BHAJI	deep-fried vegetable savoury
BHANGRA	music combining traditional Punjabi music with Western pop
BHAVAN	large house or building
BHISHTI	water-carrier
BINDI	decorative dot in middle of forehead
BOBBERY	mixed pack of hunting dogs
BUND	embankment

New Zealand words

BOOHAI	thoroughly lost

South African words

BAAS	boss
BABALAS	drunk or hungover
BAKKIE	small truck
BRAAI	grill or roast meat
BRAAIVLEIS	barbecue
BUNDU	wild, remote region

Urdu words

BAGH	garden
BALTI	spicy Indian dish stewed until most liquid has evaporated
BASTI	slum
BEGUM	woman of high rank
BIRYANI	Indian dish of highly flavoured rice mixed with meat or fish

Essential info
Value: 3 points
Number in set: 2

C

C can be a difficult letter to play (for example, it only forms one two-letter word: CH, an old dialect word for I, 7 points). However, it does form some good three-letter words including CAW, COW and COY (all 8 points) and also CAZ (short form of casual, 14 points). Worth remembering also are the short words which don't use any vowels: CLY (a word for steal, 8 points) and CWM (a Welsh word for valley, 10 points).

Two-letter word beginning with C
CH

Some three-letter words beginning with C

CAA	CEE	CIS	COX
CAG	CEL	CIT	COZ
CAM	CHA	CLY	CUM
CAW	CHE	COO	CUR
CAY	CHI	COR	CUZ
CAZ	CID	COS	CWM

Hooking requires a subtle change in a player's thought process, in that they must look at words already on the board without becoming distracted by their pronunciation.

C Some front-hooks
Two letters to three

C-AA	C-AW	C-IS	C-OS
C-AB	C-AY	C-IT	C-OW
C-AD	C-EE	C-OB	C-OX
C-AG	C-EL	C-OD	C-OY
C-AM	C-HA	C-ON	C-UM
C-AN	C-HE	C-OO	C-UP
C-AR	C-HI	C-OP	C-UR
C-AT	C-ID	C-OR	C-UT

Three letters to four

C-AGE	C-ARK	C-HID	C-IDE
C-AID	C-ART	C-HIP	C-ILL
C-AKE	C-ASH	C-HIS	C-ION
C-ALF	C-ASK	C-HIT	C-IRE
C-ALL	C-ATE	C-HOG	C-LAD
C-ALP	C-HAD	C-HOP	C-LAM
C-AMP	C-HAM	C-HOW	C-LAP
C-ANT	C-HAT	C-HUB	C-LAW
C-ANY	C-HAY	C-HUG	C-LAY
C-APE	C-HER	C-HUM	C-LEG
C-ARE	C-HEW	C-HUT	C-LIP

C-LOD	C-OCH	C-ONS	C-RED
C-LOG	C-ODA	C-ORE	C-RIB
C-LOP	C-ODE	C-OUR	C-RIM
C-LOT	C-OFF	C-OWL	C-ROW
C-LOW	C-OFT	C-RAG	C-RUE
C-LOY	C-OHO	C-RAM	C-URN
C-OAT	C-OIL	C-RAN	C-UTE
C-OBS	C-OLD	C-RAW	
C-OCA	C-ONE	C-RAY	

C

Four letters to five

C-ABLE	C-HATS	C-HORE
C-ACHE	C-HAVE	C-HOSE
C-AGED	C-HEAP	C-HOUT
C-AGER	C-HFAT	C-HOWK
C-AIRN	C-HECK	C-HUCK
C-AKED	C-HELP	C-HUFF
C-ANON	C-HERE	C-HUMP
C-APED	C-HEST	C-HUNK
C-APER	C-HICK	C-HURL
C-ARED	C-HIDE	C-INCH
C-AULD	C-HILD	C-LACK
C-AVER	C-HILI	C-LAME
C-AWED	C-HILL	C-LAMP
C-EASE	C-HIVE	C-LAMS
C-HAFF	C-HOCK	C-LANG
C-HAIN	C-HOKE	C-LANK
C-HAIR	C-HOOF	C-LASH
C-HARM	C-HOOK	C-LASS
C-HART	C-HOPS	C-LAST

C-LEAN	C-OAST	C-RAVE
C-LEAR	C-OMER	C-RAZE
C-LEFT	C-OPED	C-REAM
C-LICK	C-ORAL	C-REDO
C-LIMB	C-OUCH	C-REED
C-LING	C-OVEN	C-REEK
C-LOCK	C-OVER	C-REEL
C-LONE	C-OWED	C-REST
C-LOSE	C-RACK	C-RIPE
C-LOUD	C-RAFT	C-RISE
C-LOUT	C-RAKE	C-ROCK
C-LOVE	C-RAMP	C-ROOK
C-LOWN	C-RANK	C-RUCK
C-LUCK	C-RARE	C-RUDE
C-LUMP	C-RASH	C-RUSH
C-LUNG	C-RATE	C-RUST

Five letters to six

C-ABLED	C-HAPPY	C-LEAVE
C-ABLER	C-HASTE	C-LONER
C-ACHED	C-HEWED	C-LOSED
C-AGING	C-HIDER	C-LOSER
C-ALLOW	C-HILLY	C-LOVER
C-AMBER	C-HIPPY	C-LUCKY
C-AMPED	C-HOKEY	C-LUMPY
C-AMPLY	C-HOPPY	C-ODDER
C-APING	C-HUBBY	C-OILED
C-ASKED	C-HUFFY	C-OLDER
C-AUGHT	C-HUNKY	C-OVERT
C-EASED	C-LANKY	C-RAGGY

C-RAGGY
C-RATED
C-RATER
C-RAVED
C-RAVEN

C-RAYON
C-RAZED
C-ROWED
C-RUDER
C-RUMMY

C-RUSTY
C-UMBER
C-UPPED
C-UPPER
C-UTTER

Six letters to seven

C-ABLING
C-ACHING
C-AMPING
C-ANGLED
C-AROUSE
C-ARTFUL
C-ASHIER
C ASHING
C-ASKING
C-ASTRAL
C-AULDER
C-EASING
C-ENSURE
C-HACKED
C-HAIRED
C-HAMPER
C-HANGED
C-HANGER
C-HARING
C-HARKED
C-HARMED
C-HARMER
C-HASTEN

C-HATTED
C-HATTER
C-HAWING
C-HEAPER
C-HEATED
C-HEATER
C-HELPED
C-HEWING
C-HIDING
C-HILLED
C-HILLER
C-HIPPED
C-HIPPER
C-HIPPIE
C-HITTER
C-HOPPED
C-HOPPER
C-HUCKLE
C-HUFFED
C-HUFFER
C-HUGGED
C-HUGGER
C-HUMMED

C-HUNTER
C-INCHED
C-LACKED
C-LACKER
C-LAMBER
C-LAMMED
C-LAMMER
C-LAMPED
C-LAMPER
C-LANGER
C-LANKED
C-LAPPED
C-LAPPER
C-LASHED
C-LASHER
C-LATTER
C-LEANED
C-LEANER
C-LEANLY
C-LEARED
C-LEAVED
C-LEAVER
C-LICKED

C-LICKER	C-LUMPER	C-RESTED
C-LIMBED	C-LUNKER	C-RIBBED
C-LIMBER	C-LUSTER	C-RIBBER
C-LINGER	C-OILING	C-RICKED
C-LINKED	C-OLDEST	C-RINGED
C-LINKER	C-OLDISH	C-RINGER
C-LIPPED	C-ORACLE	C-RIPPLE
C-LIPPER	C-RACKED	C-ROCKED
C-LITTER	C-RACKER	C-ROCKET
C-LOBBER	C-RAFTED	C-ROOKED
C-LOCKED	C-RAFTER	C-ROSIER
C-LOCKER	C-RAGGED	C-ROWING
C-LOGGED	C-RAMMED	C-RUDELY
C-LOGGER	C-RAMPED	C-RUDEST
C-LOPPED	C-RANKED	C-RUMBLE
C-LOSING	C-RASHED	C-RUMPLE
C-LOTTED	C-RASHER	C-RUSHED
C-LUBBER	C-RAVING	C-RUSHER
C-LUCKED	C-REAKED	C-RUSTED
C-LUMPED	C-REAMED	C-UPPING

Highest Word Score

The highest-scoring word ever played in a Scrabble game was CAZIQUES, which achieved an enormous total of 392 points. It was played by Karl Khoshnaw of Richmond, Surrey.

Seven letters to eight

C-AMBERED	C-LAGGING	C-LUMPISH
C-ANGLING	C-LAMMING	C-OFFERED
C-ASHLESS	C-LAMPING	C-OLDNESS
C-ENSURED	C-LANKIER	C-OTTERED
C-ENTERED	C-LANKING	C-OVERAGE
C-HAIRING	C-LAPPING	C-OVERALL
C-HANDLER	C-LASHING	C-OVERTLY
C-HANGING	C-LATCHED	C-RACKING
C-HANTING	C-LAWLESS	C-RAFTING
C-HAPLESS	C-LAWLIKE	C-RAGGIER
C-HAPPIER	C-LEANEST	C-RAMMING
C-HARMFUL	C-LEANING	C-RAMPING
C-HARMING	C-LEARING	C-RANKING
C-HATTING	C-LEAVING	C-RASHING
C-HEATING	C-LICKING	C-REAMING
C-HELPING	C-LIMBING	C-REELING
C-HEWABLE	C-LINGIER	C-RESTING
C-HICKORY	C-LINKING	C-RIBBING
C-HILDING	C-LIPPING	C-RICKING
C-HILLIER	C-LOCKING	C-RIMPLED
C-HOPPING	C-LOGGING	C-RINGING
C-HUFFING	C-LOPPING	C-RIPPLED
C-HUGGERS	C-LOSABLE	C-RIPPLER
C-HUGGING	C-LOTTING	C-ROCKERY
C-HUMMING	C-LOUTING	C-RUMBLED
C-HUMPING	C-LUCKIER	C-RUMPLED
C-HUNKIER	C-LUCKING	C-RUSHING
C-INCHING	C-LUMPIER	C-RUSTIER
C-LACKING	C-LUMPING	C-RUSTILY

51

C

Some end-hooks
Two letters to three

AR-C	MI-C	RE-C
BA-C	MO-C	SI-C
DO-C	MY-C	SO-C
HI-C	OR-C	TE-C
HO-C	PA-C	TI-C
LA-C	PE-C	TO-C
MA-C	PI-C	

Three letters to four

ABA-C	DIS-C	SYN-C
ALE-C	HUI-C	TOR-C
BAN-C	MAR-C	ZIN-C
CHI-C	SAI-C	

Four letters to five

ANTI-C	ILIA-C	SERA-C
ARTI-C	LOTI-C	TARO-C
CODE-C	MAGI-C	TOPI-C
CONI-C	MALI-C	TORI-C
DURO-C	MANI-C	TRON-C
ILEA-C	RABI-C	YOGI-C

Five letters to six

ACINI-C	FILMI-C	MANIA-C
AGAMI-C	FUNDI-C	MYTHI-C
CHOLI-C	FUNGI-C	PARSE-C
CULTI-C	LIMBI-C	TRAGI-C

Six letters to seven

ALKALI-C	EMBOLI-C	SCORIA-C
CARDIA-C	NUCLEI-C	THALLI-C
COLONI-C	RHOMBI-C	TROPHI-C

Seven letters to eight

AMMONIA-C	CHIASMI-C	SYLLABI-C
AMNESIA-C	DACTYLI-C	TSUNAMI-C
BULIMIA-C	RHYTHMI-C	TYMPANI-C

Blockers

It is useful to know which words are blockers and can't therefore be extended before or after. You may want to play a blocker that your opponent can't extend, or you may want to avoid playing a blocker because you want to keep the board open.

Some three-letter blockers beginning with C

CAZ	CLY	CUZ

Some four-letter blockers beginning with C

CASH	COAX	COZY
CAVY	COPY	CRUX
CHEZ	COSH	CUED
CITY	COSY	CURT

Some five-letter blockers beginning with C (except words ending in '-ED', '-J', '-S', '-X', '-Y' or '-Z')

CACTI	CLASH	CREPT
CAJUN	CLUNG	CRUSH
CINCH	COULD	CUING
CIVIL	CRASH	CYBER

Some six-letter blockers beginning with C (except words ending in '-ED', '-J', '-S', '-X', '-Y' or '-Z')

CAGIER	CHEVAL	CONING
CAGING	CHOSEN	COSMIC
CALCIC	CISTIC	COXING
CALMER	CITING	COYEST
CANIER	CITRIC	CROUCH
CANNOT	CLENCH	CRUDER
CARDIO	CLINCH	CRUTCH
CARMAN	CLONAL	CURING
CARMEN	CLOVEN	CURTER
CATTLE	CLUING	CYANIC
CAUGHT	COGENT	CYSTIC
CAUSEN	COITAL	
CEDING	COMETH	

Bonus words

Bonus words on your rack can be hard to spot,
especially for the less experienced player. One way
to help find them is by using prefixes and suffixes.

Many larger words include a common prefix or suffix
– remembering these and using them where you
can is a good way to discover any longer words on
your rack, including any potential bonus words.
The key prefixes to remember beginning with C
are COM- and CON-.

Some words beginning with COM-
Seven-letter words

COM-BATS	COM-MENT	COM-PERE
COM-BINE	COM-MODE	COM-PILE
COM-BING	COM-MONS	COM-PLEX
COM-BUST	COM-MUTE	COM-PORT
COM-FIER	COM-PACT	COM-POSE
COM-FORT	COM-PARE	COM-POST
COM-MAND	COM-PASS	COM-POTE
COM-MEND	COM-PEND	COM-RADE

Eight-letter words

COM-BATED	COM-PADRE	COM-PLIER
COM-BINER	COM-PARED	COM-POSED
COM-BINES	COM-PILED	COM-POSER
COM-FIEST	COM-PILER	COM-POUND
COM-MONER	COM-PLAIN	COM-PRESS
COM-MUTED	COM-PLEAT	COM-PRISE
COM-MUTER	COM-PLIED	

Some words beginning with CON-
Seven-letter words

CON-CAVE	CON-FIRM	CON-SOLE
CON-CEDE	CON-FORM	CON-SORT
CON-CERT	CON-FUSE	CON-TACT
CON-CORD	CON-GEAL	CON-TAIN
CON-CUSS	CON-GEST	CON-TEND
CON-DOLE	CON-JOIN	CON-TENT
CON-DONE	CON-JURE	CON-TEST
CON-DUCE	CON-JURY	CON-TEXT
CON-DUCT	CON-NOTE	CON-TORT
CON-DUIT	CON-SENT	CON-TOUR
CON-FESS	CON-SIGN	CON-VENT
CON-FINE	CON-SIST	CON-VERT

Eight-letter words

CON-CAVED	CON-FRONT	CON-SOLED
CON-CEDED	CON-FUSED	CON-SOLER
CON-CEDER	CON-GENIC	CON-SPIRE
CON-CLAVE	CON-JOINT	CON-TEMPT
CON-DENSE	CON-JUGAL	CON-TRACT
CON-DOLED	CON-JUROR	CON-TRITE
CON-DONER	CON-QUEST	CON-VERGE
CON-FINED	CON-SERVE	CON-VERSE
CON-FOUND	CON-SIDER	CON-VEXED

Unusual letter combinations

If you have an unusual combination of letters on your rack, or want to impress your opponent with an unusual word, a few words from World English can come in handy.

Australian words

CADAGI	tropical eucalyptus tree
CARBY	carburettor
CHEWI	chewing gum
CHIACK	tease or banter
CHOOK	hen or chicken
CHOOM	Englishman
COMPO	compensation
CORREA	evergreen shrub
COUCAL	long-legged bird
COUGAN	rowdy person

CRONK   unfit or unsound
CROOL   spoil
CROWEA   pink-flowered shrub

Canadian words

CABOOSE mobile bunkhouse used by lumbermen
CANOLA   cooking oil extracted from a variety of
         rapeseed developed in Canada
CAYUSE   small Native American pony used by
         cowboys
CUSK   gadoid food fish

Hindi words

CHAI   tea, especially with added spices
CHAMPAC tree with fragrant yellow flowers
CHAPATI flat coarse unleavened bread
CHAPPAL sandal
CHARKHA spinning wheel
CHEETAH large swift feline mammal
CHELA   disciple of a religious teacher
CHINTZ   printed cotton with glazed finish
CHITAL   type of deer
CHOKEY   prison
CHOLI   short-sleeved bodice
CHOWK   marketplace
CHUDDAR large shawl or veil
CHUDDIES underpants
CHUKAR   Indian partridge

CHUKKA	period of play in polo
COWAGE	tropical climbing plant with stinging pods
CRORE	ten million
CUSHY	comfortable

New Zealand words
| COOTIE | body louse |

Urdu words
| CHARPAI | bedstead of woven webbing on a wooden frame |

D₂

Essential info
Value: 2 points
Number in set: 4

D can begin a two-letter word alongside every vowel except for U. It also forms many three-letter words, especially in combination with W or Y: DAY, DYE and DEW are all worth 7 points.

Two-letter words beginning with D

DA	DE	DI	DO

Some three-letter words beginning with D

DAE	DEV	DOM
DAG	DEX	DOO
DAH	DEY	DOP
DAK	DIB	DOR
DAL	DIF	DOW
DAN	DIS	DOY
DAP	DIT	DSO
DAW	DIV	DUH
DEB	DOB	DUN
DEE	DOC	DUP
DEF	DOD	DUX
DEG	DOF	DZO
DEI	DOH	
DEL	DOL	

Hooks

Hooking requires a subtle change in a player's thought process, in that they must look at words already on the board without becoming distracted by their pronunciation. D benefits from the past participle form of many words, providing many options when it comes to end-hooking.

Some front-hooks
Two letters to three

D-AB	D-AW	D-IN	D-ON	D-UH
D-AD	D-AY	D-IS	D-OO	D-UN
D-AE	D-EE	D-IT	D-OP	D-UP
D-AG	D-EF	D-OB	D-OR	D-YE
D-AH	D-EL	D-OD	D-OS	D-ZO
D-AL	D-EN	D-OE	D-OW	
D-AM	D-EX	D-OF	D-OY	
D-AN	D-ID	D-OH	D-SO	
D-AS	D-IF	D-OM	D-UG	

Three letters to four

D-AFT	D-EAN	D-IRE
D-ALE	D-EAR	D-IRK
D-AMP	D-ECO	D-ISH
D-ARE	D-EFT	D-OFF
D-ARK	D-ELL	D-OLE
D-ART	D-EMO	D-ONE
D-ASH	D-HOW	D-OOR
D-ATE	D-ICE	D-OPE
D-AWN	D-ILL	D-OSE

61

D-OUR	D-RAT	D-ROW
D-OWL	D-RAW	D-RUB
D-OWN	D-RAY	D-RUG
D-RAG	D-REW	D-RUM
D-RAM	D-RIP	D-ZHO

Four letters to five

D-AIRY	D-OILY	D-REAM
D-ALLY	D-ONER	D-RIFT
D-AUNT	D-OOZY	D-RILL
D-EVIL	D-RAFT	D-RINK
D-ICED	D-RAIN	D-ROLL
D-ICKY	D-RAKE	D-WELL
D-INKY	D-RANK	D-WELT
D-ITCH	D-RAWN	
D-JINN	D-READ	

Five letters to six

D-AFTER	D-EJECT	D-OFFER
D-AMPLY	D-ELUDE	D-OWNED
D-ANGER	D-EMOTE	D-OWNER
D-ANGLE	D-ICIER	D-RAYED
D-APPLE	D-ICING	D-RIVEN
D-ASHED	D-IMPLY	D-ROGUE
D-AWNED	D-INNER	D-ROVER
D-EARLY	D-OCKER	D-UMBER
D-EARTH	D-OFFED	

Six letters to seven

D-ALLIED
D-AMPING
D-ANGLED
D-ANGLER
D-ASHING
D-AWNING
D-ELATED
D-ELUDED
D-EMOTED
D-EVOLVE
D-ICIEST

D-INKIER
D-ITCHED
D-OFFING
D-OWNING
D-RAFTED
D-RAGGED
D-RAINED
D-RAWING
D-REAMED
D-REAMER
D-RIFTED

D-RILLED
D-RIPPED
D-RIPPER
D-ROLLER
D-RUBBED
D-RUBBER
D-RUGGED
D-RUMMER
D-WELLED

D

Seven letters to eight

D-ALLYING
D-ANGERED
D-ANGLING
D-EJECTED
D-ELUDING
D-ELUSION
D-EMERGED
D-EMOTING

D-EMOTION
D-ENOUNCE
D-EVOLVED
D-INKIEST
D-ITCHING
D-RAFTING
D-RAGGING
D-RAINING

D-READING
D-REAMING
D-RIFTING
D-RUBBING
D-RUGGING
D-WELLING
D-WINDLED

Some end-hooks
Two letters to three

AD-D	EN-D	MA-D	PO-D
AI-D	FA-D	ME-D	RE-D
AN-D	FE-D	MI-D	SO-D
AR-D	GI-D	MO-D	TA-D
BA-D	GO-D	MU-D	TE-D
BE-D	HA-D	NE-D	TI-D
BI-D	HI-D	NO-D	TO-D
BO-D	HO-D	OD-D	UR-D
DA-D	KI-D	OR-D	WE-D
DI-D	LA-D	OU-D	YA-D
DO-D	LI-D	PA-D	YO-D
EL-D	LO-D	PE-D	

Three letters to four

ACE-D	BOR-D	DOW-D
AGE-D	BRO-D	DUE-D
AKE-D	BUN-D	DYE-D
AMI-D	BUR-D	EAR-D
APE-D	CAR-D	ECO-D
ARE-D	CHA-D	EKE-D
AWE-D	CHI-D	ERE-D
AXE-D	COL-D	EYE-D
BAL-D	CON-D	FAN-D
BAN-D	COR-D	FAR-D
BAR-D	CRU-D	FEE-D
BEN-D	CUE-D	FEN-D
BIN-D	CUR-D	FEU-D
BON-D	DIE-D	FIN-D

FON-D	LIN-D	SEE-D
FOR-D	LOR-D	SEL-D
FOU-D	LOU-D	SEN-D
FUN-D	MAN-D	SHE-D
GAE-D	MEL-D	SIN-D
GAU-D	MEN-D	SKI-D
GEE-D	MIL-D	SOL-D
GEL-D	MOL-D	SUD-D
GIE-D	MOO-D	SUE-D
GOA-D	NEE-D	SUR-D
GOO-D	OPE-D	TAE-D
HAE-D	OWE-D	TEA-D
HAN-D	PAN-D	TEE-D
HEN-D	PAR-D	TEL-D
HFR-D	PEN-D	TEN-D
HIE-D	PIE-D	TIE-D
HIN-D	PRO-D	TIN-D
HOE-D	QUA-D	TOE-D
HOO-D	RAI-D	TYE-D
HUE-D	RAN-D	USE-D
ICE-D	RED-D	VIE-D
IRE-D	REE-D	WAI-D
KIN-D	REN-D	WAN-D
KON-D	RIN-D	WAR-D
LAR-D	ROE-D	WEE-D
LEA-D	RUE-D	WEN-D
LEE-D	RUN-D	WIN-D
LEU-D	SAI-D	WOO-D
LEW-D	SAN-D	WYN-D
LIE-D	SAR-D	YAR-D

D

Four letters to five

ABLE-D	CLUE-D	FAKE-D
ACHE-D	CODE-D	FAME-D
ACNE-D	COKE-D	FARE-D
ACRE-D	CONE-D	FATE-D
AIDE-D	COPE-D	FAZE-D
AMEN-D	CORE-D	FETE-D
AXLE-D	COVE-D	FILE-D
BAKE-D	COZE-D	FINE-D
BALE-D	CROW-D	FIRE-D
BARE-D	CUBE-D	FRAU-D
BASE-D	CURE-D	FREE-D
BEAR-D	DARE-D	FUME-D
BIDE-D	DATE-D	FUSE-D
BIKE-D	DAZE-D	GAME-D
BLUE-D	DICE-D	GAPE-D
BOAR-D	DINE-D	GATE-D
BODE-D	DIVE-D	GAZE-D
BONE-D	DOLE-D	GLUE-D
BORE-D	DOME-D	GORE-D
BRAN-D	DOPE-D	GRAN-D
CAGE-D	DOSE-D	GRIN-D
CAKE-D	DOTE-D	GUAR-D
CANE-D	DOZE-D	HARE-D
CAPE-D	DUKE-D	HATE-D
CARE-D	DUPE-D	HAZE-D
CASE-D	EASE-D	HEAR-D
CAVE-D	EDGE-D	HIKE-D
CEDE-D	FACE-D	HIRE-D
CITE-D	FADE-D	HOLE-D

HOME-D	MIME-D	RAKE-D
HONE-D	MINE-D	RARE-D
HOPE-D	MIRE-D	RATE-D
HOSE-D	MOPE-D	RAVE-D
HYPE-D	MOVE-D	RAZE-D
IDLE-D	MUSE-D	RILE-D
JADE-D	MUTE-D	ROBE-D
JAPE-D	NAME-D	ROPE-D
JIBE-D	NOSE-D	ROSE-D
JIVE-D	NOTE-D	ROVE-D
JOKE-D	NUKE-D	RULE-D
KNEE-D	OGLE-D	RUNE-D
LACE-D	OOZE-D	SATE-D
LAIR-D	PACE-D	SAVE-D
LAZE-D	PAGE-D	SHOE-D
LIKE-D	PALE-D	SIDE-D
LIME-D	PARE-D	SIRE-D
LINE-D	PAVE-D	SITE-D
LIVE-D	PIKE-D	SIZE-D
LOPE-D	PILE-D	SPIE-D
LOVE-D	PINE-D	SURE-D
LOWE-D	PIPE-D	TAME-D
LUGE-D	PLEA-D	TAPE-D
LURE-D	PLIE-D	TILE-D
LUTE-D	POKE-D	TIME-D
MACE-D	PORE-D	TIRE-D
MATE-D	POSE-D	TONE-D
MAZE-D	RABI-D	TREE-D
METE-D	RACE-D	TRIE-D
MIKE-D	RAGE-D	TUNE-D

D

67

TWEE-D	WANE-D	WIRE-D
TYPE-D	WAVE-D	YOKE-D
URGE-D	WEIR-D	ZONE-D
VOTE-D	WINE-D	
WADE-D	WIPE-D	

Five letters to six

ABASE-D	BRAKE-D	DANCE-D
ABATE-D	BRAVE-D	DELVE-D
ABIDE-D	BRIBE-D	DEUCE-D
ABUSE-D	BUDGE-D	DODGE-D
ADDLE-D	BUGLE-D	DOUSE-D
ADORE-D	BULGE-D	DOWSE-D
AGREE-D	CABLE-D	DRAPE-D
AMAZE-D	CACHE-D	DRONE-D
AMBLE-D	CARTE-D	ELATE-D
AMUSE-D	CARVE-D	ELOPE-D
ANGLE-D	CAUSE-D	ELUDE-D
ANKLE-D	CEASE-D	EMOTE-D
ARGUE-D	CHASE-D	ENSUE-D
ATONE-D	CHIME-D	ERASE-D
BARGE-D	CHOKE-D	ERODE-D
BASTE-D	CLONE-D	EVADE-D
BELIE-D	CLOSE-D	EVOKE-D
BINGE-D	CRANE-D	EXILE-D
BLAME-D	CRAVE-D	FABLE-D
BLARE-D	CRAZE-D	FENCE-D
BLAZE-D	CURSE-D	FLAKE-D
BOOZE-D	CURVE-D	FLAME-D
BRACE-D	CYCLE-D	FLARE-D

FLUKE-D	JUICE-D	PULSE-D
FORCE-D	KNIFE-D	PURGE-D
FORGE-D	LADLE-D	QUAKE-D
FRAME-D	LANCE-D	QUEUE-D
GAUGE-D	LAPSE-D	QUOTE-D
GLARE-D	LEASE-D	RAISE-D
GLAZE-D	LEAVE-D	RANGE-D
GLIDE-D	LEDGE-D	REAVE-D
GLOVE-D	LODGE-D	RETRO-D
GORGE-D	LOOSE-D	RHYME-D
GOUGE-D	LUNGE-D	RIDGE-D
GRACE-D	MERGE-D	RIFLE-D
GRADE-D	MINCE-D	RINSE-D
GRAPE-D	NUDGE-D	ROGUE-D
GRATE-D	NURSE-D	ROUTE-D
GRAVE-D	PASTE-D	SALVE-D
GRAZE-D	PAUSE-D	SAUTE-D
GRIPE-D	PHASE-D	SCALE-D
GROPE-D	PHONE-D	SCARE-D
GROVE-D	PIECE-D	SCOPE-D
GUIDE-D	PLACE-D	SCORE-D
HASTE-D	PLANE-D	SEIZE-D
HEAVE-D	POISE-D	SENSE-D
HEDGE-D	PRICE-D	SHADE-D
HINGE-D	PRIDE-D	SHAKE-D
HORSE-D	PRIME-D	SHAPE-D
HOUSE-D	PRISE-D	SHAVE-D
IMAGE-D	PROBE-D	SHINE-D
ISSUE-D	PROVE-D	SHORE-D
JUDGE-D	PRUNE-D	SHOVE-D

D

69

SHREW-D   SPICE-D   TRACE-D
SIDLE-D   SPIKE-D   TRADE-D
SIEGE-D   STAGE-D   TRUCE-D
SIEVE-D   STAKE-D   TWINE-D
SINGE-D   STALE-D   UNITE-D
SKATE-D   STARE-D   UNTIE-D
SLATE-D   STATE-D   VALUE-D
SLAVE-D   STOKE-D   VERGE-D
SLICE-D   STONE-D   VERSE-D
SLIME-D   STORE-D   VOICE-D
SLOPE-D   STYLE-D   WAIVE-D
SMILE-D   SURGE-D   WASTE-D
SMOKE-D   SWIPE-D   WEAVE-D
SNAKE-D   TABLE-D   WEDGE-D
SNARE-D   TASTE-D   WHALE-D
SNIPE-D   TEASE-D   WHINE-D
SNORE-D   TENSE-D   WHITE-D
SOLVE-D   THEME-D   WINCE-D
SPACE-D   TINGE-D
SPARE-D   TITLE-D

Six letters to seven
ACCRUE-D   ASHAME-D   BEHAVE-D
ACCUSE-D   ASSUME-D   BELATE-D
ADHERE-D   ASSURE-D   BELOVE-D
ADMIRE-D   AVENGE-D   BEMUSE-D
ADVISE-D   BABBLE-D   BERATE-D
ALLUDE-D   BAFFLE-D   BOGGLE-D
ALLURE-D   BATTLE-D   BOTTLE-D
ARRIVE-D   BEETLE-D   BOUNCE-D

70

BREEZE-D	CRUISE-D	DEPOSE-D
BRIDGE-D	CUDDLE-D	DERIDE-D
BRIDLE-D	CURDLE-D	DERIVE-D
BRONZE-D	DAMAGE-D	DESIRE-D
BROWSE-D	DANGLE-D	DETUNE-D
BRUISE-D	DAPPLE-D	DEVISE-D
BUCKLE-D	DAWDLE-D	DEVOTE-D
BUNDLE-D	DAZZLE-D	DILATE-D
BUNGLE-D	DEBASE-D	DILUTE-D
BURBLE-D	DEBATE-D	DISUSE-D
BURGLE-D	DECIDE-D	DIVIDE-D
BUSTLE-D	DECODE-D	DIVINE-D
CACKLE-D	DECREE-D	DONATE-D
CASTLE-D	DEDUCE-D	DOODLE-D
CENTRE-D	DEFACE-D	DOUBLE-D
CHANCE-D	DEFAME-D	DREDGE-D
CHANGE-D	DEFILE-D	DRUDGE-D
CHARGE-D	DEFINE-D	ELAPSE-D
CHEESE-D	DEFUSE-D	EMERGE-D
CIRCLE-D	DEGREE-D	ENABLE-D
CLEAVE-D	DELATE-D	ENCASE-D
CLICHE-D	DELETE-D	ENCODE-D
COERCE-D	DELUDE-D	ENCORE-D
CORPSE-D	DELUGE-D	ENDURE-D
COUPLE-D	DEMISE-D	ENGAGE-D
COURSE-D	DEMODE-D	ENGINE-D
CRADLE-D	DEMOTE-D	ENRAGE-D
CREASE-D	DEMURE-D	ENSURE-D
CREATE-D	DENOTE-D	ENTICE-D
CRINGE-D	DENUDE-D	EQUATE-D

ESCAPE-D	GRUDGE-D	JOSTLE-D
ESTATE-D	GUZZLE-D	JUGGLE-D
EVOLVE-D	GYRATE-D	JUMBLE-D
EXCISE-D	HANDLE-D	LIAISE-D
EXCITE-D	HECKLE-D	LOATHE-D
EXCUSE-D	HOMAGE-D	LOCATE-D
EXHALE-D	HUDDLE-D	LOUNGE-D
EXHUME-D	HUMBLE-D	MANAGE-D
EXPIRE-D	HURDLE-D	MANGLE-D
EXPOSE-D	HURTLE-D	MANURE-D
FETTLE-D	HUSTLE-D	MARBLE-D
FIDDLE-D	ICICLE-D	MATURE-D
FIGURE-D	IGNITE-D	MENACE-D
FISSLE-D	IGNORE-D	MINGLE-D
FIZZLE-D	IMPALE-D	MINUTE-D
FLEDGE-D	IMPEDE-D	MISUSE-D
FLEECE-D	IMPOSE-D	MUDDLE-D
FONDLE-D	INCITE-D	MUFFLE-D
FORAGE-D	INDUCE-D	MUMBLE-D
FRIDGE-D	INFAME-D	MUSCLE-D
FUMBLE-D	INFUSE-D	MUTATE-D
GARBLE-D	INHALE-D	MUZZLE-D
GARGLE-D	INJURE-D	NEEDLE-D
GENTLE-D	INVADE-D	NEGATE-D
GIGGLE-D	INVITE-D	NESTLE-D
GLANCE-D	INVOKE-D	NIBBLE-D
GOBBLE-D	IONISE-D	NOTICE-D
GREASE-D	JANGLE-D	NUANCE-D
GRIEVE-D	JIGGLE-D	OBLIGE-D
GROOVE-D	JINGLE-D	OPPOSE-D

PADDLE-D	RECEDE-D	SAMPLE-D
PALACE-D	RECITE-D	SAVAGE-D
PARADE-D	REDUCE-D	SCHEME-D
PAROLE-D	REFINE-D	SCRAPE-D
PEDDLE-D	REFUSE-D	SCYTHE-D
PEOPLE-D	REGALE-D	SECEDE-D
PERUSE-D	REHIRE-D	SECURE-D
PHRASE-D	RELATE-D	SEDATE-D
PICKLE-D	RELINE-D	SEDUCE-D
PIERCE-D	REMOVE-D	SEETHE-D
PIRATE-D	RENEGE-D	SEVERE-D
PLAGUE-D	REPUTE-D	SNOOZE-D
PLEASE-D	RESCUE-D	SOMBRE-D
PLEDGE-D	RESIDE-D	SOURCE-D
PLUNGE-D	RESIZE-D	SPONGE-D
POLICE-D	RESUME-D	SQUIRE-D
POOTLE-D	RETIRE-D	STABLE-D
POUNCE-D	REVERE-D	STAPLE-D
PRAISE-D	REVILE-D	STARVE-D
PRANCE-D	REVISE-D	STATUE-D
PSYCHE-D	REVIVE-D	STRIPE-D
PUDDLE-D	REVOKE-D	STRIVE-D
PUPATE-D	RIDDLE-D	STROBE-D
PURSUE-D	ROTATE-D	STROKE-D
PUZZLE-D	RUBBLE-D	SUBDUE-D
RAFFLE-D	RUFFLE-D	SUCKLE-D
RAMBLE-D	RUMBLE-D	SUPPLE-D
RATTLE-D	RUSTLE-D	SWATHE-D
RAVAGE-D	SADDLE-D	SWERVE-D
REBUKE-D	SALUTE-D	TACKLE-D

TICKLE-D	TREBLE-D	UNSURE-D
TINGLE-D	TRIFLE-D	UPDATE-D
TIPTOE-D	TRIPLE-D	VOYAGE-D
TITTLE-D	TRUDGE-D	WABBLE-D
TONGUE-D	TUMBLE-D	WHINGE-D
TOPPLE-D	TUSSLE-D	WIGGLE-D
TORQUE-D	UMPIRE-D	WINKLE-D
TOUCHE-D	UNDATE-D	WOBBLE-D
TOUSLE-D	UNLIKE-D	
TRANCE-D	UNLOVE-D	

Seven letters to eight

ABRIDGE-D	BALANCE-D	COMPILE-D
ABSOLVE-D	BANDAGE-D	COMPOSE-D
ACCURSE-D	BEGUILE-D	COMPUTE-D
ACHIEVE-D	BELIEVE-D	CONCEDE-D
ACQUIRE-D	BEREAVE-D	CONCISE-D
ADVANCE-D	BRIGADE-D	CONFIDE-D
AGITATE-D	CAPSIZE-D	CONFUSE-D
AGONISE-D	CAPTURE-D	CONJURE-D
ALLEDGE-D	CHORTLE-D	CONSOLE-D
ANALYSE-D	CHUCKLE-D	CONSUME-D
ANIMATE-D	COLLATE-D	CONVENE-D
APPROVE-D	COLLIDE-D	CORRODE-D
ARCHIVE-D	COLLUDE-D	COSTUME-D
ARRANGE-D	COMBINE-D	CRACKLE-D
ARTICLE-D	COMMUTE-D	CREMATE-D
ATOMISE-D	COMPARE-D	CRINKLE-D
ATTACHE-D	COMPERE-D	CRIPPLE-D
AVERAGE-D	COMPETE-D	CRUMBLE-D

74

CRUMPLE-D	ENCLOSE-D	INFLAME-D
CRUSADE-D	ENDORSE-D	INFLATE-D
CULTURE-D	ENFORCE-D	INSPIRE-D
DECEASE-D	ENGRAVE-D	INVOLVE-D
DECEIVE-D	ENHANCE-D	LICENCE-D
DECLARE-D	ENLARGE-D	LICENSE-D
DECLINE-D	ENTHUSE-D	MANACLE-D
DEGRADE-D	ENTITLE-D	MANDATE-D
DEPRAVE-D	EXAMINE-D	MASSAGE-D
DEPRIVE-D	EXCLUDE-D	MEASURE-D
DESERVE-D	EXECUTE-D	MESSAGE-D
DESPISE-D	EXPLODE-D	MIGRATE-D
DESTINE-D	EXPLORE-D	MISTIME-D
DEVALUE-D	FATIGUE-D	OBSCURE-D
DEVIATE-D	FEATURE-D	OBSERVE-D
DICTATE-D	FINANCE-D	OPERATE-D
DIFFUSE-D	FLOUNCE-D	OUTLINE-D
DISABLE-D	GESTATE-D	OUTRAGE-D
DISEASE-D	GESTURE-D	OUTSIZE-D
DISLIKE-D	GRUNTLE-D	OVERUSE-D
DISPOSE-D	HYDRATE-D	OZONIZE-D
DISPUTE-D	IDOLISE-D	PACKAGE-D
DIVERGE-D	IMAGINE-D	PICTURE-D
DIVORCE-D	IMITATE-D	PILLAGE-D
DRIBBLE-D	IMMERSE-D	PLACATE-D
EDUCATE-D	IMPLODE-D	POLLUTE-D
ELEVATE-D	IMPLORE-D	PRECEDE-D
EMANATE-D	IMPROVE-D	PREFACE-D
EMBRACE-D	INCLUDE-D	PREPARE-D
EMULATE-D	INDULGE-D	PRESUME-D

D

75

PRODUCE-D	RESERVE-D	SURVIVE-D
PROFILE-D	REVENGE-D	SUSPIRE-D
PROMISE-D	REVERSE-D	TEXTURE-D
PROMOTE-D	REVOLVE-D	TRAMPLE-D
PROPOSE-D	SALVAGE-D	TROUBLE-D
PROVIDE-D	SCUFFLE-D	UNHINGE-D
RAMPAGE-D	SERVICE-D	UNNERVE-D
REALISE-D	SHUFFLE-D	UPGRADE-D
REALIZE-D	SILENCE-D	UPSTAGE-D
RECEIVE-D	SMUGGLE-D	VENTURE-D
RECYCLE-D	SPARKLE-D	VIBRATE-D
REJOICE-D	SQUEEZE-D	VIOLATE-D
RELAPSE-D	STUBBLE-D	WELCOME-D
RELEASE-D	STUMBLE-D	WHISTLE-D
RELIEVE-D	SUBSIDE-D	WHITTLE-D
REPLACE-D	SUFFICE-D	WREATHE-D
REPULSE-D	SUPPOSE-D	WRESTLE-D
REQUIRE-D	SURFACE-D	WRIGGLE-D

Handy Hint

Some unusual short words it is worth remembering are DA (a Burmese knife, 3 points), DAW (a shortened form of jackdaw, 7 points), DEY (an Ottoman governor, 7 points) and DOW (an Arab ship, also 7).

Blockers

It is useful to know which words are blockers and can't therefore be extended before or after. You may want to play a blocker that your opponent can't extend, or you may want to avoid playing a blocker because you want to keep the board open.

Some three-letter blockers beginning with D

DUH DUX

Some four-letter blockers beginning with D

DAFT	DEXY	DOMY	DOWF
DAVY	DIDY	DOPY	DOXY
DEAF	DIED	DORY	DOZY
DEFT	DIEL	DOSH	DREW
DEFY	DIPT	DOSS	DUED
DEMY	DISS	DOST	DULY
DENY	DIXY	DOTH	DUSH
DESI	DOBY	DOTY	DUTY
DEUS	DOEN	DOUN	DYED
DEWY	DOGY	DOUX	

Some five-letter blockers beginning with D (except words ending in '-ED', '-J', '-S', '-X', '-Y' or '-Z')

DEALT	DOEST	DRIPT
DIACT	DONER	DUNNO
DICTA	DORIC	DURST
DINGO	DRACO	DUTCH
DINNA	DRANK	DWELT
DIRER	DRAWN	
DITCH	DREST	

Some six-letter blockers beginning with D (except words ending in '-ED', '-J', '-S', '-X', '-Y' or '-Z')

DAFTER	DEVOID	DOZIER
DANISH	DEVOUT	DREAMT
DANKER	DEWIER	DREICH
DARKER	DEWING	DRENCH
DAYLIT	DEXTRO	DRIEST
DAZING	DICIER	DRIVEN
DEAFER	DINING	DROLER
DEARER	DIREST	DRYEST
DECENT	DOABLE	DRYISH
DEEPER	DOGMAN	DUEFUL
DEFTER	DOLING	DUKING
DELISH	DOMING	DULLER
DELUXE	DOPIER	DUMBER
DENSER	DOSING	DUPING
DERMAL	DOURER	DURING
DETACH	DOVING	DYABLE

78

Bonus words

Bonus words on your rack can be hard to spot, especially for the less experienced player. One way to help find them is by using prefixes and suffixes.

Many larger words include a common prefix or suffix – remembering these and using them where you can is a good way to discover any longer words on your rack, including any potential bonus words. The key prefixes to remember beginning with D are DE- and DIS- and the key suffix is -DOM.

Some words beginning with DE-

Seven-letter words

DE-ADMAN	DE-FENCE	DE-MERIT
DE-BASED	DE-FILED	DE-NOTED
DE-BASER	DE-FINED	DE-PARTS
DE-BATED	DE-FORMS	DE-PLOYS
DE-BONED	DE-FRAUD	DE-PORTS
DE-BRIEF	DE-FROST	DE-POSED
DE-CADES	DE-FUSED	DE-POSIT
DE-CODED	DE-GRADE	DE-PRESS
DE-COYED	DE-ICING	DE-RAILS
DE-CREED	DE-LAYED	DE-RIDER
DE-CRIED	DE-LIGHT	DE-SCENT
DE-CRYPT	DE-LIVER	DE-SIGNS
DE-FACED	DE-LUGED	DE-SIRED
DE-FAULT	DE-MEANS	DE-SPITE

DE-TAILS	DE-TRACT	DE-VOTED
DE-TESTS	DE-VALUE	
DE-TOURS	DE-VICES	

Eight-letter words

DE-AERATE	DE-FINITE	DE-RAILED
DE-BASING	DE-FOREST	DE-RANGED
DE-BUGGED	DE-FORMED	DE-RIDING
DE-BUNKED	DE-GRADED	DE-SCRIBE
DE-CANTER	DE-LAYING	DE-SELECT
DE-CEASED	DE-MISTED	DE-SERVED
DE-CIPHER	DE-MOTION	DE-SIGNED
DE-CODING	DE-NOTING	DE-TAILED
DE-CRYING	DE-PARTED	DE-VOLVED
DE-DUCTED	DE-PENDED	
DE-FACING	DE-PORTED	

Some words beginning with DIS-

Seven-letter words

DIS-ABLE	DIS-GUST	DIS-POSE
DIS-ARMS	DIS-LIKE	DIS-SECT
DIS-BAND	DIS-MISS	DIS-SENT
DIS-CARD	DIS-OBEY	DIS-TILL
DIS-CUSS	DIS-OWNS	DIS-TORT
DIS-EASE	DIS-PLAY	DIS-USED

Eight-letter words

DIS-AGREE	DIS-GUISE	DIS-PLACE
DIS-ALLOW	DIS-HONOR	DIS-PROVE
DIS-APPLY	DIS-JOINT	DIS-QUIET
DIS-ARRAY	DIS-LOYAL	DIS-SOLVE
DIS-CLOSE	DIS-MOUNT	DIS-TASTE
DIS-COLOR	DIS-ORDER	DIS-TRACT
DIS-COVER	DIS-OWNED	DIS-TRUST
DIS-GORGE	DIS-PATCH	DIS-UNITY
DIS-GRACE	DIS-PERSE	

Some words ending with -DOM
Seven-letter words

BORE-DOM	FIEF-DOM	PAPA-DOM
DUKE-DOM	FREE-DOM	SERF-DOM
EARL-DOM	KING-DOM	STAR-DOM

Eight-letter words

CHIEF-DOM	LIEGE-DOM	SHEIK-DOM
CLERK-DOM	PAPPA-DOM	THANE-DOM
DEVIL-DOM	POPPA-DOM	THRAL-DOM
DUNCE-DOM	QUEEN-DOM	UNWIS-DOM
HOTEL-DOM	SAINT-DOM	

D

Unusual letter combinations

If you have an unusual combination of letters on your rack, or want to impress your opponent with an unusual word, a few words from World English can come in handy.

Australian words

DASYURE	small carnivorous marsupial
DELO	delegate
DERRO	vagrant
DINGO	wild dog
DINKUM	genuine or right
DOCO	documentary
DONGA	steep-sided gully
DORBA	stupid, inept, or clumsy person
DRACK	unattractive
DRONGO	slow-witted person
DROOB	pathetic person
DUBBO	stupid
DUGITE	venomous snake
DURRY	cigarette

Canadian words

DEKE	act or instance of feinting in ice hockey

Hindi words

DACOIT	member of a gang of armed robbers
DACOITY	robbery by an armed gang

DAK	system of mail delivery
DAL	split grain
DATURA	plant with trumpet-shaped flowers
DEKKO	look or glance
DEODAR	Himalayan cedar
DEWAN	chief minister of an Indian princedom
DHAK	tropical tree with red flowers
DHAL	curry made from lentils
DHARNA	method of obtaining justice by fasting
DHOBI	washerman
DHOTI	loincloth
DUPATTA	scarf
DURRIE	cotton carpet
DURZI	Indian tailor

South African words

| DWAAL | state of befuddlement |

Urdu words

| DAROGHA | manager |
| DHANSAK | Indian dish of meat or vegetables braised with lentils |

D

Essential info
Value: 1 point
Number in set: 12

E may be worth only one point, but it is extremely useful as it is the most common letter in the Scrabble set. Many words contain more than one E and it is worthwhile keeping these in mind, as there is a good chance you will find yourself with more than one E on your rack. Three-letter words formed by E on either side of a consonant include EYE, EWE, EVE (6 points) and EKE (7 points). E and K combine well to form a selection of other three-letter words, including ELK, EEK (7 points) and EWK (a dialect word for itch, 10 points). E is also helpful for getting rid of double consonants with words such as EGG (5 points) or EBB (7 points). E is one of the letters of the RETAIN set and is therefore a good letter to keep if trying to get a bonus word.

Two-letter words beginning with E

EA	EF	EM	ES
ED	EH	EN	ET
EE	EL	ER	EX

Some three-letter words beginning with E

EAN	EGO	ENG	EST
EAU	ELD	EON	ETA
ECH	ELL	ERE	ETH
EDH	ELT	ERF	EWK
EEK	EME	ERG	EXO
EEN	EMO	ERK	
EFF	EMU	ERN	
EFT	ENE	ESS	

Hooks

Hooking requires a subtle change in a player's thought process, in that they must look at words already on the board without becoming distracted by their pronunciation.

Some front-hooks
Two letters to three

E-AN	E-EN	E-ON
E-AR	E-GO	E-RE
E-AS	E-ME	E-ST
E-AT	E-MO	E-TA
E-CH	E-MU	E-WE
E-EL	E-NE	E-YE

Three letters to four

E-ACH	E-NOW	E-THE
E-ARD	E-PIC	E-TIC
E-AVE	E-RED	E-TUI
E-DIT	E-RES	E-UGH
E-GAD	E-REV	E-VET
E-GAL	E-SKY	E-VOE
E-KED	E-SPY	E-YEN
E-MIR	E-TAT	
E-NEW	E-TEN	

Four letters to five

E-AGER	E-LITE	E-NORM
E-ARED	E-LOGE	E-PACT
E-BONY	E-LOGY	E-POXY
E-BOOK	E-LOIN	E-PROM
E-DICT	E-LOPE	E-PROM
E-DUCE	E-LUDE	E-QUID
E-GEST	E-LUTE	E-QUIP
E-HING	E-MAIL	E-RODE
E-IKON	E-MEER	E-STOP
E-KING	E-MEND	E-TAPE
E-LAIN	E-MOTE	E-VADE
E-LAND	E-MOVE	E-VENT
E-LATE	E-MULE	E-VERY
E-LINT	E-NEWS	

Five letters to six

E-ASTER
E-CARTE
E-CHARD
E-DITED
E-GALLY
E-ITHER
E-LAPSE
E-LATED
E-LATER
E-LEGIT
E-LICIT

E-LOPED
E-LOPER
E-MERGE
E-METIC
E-MOTED
E-NERVE
E-NEWED
E-PRISE
E-QUATE
E-QUINE
E-RASED

E-RASER
E-SCAPE
E-SCARP
E-SCROW
E-SPIED
E-SPIER
E-SPRIT
E-STATE
E-VADED
E-VILER
E-VOLVE

Six letters to seven

E-ASTERN
E-BAYING
E-BONIST
E-CLOSED
E-COTYPE
E-DITING
E-LANCED
E-LAPSED
E-LECTOR
E-LEGIST
E-LOPING

E-MAILED
E-MERGED
E-MOTION
E-MOTIVE
E-MOVING
E-NERVED
E-RASING
E-RASURE
E-RODING
E-SCAPED
E-SPOUSE

E-SPYING
E-SQUIRE
E-STATED
E-TERNAL
E-VADING
E-VENTER
E-VILEST
E-VOLUTE
E-VOLVED

Seven letters to eight

E-LAPSING	E-NERVING	E-STATING
E-LECTION	E-QUALITY	E-STOPPED
E-LEVATOR	E-QUIPPED	E-STRANGE
E-MAILING	E-QUIPPER	E-TYPICAL
E-MENDING	E-RADIATE	E-VACUATE
E-MERGING	E-SCALADE	E-VALUATE
E-MERSION	E-SCAPING	E-VENTING
E-MIGRANT	E-SCARPED	E-VERSION
E-MIGRATE	E-SCRIBED	E-VOLVING
E-MISSION	E-SPECIAL	
E-MISSIVE	E-SPOUSAL	
E-NERVATE	E-SQUIRED	

Handy Hint

If you find yourself with a vowel-heavy rack, handy
short words to remember which use no consonants
are EA and EE (both 2 points) or EAU (3 points).
And there's always EUOUAE (a mnemonic used in
Gregorian chant, 6 points) and EUOI (an interjection
of Bacchic frenzy, 4 points).

Some end-hooks
Two letters to three

AG-E	DE-E	HI-E	NY-E	SH-E
AI-E	DI-E	HO-E	OB-E	TA-E
AN-E	DO-E	ID-E	OD-E	TE-E
AR-E	EM-E	JO-E	ON-E	TI-E
AT-E	EN-E	KA-E	OP-E	TO-E
AW-E	ER-E	KY-E	OR-E	UR-E
AX-E	FA-E	LI-E	OS-E	US-E
AY-E	FE-E	MA-E	OW-E	UT-E
BE-E	GI-E	ME-E	OY-E	WE-E
BY-E	GO-E	MO-E	PE-E	WO-E
CH-E	GU-E	NA-E	PI-E	YA-E
DA-E	HA-E	NE-E	RE-E	

Three letters to four

ACH-E	CAG-E	DAM-E
ADZ-E	CAM-E	DIM-E
AID-E	CAN-E	DIN-E
ANT-E	CAP-E	DIV-E
BAL-E	CAR-E	DOL-E
BAN-E	CIT-E	DOM-E
BAR-E	CON-E	DON-E
BAS-E	COP-E	DOP-E
BAT-E	COR-E	DOS-E
BID-E	COS-E	DOT-E
BIT-E	CUB-E	DUD-E
BON-E	CUR-E	DUN-E
BOR-E	CUT-E	DUP-E
BRA-E	DAL-E	EAS-E

ELS-E	KIT-E	MOR-E
FAD-E	LAC-E	MUS-E
FAR-E	LAM-E	MUT-E
FAT-E	LAT-E	NAM-E
FET-E	LIN-E	NAP-E
FIL-E	LIT-E	NIT-E
FIN-E	LOB-E	NOD-E
FIR-E	LOD-E	NON-E
FLU-E	LOP-E	NOS-E
FOR-E	LOR-E	NOT-E
FUM-E	LOS-E	OBO-E
GAL-E	LUD-E	PAC-E
GAM-E	LUG-E	PAL-E
GAP-E	LUR-E	PAN-E
GAT-E	MAC-E	PAR-E
GEN-E	MAD-E	PAT-E
GIB-E	MAG-E	PAV-E
GON-E	MAK-E	PIN-E
GOR-E	MAL-E	PIP-E
HAT-E	MAN-E	POL-E
HER-E	MAR-E	POP-E
HID-E	MAT-E	POS-E
HOM-E	MEM-E	PUR-E
HOP-E	MIC-E	RAG-E
HOS-E	MIL-E	RAT-E
HUG-E	MIM-E	RID-E
HYP-E	MIR-E	RIF-E
JAP-E	MOD-E	RIP-E
JIB-E	MOL-E	ROB-E
JUT-E	MOP-E	ROD-E

E

ROT-E	SUR-E	VAN-E
RUD-E	TAK-E	VAR-E
RUN-E	TAM-E	VAS-E
SAG-E	TAP-E	VIN-E
SAL-E	THE-E	VIS-E
SAM-E	TID-E	VOL-E
SAN-E	TIL-E	WAD-E
SAT-E	TIN E	WAG-E
SAV-E	TOM-E	WAN-E
SIN-E	TON-F	WAR-E
SIR-E	TOP-E	WIN-E
SIT-E	TOT-E	WIS-E
SOL-E	TUB-E	WOK-E
SOM-E	TUN-E	YOK-E

Four letters to five

AMID-E	CURS-E	HIRE-E
BATH-E	DOWS-E	LAPS-E
BING-E	ERAS-E	LENS-E
BLAM-E	FLAK-E	LOOS-E
BOMB-E	FLIT-E	MANS-E
BOOS-E	FORT-E	PASS-E
BRUT-E	GEES-E	PAST-E
CART-E	GLAD-E	PEAS-E
CAST-E	GLOB-E	PLAN-E
CHIV-E	GRAD-E	PLAT-E
COPS-E	GRIM-E	PLUM-E
COUP-E	GRIP-E	PRIM-E
CREW-E	HAST-E	PROS-E
CRIM-E	HING-E	PURE-E

91

QUIT-E	SNIP-E	TEAS-E
RANG-E	SPAR-E	TENS-E
SCAR-E	SPAT-E	THEM-E
SHAM-E	SPIN-E	TRAD-E
SHIN-E	SPIT-E	TRIP-E
SING-E	STAG-E	TWIN-E
SLAT-E	STAR-E	UNIT-E
SLID-E	STAT-E	WHIN-E
SLIM-E	SUED-E	WHIT-E
SLOP-E	SUIT-E	WRIT-E

Five letters to six

BLOND-E	LOCAL-E	SCRAP-E
CLOTH-E	LUPIN-E	SOOTH-E
EQUIP-E	MADAM-E	SPARS-E
FINAL-E	MORAL-E	SPRIT-E
GRAND-E	PETIT-E	STRIP-E
HEARS-E	PLEAS-E	SWATH-E
HUMAN-E	REGAL-E	TOUCH-E
IMPED-E	REPOS-E	URBAN-E
LOATH-E	RESIT-E	

Six letters to seven

ADVISE-E	ESCAPE-E	REFUGE-E
ARTIST-E	FIANCE-E	RETIRE-E
ATTACH-E	FLAMBE-E	REVERS-E
AUGUST-E	GERMAN-E	SECRET-E
BREATH-E	HEROIN-E	TARTAR-E
CORNEA-E	IMPING-E	WREATH-E
DEVOTE-E	IMPROV-E	
DIVERS-E	OBLIGE-E	

Seven letters to eight

ABSINTH-E	EMPLOYE-E	LICENCE-E
ALKALIS-E	ENDORSE-E	LICENSE-E
AMPHORA-E	ENVELOP-E	NOCTURN-E
BACKBIT-E	ESCALOP-E	OUTWRIT-E
DECLASS-E	GELATIN-E	PROTEGE-E
DIVORCE-E	INHUMAN-E	SILICON-E
DOMICIL-E	INTERNE-E	

E

Handy Hint

A good short word which uses the X and a couple of vowels is EXO (informal Australian term meaning excellent, 10 points). Note that the word could enable you to make a play that involves hooking your O onto an existing EX.

Blockers

It is useful to know which words are blockers and can't therefore be extended before or after. You may want to play a blocker that your opponent can't extend, or you may want to avoid playing a blocker because you want to keep the board open.

Some four-letter blockers beginning with E

EASY ELSE ESPY EYRY

Five-letter blocker beginning with E (except words ending in '-ED', '-J', '-S', '-X', '-Y' or '-Z')

ENLIT

Some six-letter blockers beginning with E (except words ending in '-ED', '-J', '-S', '-X', '-Y' or '-Z')

EASIER	EMDASH	ENRAPT
EFFETE	ENCASH	ENRICH
ELDEST	ENDASH	EYEING
ELVISH	ENMESH	

Bonus words

Bonus words on your rack can be hard to spot, especially for the less experienced player. One way to help find them is by using prefixes and suffixes.

Many larger words include a common prefix or suffix – remembering these and using them where you can is a good way to discover any longer words on your rack, including any potential bonus words. The key prefixes to remember beginning with E are EM-, EN- and EX- and the key suffixes are -EAUX, -ENCE, -ENCY, -EST, -ETTE and -EUR.

Some words beginning with EM-
Seven-letter words

EM-AILED	EM-IRATE	EM-PLOYS
EM-BARKS	EM-PANEL	EM-POWER
EM-BRACE	EM-PARTS	EM-PRESS
EM-BROIL	EM-PEACH	

Eight-letter words

EM-AILING	EM-BLAZED	EM-PARTED
EM-BALMED	EM-BODIED	EM-PATHIC
EM-BARKED	EM-BOLDEN	EM-PHATIC
EM-BATTLE	EM-BOSSED	EM-PLOYED
EM-BEDDED	EM-BRACED	
EM-BITTER	EM-PALING	

Some words beginning with EN-
Seven-letter words

EN-ABLED
EN-ACTED
EN-CAGED
EN-CASED
EN-CLOSE
EN-CODED
EN-CORED
EN-CRYPT

EN-DEARS
EN-FORCE
EN-GORGE
EN-RAGED
EN-SLAVE
EN-SNARE
EN-SUING
EN-SURED

EN-TAILS
EN-TIRES
EN-TITLE
EN-TRAIL
EN-TREES
EN-TRIES
EN-VYING
EN-ZYMES

Eight-letter words

EN-ABLING
EN-CAMPED
EN-CASING
EN-CHANTS
EN-CIPHER
EN-CIRCLE
EN-CLOSED
EN-CORING
EN-DANGER
EN-DEARED

EN-DURING
EN-FOLDED
EN-GENDER
EN-GORGED
EN-GRAVED
EN-GULFED
EN-JOYING
EN-LISTED
EN-QUIRED
EN-RICHED

EN-ROLLED
EN-SHRINE
EN-SIGNED
EN-SNARED
EN-SURING
EN-TAILED
EN-TITLED
EN-TRENCH
EN-VIABLE

E

Some words beginning with EX-
Seven-letter words

EX-ACTED	EX-PENDS	EX-PRESS
EX-AMINE	EX-PLAIN	EX-TENDS
EX-CITED	EX-PORTS	EX-TOLLS
EX-CLAIM	EX-POSED	EX-TRACT

Eight-letter words

EX-ACTING	EX-CITING	EX-PLAINS
EX-CELLED	EX-PANDER	EX-PORTED
EX-CESSES	EX-PERTLY	

Some words ending with -EAUX
Seven-letter words

RAT-EAUX	CAD-EAUX
BUR-EAUX	GAT-EAUX

Eight-letter words

BAND-EAUX	CHAP-EAUX	PLAT-EAUX
BATT-EAUX	CHAT-EAUX	TABL-EAUX
BORD-EAUX	MORC-EAUX	

E

Some words ending with -ENCE
Seven-letter words

ABS-ENCE	FLU-ENCE	SIL-ENCE
CAD-ENCE	LIC-ENCE	URG-ENCE
COG-ENCE	OFF-ENCE	VAL-ENCE
DEF-ENCE	POT-ENCE	
ESS-ENCE	SCI-ENCE	

Eight-letter words

AMBI-ENCE	NASC-ENCE	SENT-ENCE
AUDI-ENCE	OPUL-ENCE	SEQU-ENCE
COMM-ENCE	PATI-ENCE	SIXP-ENCE
CRED-ENCE	PRES-ENCE	TEND-ENCE
DISP-ENCE	PRET-ENCE	TENP-ENCE
EMIN-ENCE	PRUD-ENCE	TUPP-ENCE
EVID-ENCE	SALI-ENCE	VIOL-ENCE
LENI-ENCE	SAPI-ENCE	

Some words ending with -ENCY
Seven-letter words

COG-ENCY	POT-ENCY	URG-ENCY
DEC-ENCY	REC-ENCY	VAL-ENCY
FLU-ENCY	REG-ENCY	

Eight-letter words

CLEM-ENCY	LENI-ENCY	TEND-ENCY
CURR-ENCY	PUNG-ENCY	
FERV-ENCY	SOLV-ENCY	

Some words ending with -EST

Seven-letter words

AIRI-EST	HARD-EST	SUBT-EST
BALD-EST	KIND-EST	TALL-EST
BOLD-EST	LONG-EST	TEMP-EST
DAMP-EST	MEEK-EST	TENS-EST
DARK-EST	POOR-EST	WARM-EST
EARN-EST	PRET-EST	WILD-EST
FULL-EST	PROT-EST	
FUNF-EST	REQU-EST	

Eight-letter words

ACRID-EST	FLASH-EST	REDIG-EST
BLACK-EST	GAUDI-EST	SIMPL-EST
BLOND-EST	GRAND-EST	SUNNI-EST
BRIEF-EST	INERT-EST	TALKF-EST
CLEAN-EST	LOVEF-EST	TOUGH-EST
CLEAR-EST	MINUT-EST	URBAN-EST
DIVIN-EST	ORANG-EST	WASPN-EST
EAGER-EST	PEPPI-EST	WRONG-EST
EXACT-EST	QUICK-EST	

E

Some words ending with -ETTE
Seven-letter words

BLU-ETTE	GAZ-ETTE	PAL-ETTE
CAS-ETTE	LAD-ETTE	PIP-ETTE
DIN-ETTE	MIN-ETTE	POP-ETTE
FUM-ETTE	OCT-ETTE	ROS-ETTE

Eight-letter words

AMUS-ETTE	DISK-ETTE	ROQU-ETTE
BAGU-ETTE	JEAN-ETTE	ROUL-ETTE
BRUN-ETTE	MAQU-ETTE	SEPT-ETTE
CASS-ETTE	NOIS-ETTE	VIGN-ETTE
COQU-ETTE	PALL-ETTE	
CORV-ETTE	ROOM-ETTE	

Some words ending with -EUR
Seven-letter words

AMAT-EUR	PRIM-EUR	TRAC-EUR
LIQU-EUR	SABR-EUR	
MASS-EUR	SIGN-EUR	

Eight-letter words

CHASS-EUR	LONGU-EUR	SEIGN-EUR
COIFF-EUR	MONSI-EUR	VOYAG-EUR
GRAND-EUR	SABOT-EUR	
JONGL-EUR	SECAT-EUR	

Unusual letter combinations

If you have an unusual combination of letters on your rack, or want to impress your opponent with an unusual word, a few words from World English can come in handy.

Australian words

FARBASH	talk incessantly
EMU	large flightless bird
EUMUNG	type of acacia
EVO	evening
EXO	excellent

F

F 4

Essential info
Value: 4 points
Number in set: 2

F can be a useful letter for scoring with short words on premium squares. Although there are only three two-letter words beginning with F (FA and FE, 5 points each, and FY, 8 points), these are complemented with IF and OF. There are also quite a few short, high-scoring words beginning with F which use X (FAX, FIX, FOX, 13 points each), Y (FEY, FLY, FRY, 9 points each) or Z (FEZ, 15 points).

Two-letter words beginning with F

FA	FE	FY

Some three-letter words beginning with F

FAA	FEM	FOB
FAE	FEN	FOH
FAH	FER	FON
FAP	FET	FOP
FAW	FEU	FOU
FAX	FEY	FOY
FAY	FEZ	FUB
FEG	FID	FUG
FEH	FIZ	FUM

Hooks

Hooking requires a subtle change in a player's thought process, in that they must look at words already on the board without becoming distracted by their pronunciation.

Some front-hooks
Two letters to three

F-AA	F-AS	F-EM	F-OB	F-OX
F-AB	F-AT	F-EN	F-OE	F-OY
F-AD	F-AW	F-ER	F-OG	F-UG
F-AE	F-AX	F-ES	F-OH	F-UM
F-AG	F-AY	F-ET	F-ON	F-UN
F-AH	F-ED	F-ID	F-OP	F-UR
F-AN	F-EE	F-IN	F-OR	
F-AR	F-EH	F-IT	F-OU	

Three letters to four

F-ACE	F-AVE	F-ILL
F-ACT	F-AWN	F-INK
F-AFF	F-EAR	F-IRE
F-AIL	F-EAT	F-ISH
F-AIR	F-EEL	F-LAB
F-AKE	F-ELL	F-LAG
F-ALL	F-ELT	F-LAP
F-ARE	F-END	F-LAT
F-ARM	F-ERN	F-LAW
F-ASH	F-ESS	F-LAX
F-ATE	F-EST	F-LAY
F-AVA	F-ETA	F-LEA

103

F-LED	F-OIL	F-RAT
F-LEE	F-OLD	F-RAY
F-LEW	F-OOT	F-REE
F-LEX	F-ORD	F-RET
F-LIP	F-ORE	F-RIZ
F-LIT	F-ORT	F-ROM
F-LOG	F-OUR	F-RUG
F-LOP	F-OWL	F-USE
F-LOW	F-OXY	
F-LUX	F-RAG	

Four letters to five

F-ABLE	F-LAKE	F-LOWN
F-ACED	F-LAKY	F-LUFF
F-ACER	F-LAME	F-LUKE
F-AERY	F-LANK	F-LUNG
F-AIRY	F-LARE	F-LUNK
F-AKED	F-LASH	F-LUSH
F-ARED	F-LEER	F-LUTE
F-AXED	F-LEET	F-OLIO
F-AYRE	F-LICK	F-OYER
F-EAST	F-LIER	F-RAIL
F-ETCH	F-LING	F-RANK
F-EVER	F-LINT	F-REED
F-EWER	F-LITE	F-RILL
F-ILLY	F-LOCK	F-RISK
F-INCH	F-LOOR	F-RITZ
F-ITCH	F-LOSS	F-ROCK
F-LACK	F-LOUR	F-RUMP
F-LAIR	F-LOUT	F-USED

F

Five letters to six

F-ABLED	F-ICKLE	F-LOWER
F-ACING	F-INNER	F-LUTED
F-ACTOR	F-LAKED	F-LUTER
F-AILED	F-LAKER	F-LYING
F-ALLOW	F-LAMED	F-ODDER
F-ALTER	F-LAMER	F-OILED
F-AMINE	F-LAWED	F-OLDER
F-ARMED	F-LAYED	F-OUGHT
F-ARMER	F-LAYER	F-RIDGE
F-ARROW	F-LEDGE	F-RIGHT
F-AXING	F-LETCH	F-RIGID
F-EARED	F-LIGHT	F-RISKY
F-ENDED	F-LINCH	F-USING
F-ENDER	F-LINTY	F-UTILE
F-ESTER	F-LOWED	

Six letters to seven

F-ABLING	F-EARFUL	F-LAGGED
F-ACTION	F-EARING	F-LAGGER
F-ACTUAL	F-EASTER	F-LAKING
F-ADDLED	F-EATING	F-LAMING
F-AILING	F-ENDING	F-LANKER
F-AIRILY	F-ETCHED	F-LAPPED
F-AIRING	F-ETCHER	F-LAPPER
F-AIRWAY	F-ICKLER	F-LASHED
F-ANGLED	F-INCHED	F-LASHER
F-ARMING	F-INNING	F-LASKET
F-ATTEST	F-LACKED	F-LATTER
F-AWNING	F-LACKER	F-LAYING

105

F-LEDGED	F-LOPPED	F-RAILER
F-LEERED	F-LOPPER	F-RANKED
F-LEGGED	F-LOWING	F-RANKER
F-LENSED	F-LUBBER	F-RANKLY
F-LICKED	F-LUMMOX	F-RAPPED
F-LICKER	F-LUMPED	F-RAZZLE
F-LIMPED	F-LUSHED	F-RIDGED
F-LINGER	F-LUSTER	F-RINGED
F-LIPPED	F-LUTING	F-RIPPER
F-LIPPER	F-LUTIST	F-RISKED
F-LITTER	F-OILING	F-RISKER
F-LOCKED	F-OXLIKE	F-ROCKED
F-LOGGED	F-OXTAIL	F-RUSHED
F-LOGGER	F-RAGGED	F-UNFAIR

Seven letters to eight

F-ALLOWED	F-LAWLESS	
F-ALTERED	F-LETCHED	F-RANKING
F-ALTERER	F-LICKING	F-RAPPING
F-EARLESS	F-LIGHTED	F-RIDGING
F-EASTING	F-LINTING	F-RIGHTEN
F-ETCHING	F-LIPPING	F-RIGIDER
F-ICKLEST	F-LOCKING	F-RIGIDLY
F-IRELESS	F-LOGGING	F-RINGING
F-LACKING	F-LOPPING	F-RISKIER
F-LAGGING	F-LOUTING	F-RISKILY
F-LAKIEST	F-LOWERED	F-RISKING
F-LANKING	F-LUSHEST	F-ROCKING
F-LAPPING	F-RAGGING	F-UNCTION
F-LASHING	F-RANKEST	F-USELESS
		F-UTILITY

Some end-hooks
Two letters to three

AL-F	ER-F	OO-F
AR-F	GI-F	OR-F
DE-F	IF-F	RE-F
DI-F	KA-F	SI-F
DO-F	KI-F	TE-F
EF-F	NE-F	WO-F
EL-F	OF-F	

Three letters to four

BAR-F	GUL-F	RIF-F
BEE-F	HOO-F	ROO-F
CHE-F	HOW-F	SEL-F
CON-F	HUM-F	SER-F
CUR-F	LEA-F	SOW-F
DIF-F	LIE-F	SUR-F
DOF-F	LOO-F	WAI-F
FIE-F	PRO-F	WOO-F
GOO-F	REE-F	

Four letters to five

BRIE-F	KALI-F	SCUR-F
GANE-F	MOTI-F	SHEA-F
GONE-F	PILA-F	SKEE-F
HOUF-F	PROO-F	SNAR-F
HOWF-F	SCAR-F	SPIF-F

F

Five letters to six

BELIE-F	GONIF-F	RELIE-F
DECAF-F	PILAF-F	

Six letters to seven

SHERIF-F

Some two-letter blockers beginning with F

FY

Some three-letter blockers beginning with F

FAE	FAX	FEZ	FRY
FAP	FEW	FLY	

Some four-letter blockers beginning with F

FASH	FIXT	FOXY
FAUX	FLED	FROM
FEET	FLIX	FUMY
FIFI	FLUX	FURY
FILS	FOGY	

Some five-letter blockers beginning with F (except words ending in '-ED', '-J', '-S', '-X', '-Y' or '-Z')

FATAL	FEWER	FOCAL
FETAL	FINCH	FOLIC
FETCH	FLOWN	FUNGO
FETID	FLUNG	

Some six-letter blockers beginning with F (except words ending in '-ED', '-J', '-S', '-X', '-Y' or '-Z')

FACEUP	FEWEST	FLYMEN
FACILE	FEYEST	FOETAL
FAIRER	FILIAL	FOETID
FAKING	FILMIC	FONDER
FALLEN	FINEST	FOREGO
FAMING	FINISH	FORGOT
FAMISH	FINITO	FOULER
FARING	FITFUL	FOXIER
FATTER	FLAXEN	FREEST
FAXING	FLETCH	FRIGID
FAZING	FLIEST	FROZEN
FECUND	FLINCH	FRUGAL
FEEING	FLORID	FUMING
FERRIC	FLUIER	FUNGIC
FERVID	FLUISH	FUNNER
FETISH	FLYEST	FUSILE
FEUDAL	FLYMAN	FUSING

F

109

Bonus words

Bonus words on your rack can be hard to spot, especially for the less experienced player. One way to help find them is by using prefixes and suffixes.

Many larger words include a common prefix or suffix – remembering these and using them where you can is a good way to discover any longer words on your rack, including any potential bonus words. The key prefixes to remember beginning with F are FOOT- and FOR- and the key suffixes are -FISH, -FORM and -FUL.

Some words beginning with FOOT-
Seven-letter words

FOOT-AGE	FOOT-ERS	FOOT-MEN
FOOT-BAG	FOOT-LED	FOOT-PAD
FOOT-BAR	FOOT-LES	FOOT-ROT
FOOT-BOY	FOOT-MAN	FOOT-WAY

Eight-letter words

FOOT-BALL	FOOT-LIKE	FOOT-SIES
FOOT-BATH	FOOT-LING	FOOT-SORE
FOOT-ERED	FOOT-MARK	FOOT-STEP
FOOT-FALL	FOOT-NOTE	FOOT-WALL
FOOT-HILL	FOOT-PATH	FOOT-WEAR
FOOT-HOLD	FOOT-RACE	FOOT-WORK
FOOT-LESS	FOOT-REST	FOOT-WORN

Some words beginning with FOR-

Seven-letter words

FOR-AGED	FOR-FEND	FOR-MICA
FOR-AGER	FOR-GAVE	FOR-MING
FOR-AGES	FOR-GETS	FOR-RAYS
FOR-BADE	FOR-GING	FOR-SAID
FOR-BEAR	FOR-GIVE	FOR-SAKE
FOR-BIDS	FOR-GOER	FOR-SOOK
FOR-BODE	FOR-GOES	FOR-TING
FOR-CEPS	FOR-GONE	FOR-WARD
FOR-DING	FOR-KIER	FOR-WARN
FOR-DONE	FOR-KING	FOR-WENT
FOR-ESTS	FOR-LORN	FOR-WORN
FOR-EVER	FOR-MATS	

Eight-letter words

FOR-AGING	FOR-GOING	FOR-SPOKE
FOR-BODED	FOR-MATED	FOR-SWEAR
FOR-ESTER	FOR-SOOTH	FOR-SWORN
FOR-GIVEN	FOR-SPEAK	FOR-TRESS
FOR-GIVER	FOR-SPEND	FOR-TUNED

Some words ending with -FISH

Seven-letter words

BAT-FISH	DEA-FISH	GEM-FISH
BOX-FISH	DOG-FISH	HAG-FISH
CAT-FISH	FIN-FISH	HOG-FISH
COD-FISH	FOX-FISH	HUF-FISH
COW-FISH	GAR-FISH	MUD-FISH

OAR-FISH	PUP-FISH	SEL-FISH
OUT-FISH	RAF-FISH	SER-FISH
PAN-FISH	RAT-FISH	SUN-FISH
PIG-FISH	RED-FISH	
PIN-FISH	SAW-FISH	

Eight-letter words

BAIT-FISH	GOLD-FISH	SALT-FISH
BLOW-FISH	GRAY-FISH	SAND-FISH
BLUE-FISH	GRUF-FISH	SCAR-FISH
BONE-FISH	KING-FISH	SNIF-FISH
CAVE-FISH	LION-FISH	STAR-FISH
CRAW-FISH	LUNG-FISH	STIF-FISH
CRAY-FISH	MONK-FISH	SUCK-FISH
DEAL-FISH	MOON-FISH	SURF-FISH
DWAR-FISH	OVER-FISH	TOAD-FISH
FLAT-FISH	PIPE-FISH	WOLF-FISH
FOOL-FISH	ROCK-FISH	
FROG-FISH	SAIL-FISH	

Some words ending with -FORM
Seven-letter words

ACI-FORM	DEI-FORM	OVI-FORM
ALI-FORM	DIF-FORM	PER-FORM
AUS-FORM	DIS-FORM	PRE-FORM
AVI-FORM	ISO-FORM	TRI-FORM
CON-FORM	MIS-FORM	UNI-FORM

Eight-letter words

AERI-FORM	MANI-FORM	PYRI-FORM
CONI-FORM	OMNI-FORM	ROTI-FORM
CUBI-FORM	PALI-FORM	SLIP-FORM
FREE-FORM	PARA-FORM	TUBI-FORM
FUSI-FORM	PLAN-FORM	URSI-FORM
LAND-FORM	PLAT-FORM	VARI-FORM
LYRI-FORM	POST-FORM	WAVE-FORM

Some words ending with -FUL
Seven-letter words

ARMS-FUL	FORK-FUL	PAIN-FUL
BALE-FUL	FRET-FUL	PALM-FUL
BANE-FUL	GAIN-FUL	PITI-FUL
BASH-FUL	GLEE-FUL	PLAY-FUL
BOAT-FUL	GUTS-FUL	RAGE-FUL
BOWL-FUL	HAND-FUL	REST-FUL
BRIM-FUL	HARM-FUL	RISK-FUL
CARE-FUL	HATE-FUL	SACK-FUL
DARE-FUL	HEED-FUL	SKIL-FUL
DEED-FUL	HELP-FUL	SKIN-FUL
DIRE-FUL	HOPE-FUL	SOUL-FUL
DOLE-FUL	HURT-FUL	TACT-FUL
DUTI-FUL	LUNG-FUL	TANK-FUL
FACT-FUL	LUST-FUL	TEAR-FUL
FATE-FUL	MIND-FUL	TUNE-FUL
FEAR-FUL	NEED-FUL	WAKE-FUL
FIST-FUL	PAIL-FUL	WILL-FUL

F

Eight-letter words

BELLY-FUL	GLASS-FUL	SKILL-FUL
BLAME-FUL	GRACE-FUL	SPITE-FUL
BLISS-FUL	GRATE-FUL	SPOON-FUL
BOAST-FUL	GUILE-FUL	TASTE-FUL
CHEER-FUL	HASTE-FUL	THANK-FUL
COLOR-FUL	MERCI-FUL	TRUST-FUL
DIRGE-FUL	MIRTH-FUL	TRUTH-FUL
DOUBT-FUL	MOURN-FUL	UNLAW-FUL
DREAD-FUL	MOUTH-FUL	VENGE-FUL
EVENT-FUL	PEACE-FUL	WASTE-FUL
FAITH-FUL	PLATE-FUL	WATCH-FUL
FANCI-FUL	POWER-FUL	WRATH-FUL
FORCE-FUL	RIGHT-FUL	WRONG-FUL
FRUIT-FUL	SCORN-FUL	YOUTH-FUL
GHAST-FUL	SHAME-FUL	

Handy Hint

A useful way to visualise your options is to SHUFFLE (16 points) the tiles on your rack. If you rearrange tiles, place them in alphabetical order or try to form prefixes, suffixes or verb inflections you stand a better chance of thinking up good words to play.

F

Unusual letter combinations

If you have an unusual combination of letters on your rack, or want to impress your opponent with an unusual word, a few words from World English can come in handy. Here are some beginning with F.

Australian words

FASTIE   deceitful act
FESTY   dirty or smelly
FIGJAM   very conceited person
FIZGIG   frivolous or flirtatious girl
FOULIE   bad mood
FRIB   short heavy-conditioned piece of wool
FURPHY   rumour or fictitious story

F

G

₂

G begins only three two-letter words in Scrabble: GI (a suit worn by martial arts practitioners, 3 points), GO and GU (a kind of violin from Shetland, 3 points). G also combines well with Y to form quite a few short words including GAY, GEY (a Scots word for very, 7 points), GOY (a Yiddish word for a person who is not Jewish, 7 points), GUY and also GYM and GYP (9 points each).

Two-letter words beginning with G

GI	GO	GU

Some three-letter words beginning with G

GAB	GEL	GJU	GUB
GAD	GEN	GNU	GUE
GAE	GHI	GOA	GUL
GAL	GIB	GOE	GUP
GAM	GID	GON	GUR
GAN	GIE	GOO	GUV
GAR	GIF	GOR	GYM
GAT	GIO	GOV	GYP
GED	GIP	GOX	
GEE	GIT	GOY	

Hooks

Hooking requires a subtle change in a player's thought process, in that they must look at words already on the board without becoming distracted by their pronunciation.

Some front-hooks
Two letters to three

G-AB	G-AS	G-ET	G-NU	G-OX
G-AD	G-AT	G-HI	G-OB	G-OY
G-AE	G-AY	G-ID	G-OD	G-UM
G-AG	G-ED	G-IF	G-OE	G-UN
G-AL	G-EE	G-IN	G-ON	G-UP
G-AM	G-EL	G-IO	G-OO	G-UR
G-AN	G-EM	G-IS	G-OR	G-US
G-AR	G-EN	G-IT	G-OS	G-UT

Three letters to four

G-AFF	G-ASH	G-LAD
G-AGA	G-ASP	G-LAM
G-AGE	G-ATE	G-LEE
G-AIN	G-AVE	G-LIB
G-AIT	G-EAR	G-LID
G-ALA	G-EEK	G-LOB
G-ALE	G-ELD	G-LOW
G-ALL	G-ELT	G-LUG
G-APE	G-ENE	G-LUM
G-ARB	G-ILL	G-NAT

G

G-NAW	G-OWN	G-RIP
G-OAT	G-RAD	G-RIT
G-OES	G-RAM	G-ROT
G-OLD	G-RAN	G-ROW
G-ONE	G-RAY	G-RUB
G-OOF	G-REW	G-RUE
G-OON	G-RID	G-URN
G-ORE	G-RIM	
G-OUT	G-RIN	

Four letters to five

G-ABLE	G-LASS	G-ONER
G-AGED	G-LAZE	G-OOFY
G-AGER	G-LAZY	G-OOSE
G-ALLY	G-LEAM	G-OOSY
G-APED	G-LEAN	G-RACE
G-APER	G-LINT	G-RADE
G-AUNT	G-LOAM	G-RAFT
G-AVEL	G-LOBE	G-RAIL
G-EMMY	G-LODE	G-RAIN
G-HAST	G-LOOM	G-RAND
G-HOST	G-LOOP	G-RANT
G-ILLS	G-LORY	G-RASP
G-ILLY	G-LOSS	G-RATE
G-IRON	G-LOST	G-RAVE
G-LACE	G-LOUT	G-RAZE
G-LADE	G-LOVE	G-REED
G-LADY	G-LUTE	G-REEK
G-LAND	G-NOME	G-REEN
G-LARE	G-OLDY	

G

Five letters to six

G-ABLED	G-ENDER	G-RAVER
G-ABOON	G-ENTRY	G-RAYED
G-ADDED	G-INNER	G-RAZED
G-ADDER	G-LANCE	G-REAVE
G-AGGER	G-LAZED	G-REEDY
G-AGING	G-LOBED	G-RIMED
G-ALLEY	G-LOOPY	G-RIPED
G-ALLOW	G-LOSSY	G-ROPED
G-AMBIT	G-LOVED	G-ROUND
G-AMBLE	G-LOWER	G-ROUSE
G-AMINE	G-NOMIC	G-ROVED
G-AMMON	G-OLDEN	G-ROWER
G-APING	G-OLDER	G-RUBBY
G-ARGLE	G-RACED	G-RUING
G-ASHED	G-RAINY	G-RUMPY
G-ASPER	G-RANGE	G-UNMAN
G-ASTER	G-RATED	G-URNED
G-AUGER	G-RATER	G-USHER
G-EARED	G-RAVED	G-UTTER
G-ELATE	G-RAVEL	
G-ELDER	G-RAVEN	

G

Six letters to seven

G-ABLING	G-LINTED	G-RIDDED
G-ADDING	G-LISTEN	G-RIDDER
G-ALLIED	G-LISTER	G-RIDDLE
G-AMBLED	G-LITTER	G-RIFTED
G-AMBLER	G-LOOMED	G-RILLED
G-ASHING	G-LOOPED	G-RIMMER
G-AUNTLY	G-LOVING	G-RINDED
G-EARING	G-LOWING	G-RIPING
G-ELATED	G-OLDEST	G-RIPPED
G-ELDING	G-OLDISH	G-RIPPER
G-ESTATE	G-OWNING	G-ROOMED
G-HOSTED	G-RACING	G-ROOMER
G-HOSTLY	G-RAFTED	G-ROPING
G-IGGING	G-RAFTER	G-ROUSED
G-IZZARD	G-RAINED	G-ROUSER
G-LACIER	G-RANGER	G-ROUTED
G-LADDER	G-RANTED	G-ROUTER
G-LANCED	G-RANTER	G-ROWING
G-LANCER	G-RAPIER	G-RUBBED
G-LAZIER	G-RAPING	G-RUBBER
G-LAZILY	G-RASPED	G-RUFFED
G-LAZING	G-RASPER	G-RUFFLY
G-LEAMED	G-RATIFY	G-RUMBLE
G-LEANED	G-RATING	G-RUMMER
G-LEANER	G-RAVING	G-RUMPED
G-LEEING	G-RAYING	G-RUNTED
G-LIBBED	G-RAZING	G-UNLESS
G-LIBBER	G-REAVED	G-UNSHOT
G-LIMMER	G-REEKED	

Seven letters to eight

G-ALLOWED
G-AMBLING
G-ANGLING
G-ARGLING
G-EARLESS
G-ELASTIC
G-ELATING
G-ESTATED
G-HASTING
G-HOSTING
G-LANCING
G-LAZIEST
G-LEAMING
G-LEANERS
G-LEANING
G-LIBBING
G-LINTIER
G-LINTING

G-LITTERY
G-LOAMING
G-LOOMING
G-LOOPIER
G-LOOPING
G-LOWERED
G-LUGGING
G-NATTIER
G-OATLIKE
G-OFFERED
G-OLDENED
G-ONENESS
G-RAFTING
G-RAINIER
G-RAINING
G-RANTING
G-RANULAR
G-RASPING

G-RAVELLY
G-REEDIER
G-REEDILY
G-RIDDLED
G-RIEVING
G-RIFTING
G-RILLING
G-RIPPING
G-ROOMING
G-ROUNDED
G-ROUNDER
G-ROUSING
G-ROUTING
G-ROWABLE
G-RUMBLED
G-UNMAKER
G-UNSTOCK
G-UTTERED

G

Handy Hint

Some unusual and high-scoring words beginning with G are GJU (a variant spelling of GU, 11 points), GOX (form of gaseous oxygen, 11 points), GUANXI (Chinese social concept based on the exchange of favours, 14 points) and GYOZA (Japanese fried dumplings, 18 points).

Some end-hooks
Two letters to three

BA-G	FA-G	MA-G	RE-G
BE-G	FE-G	ME-G	SO-G
BI-G	GI-G	MI-G	TA-G
BO-G	HA-G	MO-G	TE-G
DA-G	HO-G	MU-G	TI-G
DE-G	JA-G	NA-G	TO-G
DI-G	JO-G	NE-G	WO-G
DO-G	LA-G	NO-G	YA-G
EN-G	LI-G	PE-G	YU-G
ER-G	LO-G	PI-G	ZA-G

Three letters to four

AGO-G	FRO-G	RAN-G
BAN-G	GAN-G	RIN-G
BIN-G	GON-G	RUN-G
BIO-G	HAN-G	SAN-G
BON-G	HUN-G	SIN-G
BRA-G	KIN-G	SON-G
BUN-G	LIN-G	SUN-G
BUR-G	MAR-G	TAN-G
DAN-G	MUN-G	TIN-G
DIN-G	PAN-G	TON-G
DON-G	PIN-G	WIN-G
DUN-G	PLU-G	ZIN-G
FAN-G	PRO-G	
FRA-G	QUA-G	

Four letters to five

AGIN-G	GULA-G	THIN-G
BEIN-G	RUIN-G	THON-G
BLIN-G	SPAN-G	TYIN-G
BRIN-G	STUN-G	
CLAN-G	SWAN-G	

Five letters to six

ACTIN-G	LAWIN-G	RAVIN-G
BASIN-G	LAYIN-G	RICIN-G
BELON-G	LIKIN-G	ROBIN-G
CONIN-G	LININ-G	ROSIN-G
COVIN-G	MATIN-G	SAVIN-G
ELFIN-G	MIRIN-G	SEWIN-G
GAMIN-G	PAVIN-G	TAKIN-G
LAKIN-G	PURIN-G	TAMIN-G

Six letters to seven

BOBBIN-G	HOGGIN-G	OUTWIN-G
BUGGIN-G	JERKIN-G	OVERDO-G
BUSKIN-G	MERLIN-G	PARKIN-G
COPPIN-G	MUFFIN-G	PIPPIN-G
CUFFIN-G	MUNTIN-G	PUFFIN-G
CYCLIN-G	MURLIN-G	RAISIN-G
DENTIN-G	NOGGIN-G	RENNIN-G
DUBBIN-G	OUTRAN-G	ROBBIN-G
GRADIN-G	OUTRUN-G	TANNIN-G
GRATIN-G	OUTSIN-G	TIFFIN-G

G

Seven letters to eight

ASPIRIN-G	MAHJONG-G	RESILIN-G
CHITLIN-G	MORPHIN-G	SCULPIN-G
CREATIN-G	PUMPKIN-G	SPELDIN-G
CRISPIN-G	RATTLIN-G	SPONGIN-G
GELATIN-G	RAVELIN-G	UNDERDO-G
LITTLIN-G	RELAXIN-G	

Blockers

It is useful to know which words are blockers and can't therefore be extended before or after. You may want to play a blocker that your opponent can't extend, or you may want to avoid playing a blocker because you want to keep the board open.

Some three-letter blockers beginning with G

GEY	GOX

Some four-letter blockers beginning with G

GAGA	GAZY	GIZZ
GAMY	GEED	GORY
GASH	GEEZ	

Some five-letter blockers beginning with G (except words ending in '-ED', '-J', '-S', '-X', '-Y' or '-Z')

GEESE	GLIAL	GOYIM
GELID	GNASH	GREEK
GENAL	GNAWN	GROWN
GEYER	GONNA	GULCH
GHEST	GONZO	GURSH
GINZO	GOTTA	GYRAL

Some six-letter blockers beginning with G (except words ending in '-ED', '-J', '-S', '-X', '-Y' or '-Z')

GAMEST	GEEING	GOOIER
GAMIER	GEMINI	GORIER
GARDAI	GENIAL	GOTTEN
GARISH	GIBING	GRAVEN
GASHER	GIDDUP	GRAYER
GASLIT	GLOBAL	GREEBO
GASMAN	GLUIER	GREYER
GASMEN	GLUING	GRINCH
GAYEST	GNOMIC	GUNMAN
GEDDIT	GOLDER	GUNMEN

G

Bonus words

Bonus words on your rack can be hard to spot, especially for the less experienced player. One way to help finding them is by using prefixes and suffixes.

Many larger words include a common prefix or suffix – remembering these and using them where you can is a good way to discover any longer words on your rack, including any potential bonus words. The key suffixes to remember ending with G are -GEN and -GRAM.

Some words ending with -GEN
Seven-letter words

ANTI-GEN	INDI-GEN	PYRO-GEN
CRYO-GEN	LOXY-GEN	SMID-GEN
ENDO-GEN	MUTA-GEN	TRUD-GEN
HALO-GEN	ONCO-GEN	TWIG-GEN

Eight-letter words

ABORI-GEN	ENLAR-GEN	NITRO-GEN
ALLER-GEN	ESTRO-GEN	PATHO-GEN
ANDRO-GEN	HISTO-GEN	PHOTO-GEN
COLLA-GEN	HYDRO-GEN	
CYANO-GEN	MISCE-GEN	

Some words ending with -GRAM
Seven-letter words

ANA-GRAM	ISO-GRAM	TAN-GRAM
DIA-GRAM	MYO-GRAM	TRI-GRAM
EPI-GRAM	PAN-GRAM	
GRO-GRAM	PRO-GRAM	

Eight-letter words

AERO-GRAM	HEXA-GRAM	LEXI-GRAM
DECA-GRAM	HOLO-GRAM	MONO-GRAM
DECI-GRAM	IDEO-GRAM	NANO-GRAM
ETHO-GRAM	IDIO-GRAM	SONO-GRAM
GENO-GRAM	KILO-GRAM	TELE-GRAM

G

Unusual letter combinations

If you have an unusual combination of letters on your rack, or want to impress your opponent with an unusual word, a few words from World English can come in handy.

Australian words

GALAH	grey-and-pink cockatoo
GARBO	dustman
GEEBUNG	tree with edible but tasteless fruit
GIDGEE	small acacia tree that sometimes emits an unpleasant smell
GILGAI	natural water hole
GING	child's catapult

GNOW	ground-dwelling bird
GOANNA	monitor lizard
GOOG	egg
GUNYAH	bush hut or shelter
GYMPIE	tall tree with stinging hairs on its leaves

Canadian words

| GROWLER | small iceberg that has broken off from a larger iceberg or glacier |

Hindi words

GAUR	large wild cow
GARIAL	fish-eating crocodilian with long slender snout
GHARRI	horse-drawn vehicle for hire
GHAT	stairs or passage leading down to a river
GHEE	clarified butter
GHERAO	industrial action in which workers imprison their employers
GINGILI	oil obtained from sesame seeds
GORAL	small goat antelope
GUAR	plant that produces gum
GUNNY	coarse fabric used for sacks

New Zealand words

| GRAUNCH | crush or destroy |

South African words

| GEELBEK | yellow-jawed fish |

H₄

Essential info
Value: 4 points
Number in set: 2

H begins a two-letter word with every vowel except for U (although it can form UH, a sound that people make when they are unsure about something, 5 points), making it very useful for forming short words in different directions. As H is worth 4 points, these words can return very high scores in conjunction with premium squares despite their brevity: HA, HE, HI and HO are all worth 5 points.

Two-letter words beginning with H

HA   HE   HI   HM   HO

Some three-letter words beginning with H

HAE	HET	HOA	HOY
HAH	HEW	HOC	HUB
HAJ	HEX	HOD	HUH
HAN	HEY	HOH	HUN
HAO	HIC	HOI	HUP
HAP	HIE	HOM	HYE
HAW	HIN	HON	HYP
HEH	HIS	HOO	
HEP	HMM	HOX	

129

Hooks

Hooking requires a subtle change in a player's thought process, in that they must look at words already on the board without becoming distracted by their pronunciation.

Some front-hooks
Two letters to three

H-AD	H-EM	H-OB	H-OX
H-AE	H-EN	H-OD	H-OY
H-AG	H-ER	H-OE	H-UG
H-AH	H-ES	H-OH	H-UH
H-AM	H-ET	H-OI	H-UM
H-AN	H-EX	H-OM	H-UN
H-AS	H-ID	H-ON	H-UP
H-AT	H-IN	H-OO	H-UT
H-AW	H-IS	H-OP	H-YE
H-AY	H-IT	H-OS	
H-EH	H-MM	H-OW	

Three letters to four

H-AFT	H-ALF	H-ART
H-AHA	H-ALL	H-ASP
H-AIL	H-ALT	H-ATE
H-AIN	H-AND	H-AVE
H-AIR	H-ARD	H-EAR
H-AKA	H-ARE	H-EAT
H-AKE	H-ARK	H-EEL
H-ALE	H-ARM	H-EFT

H-ELL	H-ISH	H-OOP
H-ELM	H-OAR	H-OOT
H-ERE	H-OBO	H-OPE
H-ICK	H-OLD	H-OSE
H-IDE	H-OLE	H-OUR
H-ILL	H-ONE	H-OWL
H-IRE	H-OOF	H-UMP

Four letters to five

H-AIRY	H-EAST	H-INKY
H-ARDS	H-EATH	H-IRED
H-ARED	H-EAVE	H-ITCH
H-ASHY	H-ECHT	H-OARY
H-AULD	H-EDGE	H-OAST
H-AUNT	H-EDGY	H-ONER
H-AVER	H-EXED	H-OVEN
H-AWED	H-EXES	H-OVER
H-EARD	H-EYED	

Five letters to six

H-ACKER	H-ASHED	H-ILLER
H-AILED	H-AUGHT	H-INTER
H-AIRED	H-AWING	H-IRING
H-ALLOW	H-EARTH	H-ITCHY
H-ALTER	H-EATER	H-OLDEN
H-ANGER	H-EAVED	H-OLDER
H-ARBOR	H-EDGED	H-OTTER
H-ARMED	H-EDGER	H-OWLED
H-ARMER	H-EIGHT	H-OWLER
H-ARROW	H-EXING	H-USHER

Six letters to seven

H-AILING	H-ASHIER	H-EDGING
H-AIRIER	H-ASHING	H-EIGHTH
H-AIRING	H-AUNTER	H-ERRING
H-AMBLED	H-AUTEUR	H-INKIER
H-ARBOUR	H-EARING	H-ITCHED
H-ARKING	H-EATING	H-OVERED
H-ARMFUL	H-EAVING	H-OWLING
H-ARMING	H-EDGIER	H-UPPING

Seven letters to eight

H-AIRIEST	H-ARBORED	H-ITCHILY
H-AIRLESS	H-ARMLESS	H-ITCHING
H-AIRLIKE	H-ARROWED	H-OVERFLY
H-AIRLINE	H-EATABLE	H-OVERING
H-AIRLOCK	H-EDGIEST	H-USHERED
H-ALLOWED	H-INKIEST	
H-ALTERED	H-ITCHIER	

Some end-hooks
Two letters to three

AA-H	ET-H	LA-H	RE-H
AS-H	FA-H	NA-H	SH-H
BA-H	FE-H	NO-H	SO-H
BO-H	HA-H	OO-H	UG-H
DA-H	HE-H	PA-H	YA-H
DO-H	HO-H	PE-H	YE-H
ED-H	IS-H	PO-H	

Three letters to four

ARC-H	GAS-H	MAT-H	POS-H
BAC-H	GOS-H	MES-H	PUS-H
BAS-H	GOT-H	MET-H	RAS-H
BAT-H	GUS-H	MOS-H	SHA-H
BOO-H	HAS-H	MOT-H	SIT-H
BOT-H	HAT-H	MUS-H	SUK-H
BUS-H	HET-H	NIS-H	TAS-H
COS-H	HIS-H	NOS-H	TEC-H
DAS-H	HOG-H	OAT-H	UMP-H
DIS-H	KIT-H	PAS-H	WAS-H
DOS-H	LAS-H	PAT-H	WIS-H
DOT-H	LAT-H	PEC-H	WIT-H
EAT-H	MAC-H	PIT-H	YEA-H
FAS H	MAS-H	POO-H	

Four letters to five

BOOT-H	HUMP-H	SOUT-H
BRAS-H	LEAS-H	SWAT-H
BRUS-H	MARC-H	SYNC-H
BUMP-H	MARS-H	TENT-H
BURG-H	MERC-H	THIG-H
CLOT-H	MYNA-H	TOOT-H
CRUS-H	NEAT-H	TORA-H
FLUS-H	PLUS-H	TORC-H
FORT-H	SCAT-H	WOOS-H
FRIT-H	SLOT-H	WORT-H
GIRT-H	SMIT-H	
HEAT-H	SOOT-H	

Five letters to six

COMET-H	HOOKA-H	POLIS-H
DELIS-H	HURRA-H	PUNKA-H
EIGHT-H	HUZZA-H	SHEIK-H
FATWA-H	LOOFA-H	SHIVA-H
FELLA-H	MULLA-H	SUNNA-H
FINIS-H	PARIS-H	WALLA-H
HEART-H	PERIS-H	

Six letters to seven

AARRGH-H	OUTWIT-H	SABBAT-H
HAGGIS-H	QABALA-H	

Seven letters to eight

BEGORRA-H	MADRASA-H	PEISHWA-H
HOSANNA-H	MESHUGA-H	SAVANNA-H
HYDRANT-H	NARGILE-H	SCAMPIS-H
KHALIFA-H	OCTOPUS-H	VERANDA-H

Blockers

It is useful to know which words are blockers and can't therefore be extended before or after. You may want to play a blocker that your opponent can't extend, or you may want to avoid playing a blocker because you want to keep the board open.

Some three-letter blockers beginning with H

HEX	HMM	HOX

Some four-letter blockers beginning with H

HAZY	HOAX	HUNG
HELD	HOLY	
HIYA	HUED	

Some five-letter blockers beginning with H (except words ending in '-ED', '-J', '-S', '-X', '-Y' or '-Z')

HARSH	HOOCH	HUNCH
HAULT	HOVEN	HUTCH
HAUTE	HUGER	
HOING	HUMID	

Some six-letter blockers beginning with H (except words ending in '-ED', '-J', '-S', '-X', '-Y' or '-Z')

HABILE	HITMEN	HOSING
HARDER	HOLDEN	HOWZAT
HATING	HOLIER	HUGEST
HAUNCH	HOOTCH	HYENIC
HAZIER	HOOVEN	HYMNIC
HIKING	HOPING	
HITMAN	HORRID	

H

Bonus words

Bonus words on your rack can be hard to spot, especially for the less experienced player. One way to help find them is by using prefixes and suffixes.

Many larger words include a common prefix or suffix – remembering these and using them where you can is a good way to discover any longer words on your rack, including any potential bonus words. The key suffixes to remember ending with H are -HOLE, -HOOD and -HORN.

Some words ending with -HOLE
Seven-letter words

AIR-HOLE	KEY-HOLE	PIN-HOLE
ARM-HOLE	LUG-HOLE	POT-HOLE
EYE-HOLE	MAN-HOLE	SPY-HOLE
FOX-HOLE	PIE-HOLE	

Eight-letter words

BLOW-HOLE	HELL-HOLE	PORT-HOLE
BOLT-HOLE	KNOT-HOLE	SINK-HOLE
BORE-HOLE	LOOP-HOLE	WELL-HOLE
BUNG-HOLE	PEEP-HOLE	WOOD-HOLE
FEED-HOLE	PLUG-HOLE	WORM-HOLE

Some words ending with -HOOD
Seven-letter words

BOY-HOOD	LAD-HOOD	SON-HOOD
GOD-HOOD	MAN-HOOD	

Eight-letter words

AUNT-HOOD	LADY-HOOD	PUMP-HOOD
BABY-HOOD	MAID-HOOD	SELF-HOOD
DOLL-HOOD	MISS-HOOD	SERF-HOOD
GIRL-HOOD	MONK-HOOD	WIFE-HOOD
IDLE-HOOD	PAGE-HOOD	WIVE-HOOD
KING-HOOD	POPE-HOOD	

Some words ending with -HORN
Seven-letter words

ALP-HORN	FOG-HORN	TIN-HORN
BET-HORN	INK-HORN	UNS-HORN
BIG-HORN	LEG-HORN	
DIS-HORN	SAX-HORN	

Eight-letter words

BOXT-HORN	DEER-HORN	RAMS-HORN
BUCK-HORN	HAWT-HORN	SHOE-HORN
BULL-HORN	LONG-HORN	STAG-HORN

Unusual letter combinations

If you have an unusual combination of letters on your rack, or want to impress your opponent with an unusual word, a few words from World English can come in handy.

Australian words

HAKEA	type of shrub or tree
HOVEA	plant with purple flowers
HUTCHIE	groundsheet draped over an upright stick as a shelter

Canadian words

HONKER Canada goose

Hindi words

HARTAL	act of closing shop or stopping work as a political protest
HOWDAH	seat for riding on an elephant's back

New Zealand words

Many Maori words start with the letter H, and if you have an H alongside a selection of vowels you may be able to play some of the following:

HAKA	war dance
HANGI	open-air cooking pit
HAPU	subtribe
HAPUKA	large fish
HEITIKI	neck ornament

HIKOI	protest march
HOKONUI	illicit whisky
HONGI	nose-touching greeting
HUHU	hairy beetle
HUI	conference or meeting
HUIA	extinct New Zealand bird

H

Handy Hint

Some short, useful words starting with H and using power tiles are HAJ (Muslim pilgrimage to Mecca, 13 points, also its variant forms HAJJ and HADJ), HAZF (16 points), HAZY (19 points), HEX (a curse or spell, 13 points) and HOX (a Shakespearean word meaning to cut a horse's hamstring, also 13).

Essential info
Value: 1 point
Number in set: 9

I can be a tricky letter to use in multiples so you need to try and use an I as soon as you can to avoid getting two of them. There are plenty of two-letter words beginning with I to help you make good-scoring parallel plays as shown below. The higher-scoring three letter words beginning with I are worth making note of, such as ICY (8 points), IVY (9 points) and IMP (7 points). The I can also be vital for reaping points with a Q or X with QI or XI. The I is also one of the letters of the RETAIN set and is therefore a good letter to keep if trying to get a bonus word.

Two-letter words beginning with I

ID	IF	IN	IO	IS	IT

Some three-letter words beginning with I

ICH	ION	ISO
ICK	IRE	ITA
IDE	ISH	
IFF	ISM	

Hooks

Hooking requires a subtle change in a player's thought process, in that they must look at words already on the board without becoming distracted by their pronunciation.

Some front-hooks
Two letters to three

I-CH	I-OS	I-SO
I-DE	I-RE	I-TA
I-ON	I-SH	

Three letters to four

I-BIS	I-KON	I-RES
I-CON	I-LEA	I-RID
I-DEE	I-LEX	I-SIT
I-DOL	I-MAM	I-SOS
I-GAD	I-MID	I-TAS
I-KAT	I-RED	I-URE

Four letters to five

I-DANT	I-MAGE	I-RATE
I-DEAL	I-MINE	I-RING
I-DEES	I-MINO	I-RONE
I-DENT	I-NANE	I-SLED
I-GAPO	I-ODIC	I-VIED
I-LEAL	I-RADE	

Five letters to six

I-CONIC	I-ODISM	I-SATIN
I-GUANA	I-ONIUM	I-SLING
I-LEXES	I-RATER	I-TEMED
I-NYALA	I-RISES	

Six letters to seven

I-MAGISM	I-RISING	I-SOLATE

Seven letters to eight

I-CONICAL	I-SLANDER
I-SABELLA	I-SOLATED

I

Handy Hint

If you have enough letters to form the suffix -ING, you could be well on the way to scoring a bonus word for 50 points. Look at the other letters on your rack and try to form a word ending in -ING (there are thousands!). But don't hang on to -ING at all costs, as by doing so you are restricting yourself to playing with just four letters, with the consequent likelihood of low scores.

Some end-hooks

Two letters to three

AH-I	HO-I	PO-I
AM-I	JA-I	RE-I
AN-I	KA-I	TA-I
BO-I	KO-I	UN-I
CH-I	MO-I	
DE-I	OB-I	

Three letters to four

ANT-I	HAJ-I	PEN-I
ART-I	IMP-I	PER-I
BAN-I	KAK-I	PIP-I
BEN-I	LOB-I	PUR-I
BID-I	LOT-I	QUA-I
BUD-I	MAG-I	RAG-I
CAD-I	MAL-I	RAM-I
CAP-I	MAN-I	RAN-I
CHA-I	MAX-I	ROT-I
CON-I	MID-I	SAD-I
DAL-I	MIR-I	SAR-I
DEF-I	MOD-I	SAT-I
DEL-I	MOM-I	SIR-I
DEN-I	MOT-I	TAB-I
DIV-I	MUN-I	TAX-I
FEN-I	NID-I	TIP-I
FIN-I	NOD-I	TOP-I
GAD-I	NON-I	TOR-I
GAR-I	PAD-I	

Four letters to five

BASS-I	FAST-I	MACH-I
BAST-I	FERM-I	MYTH-I
BEST-I	FILM-I	PARK-I
BIND-I	FUND-I	PART-I
BUFF-I	FUNG-I	POOR-I
CAMP-I	GLOB-I	PRIM-I
CARD-I	HADJ-I	PULL-I
CARP-I	HAJJ-I	PUTT-I
CELL-I	HANG-I	ROST-I
COAT-I	HONG-I	SENS-I
COMB-I	HOUR-I	SENT-I
CORN-I	JINN-I	SWAM-I
CROC-I	LASS-I	TANG-I
CULT-I	LENT-I	TARS-I
CURL-I	LIMB-I	TEMP-I
DILL-I	LOGO-I	VILL-I
DISC-I	LUNG-I	VOLT-I

Five letters to six

ANNUL-I	FRACT-I	SCAMP-I
AVANT-I	GARDA-I	SENSE-I
CAROL-I	GLUTE-I	SHALL-I
CHICH-I	HAIKA-I	SILEN-I
CHILL-I	JEHAD-I	SMALT-I
COLON-I	JIHAD-I	SOLID-I
CUBIT-I	KAIKA-I	STELA-I
DENAR-I	MANAT-I	TAPET-I
DJINN-I	POLYP-I	YOGIN-I
EQUAL-I	RHOMB-I	

144

Six letters to seven

ACANTH-I	DENARI-I	REVERS-I
AFGHAN-I	HALLAL-I	RHYTHM-I
BANDAR-I	JAMPAN-I	SECOND-I
CHIASM-I	MARTIN-I	SHIKAR-I
DACTYL-I	PAESAN-I	SIGNOR-I
DEMENT-I	QAWWAL-I	TYMPAN-I

Seven letters to eight

BRAHMAN-I	CONDUCT-I	MARCHES-I
CALAMAR-I	DRACHMA-I	PARCHES-I
CAPITAN-I	FASCISM-I	PERFECT-I
CONCEPT-I	FASCIST-I	SIGNIOR-I
CONCERT-I	HETAIRA-I	TANDOOR-I

Blockers

It is useful to know which words are blockers and can't therefore be extended before or after. You may want to play a blocker that your opponent can't extend, or you may want to avoid playing a blocker because you want to keep the board open.

Some four-letter blockers beginning with I

IBIS	IDLY	INLY

Some five-letter blockers beginning with I (except words ending in '-ED', '-J', '-S', '-X', '-Y' or '-Z')

ICTIC	IMINO	INEPT	INUST
ILEAC	IMSHI	INERM	IODIC
ILEAL	INAPT	INFRA	ISNAE
ILIAC	INBYE	INTIL	
IMIDO	INCUT	INTRA	

Some six-letter blockers beginning with I (except words ending in '-ED', '-J', '-S', '-X', '-Y' or '-Z')

ICEMEN	INFIMA	INWITH
ICONIC	INGRAM	INWORN
IDLEST	INKJET	IRATER
INANER	INLAID	IRIDAL
INBENT	INMESH	IRIDIC
INBORN	INMOST	IRITIC
INCUBI	INRUSH	IRREAL
INFELT	INTACT	ITSELF
INFERE	INTIRE	

I

Bonus words

Bonus words on your rack can be hard to spot, especially for the less experienced player. One way to help find them is by using prefixes and suffixes.

Many larger words include a common prefix or suffix – remembering these and using them where you can is a good way to discover any longer words on your rack, including any potential bonus words. The key prefixes to remember beginning with I are IM-, IN- and ISO- and the key suffixes are -IBLE, -IFY, -INGS, -ISE, -ISH, -ISM, -IST, -ITY and -IUM.

Some words beginning with IM-
Seven-letter words

IM-AGERS	IM-PALER	IM-PLIED
IM-AGING	IM-PANEL	IM-PORTS
IM-BURSE	IM-PARTS	IM-POSED
IM-MENSE	IM-PASSE	IM-POUND
IM-MORAL	IM-PEACH	IM-PRESS
IM-PACTS	IM-PEDES	IM-PRINT
IM-PAIRS	IM-PENDS	IM-PROVE
IM-PALAS	IM-PERIL	IM-PULSE
IM-PALED	IM-PLANT	IM-PURER

Eight-letter words

IM-BARKED	IM-PARTED	IM-PROPER
IM-BODIED	IM-PENDED	IM-PROVED
IM-MATURE	IM-PLYING	IM-PROVER
IM-MOBILE	IM-POLITE	IM-PUDENT
IM-MODEST	IM-PORTED	IM-PURELY
IM-MORTAL	IM-POSING	IM-PUREST
IM-PAIRED	IM-POSTER	IM-PURITY
IM-PALING	IM-POTENT	
IM-PARITY	IM-PRISON	

Some words beginning with IN-
Seven-letter words

IN-BOUND	IN-FIRMS	IN-QUIRE
IN-BUILT	IN-FLAME	IN-ROADS
IN-CASED	IN-FORCE	IN-SANER
IN-CENSE	IN-FORMS	IN-SECTS
IN-CITED	IN-FRACT	IN-SIDER
IN-COMER	IN-FUSED	IN-SIGHT
IN-DENTS	IN-GESTS	IN-SISTS
IN-DEXES	IN-GRAIN	IN-SNARE
IN-DICES	IN-GRATE	IN-SOFAR
IN-DICTS	IN-GROWN	IN-SOLES
IN-DOORS	IN-HABIT	IN-SPIRE
IN-DORSE	IN-HALED	IN-STALL
IN-DUCTS	IN-HUMAN	IN-STATE
IN-EXACT	IN-LAYER	IN-STEAD
IN-FAMED	IN-MATES	IN-STEPS
IN-FESTS	IN-NARDS	IN-STILL
IN-FIGHT	IN-QUEST	IN-SURED

IN-TAKES   IN-TONER   IN-VERSE
IN-TENDS   IN-VADED   IN-VESTS
IN-TENSE   IN-VALID   IN-VOLVE
IN-TERNS   IN-VENTS   IN-WARDS

Eight-letter words

IN-ACTION   IN-EQUITY   IN-PUTTED
IN-ACTIVE   IN-EXPERT   IN-SANELY
IN-BREEDS   IN-FAMOUS   IN-SANITY
IN-CENSED   IN-FESTER   IN-SCRIBE
IN-CITING   IN-FILLED   IN-SECURE
IN-CLOSED   IN-FINITE   IN-SHRINE
IN-COMING   IN-FIRMER   IN-SISTER
IN-CREASE   IN-FLIGHT   IN-STANCE
IN-CURRED   IN-FORMAL   IN-STATED
IN-DEBTED   IN-FORMED   IN-TERNAL
IN-DECENT   IN-FRINGE   IN-THRALL
IN-DENTED   IN-FUSION   IN-TREPID
IN-DIGEST   IN-GROUND   IN-VENTED
IN-DIRECT   IN-GROWTH   IN-VIABLE
IN-DOLENT   IN-HUMANE
IN-EDIBLE   IN-JURIES

Some words beginning with ISO-

Seven-letter words

ISO-BARS	ISO-LATE	ISO-TOPE
ISO-DOSE	ISO-MERE	ISO-TRON
ISO-FORM	ISO-PODS	ISO-TYPE
ISO-GRAM	ISO-TONE	

Eight-letter words

ISO-BARIC	ISO-GRAPH	ISO-TONIC
ISO-BUTYL	ISO-LATED	ISO-TOPIC
ISO-GAMIC	ISO-MORPH	ISO-TYPIC
ISO-GENIC	ISO-NOMIC	
ISO-GRAFT	ISO-THERM	

Some words ending with -IBLE

Seven-letter words

ADD-IBLE	FUS-IBLE	RIS-IBLE
AUD-IBLE	LEG-IBLE	VIS-IBLE
DEL-IBLE	MIX-IBLE	
DOC-IBLE	PAT-IBLE	

Eight-letter words

CRED-IBLE	GULL-IBLE	SENS-IBLE
CRUC-IBLE	HORR-IBLE	TANG-IBLE
ELIG-IBLE	INED-IBLE	TENS-IBLE
FALL-IBLE	MAND-IBLE	TERR-IBLE
FEAS-IBLE	POSS-IBLE	VINC-IBLE
FLEX-IBLE	RINS-IBLE	
FORC-IBLE	RUNC-IBLE	

I

Some words ending with -IFY
Seven-letter words

ACID-IFY	GRAT-IFY	REUN-IFY
AMPL-IFY	HORR-IFY	SACR-IFY
BEAT-IFY	JUST-IFY	SALS-IFY
CERT-IFY	LIQU-IFY	SCAR-IFY
CLAR-IFY	MAGN-IFY	SIGN-IFY
CRUC-IFY	MORT-IFY	SPEC-IFY
DIGN-IFY	NULL-IFY	TERR-IFY
FALS-IFY	PETR-IFY	TEST-IFY
FORT-IFY	QUAL-IFY	YUPP-IFY
GLOR-IFY	RECT-IFY	ZOMB-IFY

Eight-letter words

BEAUT-IFY	PRETT-IFY	SANCT-IFY
CLASS-IFY	QUANT-IFY	SIMPL-IFY
DETOX-IFY	REMOD-IFY	SOLID-IFY
EMULS-IFY	RENOT-IFY	STRAT-IFY
GENTR-IFY	REPUR-IFY	STULT-IFY
HUMID-IFY	RESIN-IFY	
IDENT-IFY	RIGID-IFY	

Some words ending with -INGS
Seven-letter words

ACH-INGS	FAD-INGS	RAG-INGS
ARM-INGS	FIX-INGS	RAT-INGS
BID-INGS	GAP-INGS	SAY-INGS
BUS-INGS	GAT-INGS	SPY-INGS
CAN-INGS	HID-INGS	TIM-INGS
COD-INGS	INN-INGS	TOY-INGS
COM-INGS	LAD-INGS	TRY-INGS
DAT-INGS	MER-INGS	TUB-INGS
DRY-INGS	OUT-INGS	WAD-INGS
EAR-INGS	PAR-INGS	WAN-INGS
END-INGS	PAY-INGS	

Eight-letter words

BAIT-INGS	DRAW-INGS	HEAR-INGS
BANG-INGS	EARN-INGS	HINT-INGS
BEAR-INGS	EDIT-INGS	HUNT-INGS
BEAT-INGS	ETCH-INGS	JUMP-INGS
BOMB-INGS	EVEN-INGS	KILL-INGS
BOND-INGS	FAIL-INGS	LAND-INGS
BOWL-INGS	FAST-INGS	LASH-INGS
BUCK-INGS	FEED-INGS	LEAN-INGS
CAMP-INGS	FIND-INGS	LIMP-INGS
CAST-INGS	FISH-INGS	LIST-INGS
COAT-INGS	FOOT-INGS	LOAN-INGS
COIN-INGS	GASP-INGS	LONG-INGS
COMB-INGS	GELD-INGS	MALT-INGS
DAWN-INGS	GOLF-INGS	MEAN-INGS
DEAL-INGS	HEAD-INGS	MEET-INGS

MOOR-INGS	ROCK-INGS	TRAD-INGS
MORN-INGS	ROLL-INGS	TWIN-INGS
NEST-INGS	ROOF-INGS	UNDO-INGS
ONGO-INGS	ROUT-INGS	UNIT-INGS
OUTS-INGS	SACK-INGS	WARN-INGS
PAIR-INGS	SEAL-INGS	WASH-INGS
PARK-INGS	SEAT-INGS	WEEP-INGS
PAST-INGS	SHOW-INGS	WHIN-INGS
PELT-INGS	SIGN-INGS	WHIT-INGS
PRIM-INGS	SING-INGS	WIND-INGS
RAIL-INGS	SLID-INGS	WORK-INGS
READ-INGS	SNIP-INGS	WRIT-INGS
REEL-INGS	STAG-INGS	
RING-INGS	STAR-INGS	

Some words ending with -ISE
Seven-letter words

AGON-ISE	IRON-ISE	PREC-ISE
ATOM-ISE	ITEM-ISE	PREM-ISE
BAPT-ISE	LION-ISE	PROM-ISE
CONC-ISE	MORT-ISE	REAL-ISE
DUAL-ISE	ODOR-ISE	REPR-ISE
ICON-ISE	OXID-ISE	UNIT-ISE
IDOL-ISE	POET-ISE	

Eight-letter words

ACTIV-ISE	FINAL-ISE	PENAL-ISE
BANAL-ISE	HUMAN-ISE	POLAR-ISE
CALOR-ISE	IDEAL-ISE	PRACT-ISE
CANON-ISE	IMMUN-ISE	SANIT-ISE
CIVIL-ISE	LEGAL-ISE	SATIR-ISE
COLON-ISE	LOCAL-ISE	TREAT-ISE
COLOR-ISE	MAXIM-ISE	UNION-ISE
DEMON-ISE	MINIM-ISE	VAPOR-ISE
DEPUT-ISE	MORAL-ISE	VITAL-ISE
EQUAL-ISE	MOTOR-ISE	VOCAL-ISE
ETHER-ISE	ORGAN-ISE	VOWEL-ISE
EXERC-ISE	PARAD-ISE	

Some words ending with -ISH
Seven-letter words

BOOK-ISH	HAWK-ISH	RUBB-ISH
BULL-ISH	HOTT-ISH	SELF-ISH
COLD-ISH	LEFT-ISH	SLAV-ISH
DARK-ISH	LONG-ISH	SLOW-ISH
FOOL-ISH	MORE-ISH	SOFT-ISH
FOPP-ISH	PECK-ISH	TALL-ISH
GIRL-ISH	PEEV-ISH	VARN-ISH
GOOD-ISH	REDD-ISH	WAIF-ISH

Eight-letter words

BLACK-ISH	FEVER-ISH	ROUGH-ISH
BLOKE-ISH	FIEND-ISH	SHARP-ISH
BLOND-ISH	GOLDF-ISH	SHEEP-ISH
BLUNT-ISH	LIGHT-ISH	SMALL-ISH
CHILD-ISH	NANNY-ISH	SWEET-ISH
CLOWN-ISH	PLAIN-ISH	THICK-ISH
DEVIL-ISH	REFIN-ISH	YOUNG-ISH

Some words ending with -ISM
Seven-letter words

BRUT-ISM	EGOT-ISM	SIZE-ISM
CULT-ISM	FASC-ISM	TOUR-ISM
DADA-ISM	IDOL-ISM	
DUAL-ISM	REAL-ISM	

Eight-letter words

ACTIV-ISM	FEMIN-ISM	NIHIL-ISM
ALARM-ISM	FUTUR-ISM	OPTIM-ISM
ALIEN-ISM	HEDON-ISM	ORGAN-ISM
ANEUR-ISM	HUMAN-ISM	PACIF-ISM
BOTUL-ISM	IDEAL-ISM	POPUL-ISM
CLASS-ISM	JINGO-ISM	ROYAL-ISM
CRONY-ISM	LOCAL-ISM	STOIC-ISM
CYNIC-ISM	LOYAL-ISM	TOKEN-ISM
DYNAM-ISM	LYRIC-ISM	UNION-ISM
EMBOL-ISM	MINIM-ISM	VEGAN-ISM
ESCAP-ISM	MORAL-ISM	
FATAL-ISM	NATIV-ISM	

Some words ending with -IST
Seven-letter words

ATOM-IST	DIET-IST	LEFT-IST
BASS-IST	DUAL-IST	PALM-IST
CELL-IST	DUEL-IST	PERS-IST
CHEM-IST	FLOR-IST	REAL-IST
DIAR-IST	HARP-IST	TOUR-IST

Eight-letter words

ALARM-IST	IDEAL-IST	PACIF-IST
ARSON-IST	JIHAD-IST	PANEL-IST
BANJO-IST	JINGO-IST	POPUL-IST
CANOE-IST	LOBBY-IST	PUGIL-IST
CHART-IST	LOYAL-IST	RALLY-IST
CLASS-IST	LYRIC-IST	REGAL-IST
COLOR-IST	MEDAL-IST	RIGHT-IST
ESSAY-IST	MINIM-IST	ROYAL-IST
FINAL-IST	MORAL-IST	SHOOT-IST
HOBBY-IST	MOTOR-IST	STOCK-IST
HUMAN-IST	OPTIM-IST	TOTAL-IST
HUMOR-IST	ORGAN-IST	TOTEM-IST

Some words ending with -ITY
Seven-letter words

ACID-ITY	DUAL-ITY	QUAL-ITY
AMEN-ITY	JOLL-ITY	REAL-ITY
ARID-ITY	NULL-ITY	TENS-ITY
CHAR-ITY	OBES-ITY	TRIN-ITY
DENS-ITY	PRIV-ITY	UTIL-ITY
DIGN-ITY	PROB-ITY	VACU-ITY

Eight-letter words

ACRID-ITY	HUMID-ITY	REGAL-ITY
ACTIV-ITY	HUMIL-ITY	RIGID-ITY
AFFIN-ITY	IDENT-ITY	RURAL-ITY
BANAL-ITY	IMMUN-ITY	SANCT-ITY
CALAM-ITY	INSAN-ITY	SECUR-ITY
CHAST-ITY	LEGAL-ITY	SENIL-ITY
CONIC-ITY	LIVID-ITY	SEREN-ITY
CUBIC-ITY	LOCAL-ITY	SEVER-ITY
ENORM-ITY	LUCID-ITY	SOLID-ITY
EQUAL-ITY	MAJOR-ITY	TIMID-ITY
FACIL-ITY	MINOR-ITY	TONAL-ITY
FATAL-ITY	MOBIL-ITY	TONIC-ITY
FIDEL-ITY	MORAL-ITY	TOTAL-ITY
FINAL-ITY	NATIV-ITY	TOXIC-ITY
FLUID-ITY	POLAR-ITY	VALID-ITY
FUTIL-ITY	PRIOR-ITY	VITAL-ITY
GRATU-ITY	RABID-ITY	
HUMAN-ITY	RAPID-ITY	

Some words ending with -IUM
Seven-letter words

CALC-IUM	IRID-IUM	RHOD-IUM
CRAN-IUM	LITH-IUM	STAD-IUM
FERM-IUM	PALL-IUM	TERT-IUM
GALL-IUM	PLAG-IUM	TRIT-IUM
HASS-IUM	PREM-IUM	URAN-IUM
HOLM-IUM	PROT-IUM	YTTR-IUM

Eight-letter words

ACTIN-IUM	EULOG-IUM	ROSAR-IUM
AEROB-IUM	FRANC-IUM	RUBID-IUM
ALLUV-IUM	GERAN-IUM	SELEN-IUM
AMMON-IUM	IMPER-IUM	SOLAR-IUM
AQUAR-IUM	INGEN-IUM	SOLAT-IUM
BRACH-IUM	MOTOR-IUM	THALL-IUM
CHROM-IUM	NOBEL-IUM	TITAN-IUM
CORON-IUM	OSSAR-IUM	TRILL-IUM
DELIR-IUM	PHORM-IUM	VIVAR-IUM
DILUV-IUM	POLON-IUM	
EMPOR-IUM	REFUG-IUM	

Unusual letter combinations

If you have an unusual combination of letters on your rack, or want to impress your opponent with an unusual word, a few words from World English can come in handy. Here are some beginning with I.

New Zealand words
IWI   a Maori tribe

Canadian words
ICEWINE   dessert wine made from frozen grapes

Urdu words
INQILAB   revolution

J
8

Essential info
Value: 8 points
Number in set: 1
Power Tile

J alone is worth 8 points, making it an extremely valuable tile. However, it can be difficult to play: for example, there are only two two-letter words beginning with J (JA, a South African word for yes, and JO, a Scots word for sweetheart, both 9 points). When used in conjunction with the other power tiles X and Z, however, there is scope for huge scoring, especially if words are played judiciously on double- or triple-letter squares. Good short words to remember which use J alongside X and Z include JINX (18 points) and JAZY (23 points). Remember, as there is only one J tile in the Scrabble set, you will need a blank tile to take advantage of words with two Js (e.g. HAJJ, 13 points) or indeed a J and two of the same power tile letters (e.g. JAZZES, 21 points).

Two-letter words beginning with J
JA   JO

Some three-letter words beginning with J
| JAG | JAK | JAY |
| JAI | JAP | JEE |

JEU	JIZ	JOW
JEW	JOE	JUD
JIB	JOL	JUN
JIN	JOR	JUS

Some three-letter words using J

GJU	HAJ	RAJ	TAJ

Some four-letter words using J

Some four-letter words using J that you may not know are DOJO (room or hall for the practice of martial arts, 12 points), JEHU (a fast driver, 14 points), JIAO (Chinese currency unit, 11 points) and JIRD (another word for gerbil, 12 points)

AJAR	JANE	JAZZ	JESS
DJIN	JANN	JEAN	JEST
DOJO	JAPE	JEAT	JETE
FUJI	JARK	JEDI	JEUX
HADJ	JARL	JEED	JIAO
HAJJ	JARP	JEEL	JIBB
JAAP	JASP	JEEP	JIBE
JACK	JASS	JEER	JIFF
JADE	JASY	JEEZ	JILL
JAFA	JATO	JEFE	JILT
JAGA	JAUK	JEFF	JIMP
JAGG	JAUP	JEHU	JINK
JAIL	JAVA	JELL	JINN
JAKE	JAXY	JEON	JINS
JAMB	JAZY	JERK	JINX

160

JIRD	JOLL	JUBE	JURE
JIVE	JOLT	JUCO	JURY
JIVY	JOMO	JUDO	JUST
JOBE	JONG	JUDY	JUTE
JOCK	JOOK	JUGA	JUVE
JOCO	JOSH	JUJU	JYNX
JOEY	JOSS	JUKE	KOJI
JOHN	JOTA	JUKU	MOJO
JOIN	JOUK	JUMP	RAJA
JOKE	JOUR	JUNK	SOJA
JOKY	JOWL	JUPE	
JOLE	JUBA	JURA	

Hooks

Hooking requires a subtle change in a player's thought process, in that they must look at words already on the board without becoming distracted by their pronunciation.

Some front-hooks
Two letters to three

J-AB	J-EE	J-OY
J-AG	J-ET	J-UG
J-AI	J-IN	J-UN
J-AM	J-OB	J-US
J-AR	J-OE	J-UT
J-AW	J-OR	
J-AY	J-OW	

Three letters to four

J-AGA	J-EAT	J-IVY
J-AIL	J-EEL	J-OBE
J-AKE	J-EFF	J-OKE
J-ANE	J-ELL	J-OLE
J-ANN	J-ERK	J-OUK
J-APE	J-ESS	J-OUR
J-ARK	J-EST	J-OWL
J-ASP	J-IFF	J-UDO
J-ASS	J-ILL	J-UKE
J-AUK	J-IMP	J-UMP
J-AVA	J-INK	J-URE
J-EAN	J-INN	J-UTE

Four letters to five

J-AGER	J-EMMY	J-OWED
J-ALAP	J-ESSE	J-OWLY
J-AMBO	J-IFFY	J-UMBO
J-APED	J-ILLS	J-UMPY
J-APER	J-IMMY	J-UNCO
J-AUNT	J-INGO	J-UNTO
J-AVEL	J-NANA	J-UPON
J-AWED	J-OINT	
J-EELY	J-OUST	

J

Five letters to six

J-ABBED	J-ASSES	J-OTTER
J-ACKER	J-AUNTY	J-OUNCE
J-AGGER	J-AWING	J-OWING
J-AILED	J-EANED	J-OWLED
J-AMBER	J-EFFED	J-OWLER
J-ANGLE	J-ESSES	J-UDDER
J-ANKER	J-ESTER	J-UGGED
J-APERY	J-IGGED	J-UMBLE
J-APING	J-IMPLY	J-UMPED
J-ARGON	J-INGLE	J-UNKED
J-ARRAH	J-INKED	J-UNKET
J-ASPER	J-INKER	

Six letters to seven

J-AGGIES	J-IMMIES	J-OUSTER
J-AILING	J-INGOES	J-OWLIER
J-ANGLED	J-INKING	J-OWLING
J-ANGLER	J-OCULAR	J-UGGING
J-AUNTIE	J-OINTED	J-UMPING
J-AWLESS	J-OLLIES	J-UNCATE
J-EFFING	J-OSTLER	J-UNCOES
J-IGGING	J-OUSTED	J-UNKING

Seven letters to eight

J-ANGLING	J-OUSTING	J UNCTION
J-APERIES	J-OWLIEST	
J-OINTING	J-UDDERED	

J

Some end-hooks
Two letters to three

HA-J   TA-J

Three letters to four

BEN-J   HAD-J   HAJ-J

Blockers

It is useful to know which words are blockers and
can't therefore be extended before or after. You may
want to play a blocker that your opponent can't
extend, or you may want to avoid playing a blocker
because you want to keep the board open.

Some four-letter blockers beginning with J

JASS	JEON	JOSH
JASY	JEUX	JOSS
JAZY	JINX	JURY
JEED	JIVY	JYNX
JEEZ	JOKY	

Some five-letter blockers beginning with J
(except words ending in '-ED', '-J', '-S', '-X',
'-Y' or '-Z')

JEUNE	JIRRE	JOMON
JINGO	JOKOL	JURAL

Some six-letter blockers beginning with J (except words ending in '-ED', '-J', '-S', '-X', '-Y' or '-Z')

JACENT	JINNEE	JOLING
JADING	JIVIER	JOVIAL
JADISH	JIVING	JOWING
JEEING	JOBING	JOYFUL
JEJUNE	JOCOSE	JOYING
JIBING	JOCUND	JUBATE
JIMPER	JOKIER	JUGATE
JIMSON	JOKING	JUKING

J

Handy Hint

When holding a power tile try looking beyond the easy two and three-letter words that might jump out at you. Also look for words that might score more embedding the power tile rather than starting with it – a few containing a J are RAJA (11 points), MAJOR (14), CAJOLE (15), OUIJA (12), BANJO (14).

Bonus words
Seven-letter words

JABBERS
JABBING
JACKALS
JACKASS
JACKDAW
JACKERS
JACKETS
JACKING
JACKPOT
JACKSIE
JADEDLY
JAGGERS
JAGGERY
JAGGIER
JAGGIES
JAGGING
JAGUARS
JAILERS
JAILING
JAILORS
JAMJARS
JAMLIKE
JAMMERS
JAMMIER
JAMMIES
JAMMING
JAMPOTS

JANDALS
JANGLED
JANGLER
JANGLES
JANITOR
JARFULS
JARGONS
JARGONY
JARHEAD
JARPING
JARRAHS
JARRING
JASMINE
JASPERS
JASPERY
JAUNTED
JAUNTEE
JAUNTIE
JAUPING
JAVELIN
JAWBONE
JAWINGS
JAWLESS
JAWLINE
JAYBIRD
JAYWALK
JAZZIER

JAZZILY
JAZZING
JAZZMAN
JAZZMEN
JEALOUS
JEEPERS
JEEPING
JEERERS
JEERING
JEHADIS
JELLIED
JELLIFY
JELLING
JEMIMAS
JEMMIED
JEMMIER
JEMMIES
JENNIES
JEOPARD
JERBILS
JERBOAS
JEREEDS
JERKERS
JERKIER
JERKIES
JERKILY
JERKING

JERKINS	JIGSAWS	JOINERS
JERRIES	JIHADIS	JOINERY
JERSEYS	JILTERS	JOINING
JESSIES	JILTING	JOINTED
JESTEES	JIMJAMS	JOINTER
JESTERS	JIMMIED	JOINTLY
JESTFUL	JIMMIES	JOISTED
JESTING	JIMMINY	
JESUITS		JOJOBAS
	JINGLED	
JETLAGS	JINGLER	JOKIEST
JETLIKE	JINGLET	JOLLEYS
JETSAMS	JINGOES	JOLLIED
JETSOMS	JINXING	JOLLIER
JETTIED	JITTERS	JOLLIES
JETTIER	JITTERY	JOLLIFY
JETTIES	JIVIEST	JOLLILY
JETTING		JOLLITY
	JOANNAS	JOLTILY
JEWELED	JOBBERS	JOLTING
JEWELER	JOBBING	
JEWELRY	JOBLESS	JONESED
		JONESES
JEZEBEL	JOCKEYS	
	JOCULAR	JOSHERS
JIBBERS		JOSHING
JIBBING	JODHPUR	JOSTLED
		JOSTLER
JIFFIES	JOGGERS	
	JOGGING	JOTTERS
JIGGERS		JOTTING
JIGGIER	JOHNNIE	
JIGGING	JOHNSON	JOURNAL
JIGGLED		JOURNEY

167

JOURNOS
JOUSTED
JOUSTER
JOWLIER
JOWLING
JOYLESS
JOYRIDE
JUBILEE
JUDASES
JUDDERS
JUDGERS
JUDGING
JUDOIST
JUGFULS
JUGGLED
JUGGLER

JUGHEAD
JUGSFUL
JUGULAR
JUICERS
JUICIER
JUICILY
JUICING
JUJITSU
JUJUIST
JUKEBOX
JUMBLED
JUMBLER
JUMBUCK
JUMPERS
JUMPIER
JUMPILY

JUMPING
JUNGLED
JUNGLES
JUNIORS
JUNIPER
JUNKETS
JUNKIER
JUNKMAN
JUNKMEN
JURISTS
JURYING
JURYMAN
JURYMEN
JUSTICE
JUSTIFY
JUTTING

Eight-letter words

JABBERED
JABBERER
JACKAROO
JACKBOOT
JACKEROO
JACKETED
JADELIKE
JAGGEDER
JAGGEDLY

JAGGIEST
JAILABLE
JAILBAIT
JAILBIRD
JAILLESS
JALAPENO
JAMBOREE
JAMMABLE
JAMMIEST

JANGLIER
JANGLING
JANITRIX
JAPANISE
JAPANIZE
JAPINGLY
JARGONED
JAUNDICE
JAUNTIER

J

AUNTILY	JIHADISM	JONESING
AUNTING	JIHADIST	JONGLEUR
AVELINA	JILLAROO	JOSTLING
AWBONED	JIMCRACK	JOUNCIER
AWBONER	JIMMYING	JOUNCING
AZZIEST	JINGLIER	JOUSTING
AZZLIKE	JINGLING	JOVIALLY
EALOUSY	JINGOISM	JOVIALTY
EANETTE	JINGOIST	JOWLIEST
EHADISM	JITTERED	JOYFULLY
EHADIST	JOBSHARE	JOYOUSLY
ELLYING	JOCKETTE	JOYRIDER
EMMIEST	JOCKEYED	JOYSTICK
EMMYING	JOGGLING	
EOPARDY	JOINABLE	JUBILANT
ERKIEST	JOINTING	JUBILATE
EROBOAM	JOINTURE	JUDDERED
ERRICAN	JOISTING	JUDGMENT
ERRYCAN	JOKESOME	JUDICIAL
ERSEYED	JOKESTER	JUGGLERY
ESTBOOK	JOKINESS	JUGGLING
ESUITIC	JOKINGLY	JUGULATE
ESUITRY	JOLLEYER	JUICIEST
IGGLIER	JOLLIEST	JULIENNE
IGGLING	JOLLYING	JUMBLIER
IGSAWED	JOLTHEAD	JUMBLING
	JOLTIEST	JUMPABLE

J

169

JUMPIEST	JUNKETER	JURYMAST
JUMPSUIT	JUNKIEST	JUSTICER
JUNCTION	JUNKYARD	JUSTLING
JUNCTURE	JURASSIC	JUSTNESS
JUNGLIER	JURATORY	JUTELIKE
JUNGLIST	JURISTIC	JUTTYING
JUNKETED	JURYLESS	JUVENILE

Unusual letter combinations

If you have an unusual combination of letters on your rack, or want to impress your opponent with an unusual word, a few words from World English can come in handy.

Australian words

JARRAH	type of eucalyptus tree
JEFF	downsize or close down an organization
JUMBUCK	sheep

Canadian words

| JOUAL | nonstandard Canadian French dialect |

Hindi words

| JAGGERY | coarse brown sugar |
| JAI | victory |

Essential info
Value: 5 points
Number in set: 1

K is a valuable tile at 5 points and is particularly useful if you also have a C on your rack because of the abundance of words ending in -CK. There is a selection of useful two-letter words beginning with K: KA, KI, KO (6 points each) and KY (9 points). Three-letter words beginning with K include common words such as KEG and KID (8 points) KIP (9 points), and KFY (10 points). Others tend to be more unusual words but nevertheless very useful: KEB (9 points). KEX (14 points), KIF (10 points).

K

Two-letter words beginning with K

KA   KI   KO   KY

Some three-letter words beginning with K

KAB	KEA	KHI	KOP
KAE	KEB	KIF	KOR
KAF	KED	KIN	KOW
KAI	KEF	KIR	KYF
KAM	KEN	KOA	KYU
KAT	KEP	KOB	
KAW	KET	KOI	
KAY	KEX	KON	

171

Hooks

Hooking requires a subtle change in a player's thought process, in that they must look at words already on the board without becoming distracted by their pronunciation.

Some front-hooks
Two letters to three

K-AB	K-AW	K-ET	K-IS	K-OR
K-AE	K-AY	K-EX	K-IT	K-OS
K-AI	K-EA	K-HI	K-OB	K-OW
K-AM	K-ED	K-ID	K-OI	K-YE
K-AS	K-EF	K-IF	K-ON	K-YU
K-AT	K-ET	K-IN	K-OP	

Three letters to four

K-AGO	K-AVA	K-HET	K-NOT
K-AID	K-AWA	K-ICK	K-NOW
K-AIL	K-BAR	K-IFF	K-NUB
K-AIM	K-EEK	K-ILL	K-NUR
K-AIN	K-EEL	K-INK	K-NUT
K-AKA	K-EEN	K-IRK	K-OBO
K-ALE	K-ELL	K-ISH	K-OFF
K-AMA	K-ELT	K-IWI	K-ORA
K-AMI	K-ERF	K-LAP	K-ORE
K-ANA	K-ERN	K-NAG	K-SAR
K-ANE	K-EST	K-NAP	K-UDO
K-ANT	K-ETA	K-NEE	K-UTA
K-ARK	K-HAN	K-NEW	K-UTU
K-ART	K-HAT	K-NIT	K-YAK

172

Four letters to five

K-ALIF	K-INKY	K-NURL
K-ANGA	K-LANG	K-NURR
K-ARSY	K-LAPS	K-OKRA
K-ARTS	K-LICK	K-OMBU
K-AVAS	K-LONG	K-RAFT
K-AWED	K-LOOF	K-RAIT
K-EDGE	K-LUGE	K-RANG
K-EDGY	K LUTZ	K-RILL
K-EECH	K-NAVE	K-RONE
K-EMPT	K-NEED	K-ROON
K-ERNE	K-NIFE	K-ULAN
K-ETCH	K-NISH	K-VELL
K-EVIL	K-NOCK	K-YACK
K-EYED	K-NOLL	K-YANG
K-HETH	K-NOUT	
K-ICKY	K-NOWN	

Five letters to six

K-AINGA	K-EGGED	K-INGLE
K-ALONG	K-EGGER	K-INKED
K-ANTAR	K-EIGHT	K-INKLE
K-ANTED	K-EMBED	K-IRKED
K-ARKED	K-ENTIA	K-ISHES
K-ARRIS	K-ERNED	K-LATCH
K-ARSEY	K-ETTLE	K-LUGED
K-AWING	K-EYING	K-NAGGY
K-EBBED	K-ICKER	K-NIGHT
K-EDGED	K-ILLER	K-RATER
K-EDGER	K-INDIE	K-VETCH

173

Six letters to seven

K-ANTING
K-ARKING
K-EBBING
K-EDGERS
K-EDGIER
K-EDGING
K-EECHES
K-EGGING
K-ENOSIS
K-ERNING
K-ICKIER
K-IDLING

K-INKIER
K-INKING
K-INSHIP
K-IRKING
K-LAPPED
K-LINKER
K-LISTER
K-LUGING
K-LUTZES
K-NAPPED
K-NAPPER
K-NICKER

K-NISHES
K-NOBBLE
K-NOCKED
K-NUBBLE
K-NUBBLY
K-NURLED
K-ONNING
K-RATERS
K-RIMMER
K-RISING
K-VETCHY

Seven letters to eight

K-ALEWIFE
K-EDGIEST
K-ETAMINE
K-ETCHING
K-ICKIEST
K-INKIEST
K-INSHIPS

K-LAPPING
K-LATCHES
K-NAGGIER
K-NAPPING
K-NIGHTED
K-NIGHTLY
K-NOBBIER

K-NOBBLED
K-NOCKING
K-NUBBIER
K-NUBBLED
K-NURLING
K-OSMOSES

K

Some end-hooks
Two letters to three

AR-K	IN-K	SI-K
AS-K	JA-K	TA-K
BO-K	KA-K	WO-K
DA-K	MA-K	YA-K
EE-K	NE-K	YO-K
EL-K	OI-K	YU-K
ER-K	OU-K	

Three letters to four

BAC-K	DIS-K	HUN-K
BAL-K	DOC-K	JAR-K
BAN-K	DOR-K	JUN-K
BAR-K	DUN-K	KIN-K
BAS-K	FAN-K	KIR-K
BON-K	FIN-K	LAC-K
BOO-K	FIR-K	LAR-K
BUN-K	FOR-K	LAW-K
BUR-K	FUN-K	LEA-K
BUS-K	GEE-K	LEE-K
CAR-K	GIN-K	LIN-K
CAW-K	GON-K	LIS-K
CHI-K	GUN-K	LOO-K
CON-K	HAN-K	LUR-K
COO-K	HIC-K	MAC-K
COR-K	HOC-K	MAR-K
COW-K	HON-K	MAS-K
DAN-K	HOO-K	MAW-K
DIN-K	HOW-K	MEE-K

K

175

MIL-K	PIC-K	SOC-K
MIR-K	PIN-K	SUN-K
MOC-K	PUN-K	TAN-K
MON-K	RAN-K	TAS-K
MOO-K	REE-K	TEA-K
MUS-K	RIN-K	TEE-K
NOO-K	ROC-K	TIC-K
NOR-K	ROO-K	TOC-K
PAC-K	RUC-K	TON-K
PAR-K	SAC-K	TOO-K
PEA-K	SAN-K	WEE-K
PEC-K	SEE-K	WIN-K
PEE-K	SIC-K	
PER-K	SIN-K	

K

Four letters to five

ABAC-K	CLON-K	SKIN-K
ALEC-K	CRAN-K	SLEE-K
BLIN-K	CREE-K	SMIR-K
BLOC-K	CROC-K	SPAN-K
BRAN-K	FLAN-K	SPAR-K
BRIN-K	FLIC-K	SPEC-K
BRIS-K	FLOC-K	SPIN-K
BROO-K	FRIS-K	STAR-K
BRUS-K	GREE-K	STIR-K
CHAL-K	PLAN-K	STUN-K
CHIC-K	SCUL-K	SWAN-K
CHIN-K	SHAN-K	THAN-K
CHOC-K	SHIR-K	THIN-K
CLAN-K	SHOO-K	TWIN-K

Five letters to six

ANTIC-K	KALPA-K	RESEE-K
ASPIC-K	MEDIC-K	SQUAW-K
BEGUN-K	MELIC-K	UMIAC-K
DEBAR-K	MUSIC-K	UNBAR-K
EMBAR-K	PACHA-K	ZEBEC-K
IMBAR-K	PANIC-K	
JAMBO-K	REBEC-K	

Six letters to seven

AMTRAC-K	FINNAC-K	OUTBAR-K
BOOBOO-K	GWEDUC-K	OUTRAN-K
CALPAC-K	LIMBEC-K	TIETAC-K
DISBAR-K	OOMIAC-K	TOMBAC-K

Seven letters to eight

ALMANAC-K	OVERRAN-K	SHOEPAC-K
BALDRIC-K	POLITIC-K	TAMARIS-K
BAUDRIC-K	PRACTIC-K	
FORERAN-K	SHELLAC-K	

K

Blockers

It is useful to know which words are blockers and can't therefore be extended before or after. You may want to play a blocker that your opponent can't extend, or you may want to avoid playing a blocker because you want to keep the board open.

Three-letter blocker beginning with K
KEX

Some four-letter blockers beginning with K

KEPT   KEWL   KILD   KISH   KNEW   KRIS

Some five-letter blockers beginning with K (except words ending in '-ED', '-J', '-S', '-X', '-Y' or '-Z')

KEECH	KIDGE	KNISH	KRONA
KEMPT	KINDA	KORAI	
KENCH	KNELT	KOTCH	

Some six-letter blockers beginning with K (except words ending in '-ED', '-J', '-S', '-X', '-Y' or '-Z')

KAPUTT	KIPPEN	KOTUKU
KARMIC	KIRSCH	KRONEN
KAWING	KLATCH	KRONER
KEPPIT	KNITCH	KULAKI
KEWLER	KONAKI	KUTCHA
KIBOSH	KOTARE	KYBOSH

178

Bonus words

Bonus words on your rack can be hard to spot, especially for the less experienced player. One way to help find them is by using prefixes and suffixes.

Many larger words include a common prefix or suffix – remembering these and using them where you can is a good way to discover any longer words on your rack, including any potential bonus words. The key suffix to remember beginning with K is -KIN.

Some words ending with -KIN
Seven-letter words

BUMP-KIN	LADY-KIN	MINI-KIN
CATS-KIN	LAMB-KIN	OILS-KIN
COWS-KIN	LORD-KIN	PIGS-KIN
DOES-KIN	LUMP-KIN	PUMP-KIN
FOXS-KIN	MANA-KIN	RAMA-KIN
GHER-KIN	MANI-KIN	WOLF-KIN

Eight-letter words

BEARS-KIN	FISHS-KIN	MUNCH-KIN
BOOTI-KIN	GOATS-KIN	SEALS-KIN
BUCKS-KIN	LAMBS-KIN	SWANS-KIN
CALFS-KIN	LARRI-KIN	TURNS-KIN
CIDER-KIN	MANNI-KIN	WINES-KIN
DEERS-KIN	MOLES-KIN	WOLFS-KIN
DEVIL-KIN	MOUSE-KIN	WOOLS-KIN

Unusual letter combinations

If you have an unusual combination of letters on your rack, or want to impress your opponent with an unusual word, a few words from World English can come in handy.

Australian words

KARRI	type of eucalyptus tree
KOALA	slow-moving arboreal marsupial
KYBO	temporary lavatory
KYLIE	boomerang that is flat on one side and convex on the other

Hindi words

KHADDAR	cotton cloth
KHEDA	enclosure for captured elephants
KOEL	parasitic cuckoo
KOS	Indian unit of distance
KRAIT	brightly coloured venomous snake
KULFI	Indian dessert
KURTA	long loose garment

K

New Zealand words

KAHAWAI	large fish
KAI	food
KARANGA	call or chant of welcome
KATIPO	small venomous spider
KAUPAPA	strategy, policy or cause
KAURI	coniferous tree
KAWA	protocol or etiquette
KIWI	flightless bird with long beak and no tail
KOHA	gift or donation
KORU	curved pattern
KOWHAI	small tree
KUIA	female elder
KURI	mongrel dog
KUTU	body louse

South African words

KEREL	chap or fellow
KRAAL	stockaded village
KWAITO	type of pop music

K

Urdu words

KAMEEZ	long tunic
KEBAB	dish of meat, onions, etc, grilled on skewers
KHARIF	crop harvested at beginning of winter
KHAYAL	kind of Indian classical vocal music
KINCOB	fine silk fabric embroidered with gold or silver threads
KOFTA	Indian dish of seasoned minced meat shaped into balls
KOFTGAR	person skilled in inlaying steel with gold
KOFTGARI	art of inlaying steel with gold
KORMA	Indian dish of meat or vegetables braised with yoghurt or cream

K

Handy Hint

The letter K features prominently in many variants of World English. Along with its frequency of use in the Maori-derived words of New Zealand English, the use of a double K is common in Australian English (QUOKKA, 18 points), Hindi (PUKKA, 10 points), Inuit words (MUKTUK, 11 points) and Urdu (KHAKI, 11 points). As there is only one K in the Scrabble set, you will need to have a handy blank tile to play these fascinating words.

Essential info
Value: 1 points
Number in set: 4

The **L** is a very flexible letter for playing words because it combines with many other consonants such as BL-, CL-, FL-, PL-. If you have two of them there are also many words enging in -LL to help you out. Be aware of the following two-letter words for making parallel plays involving an L: LA (in music, the sixth note of a major scale, 2 points), LI (a Chinese unit of length, 2 points) and LO (a command that means look, 2 points). There's a great selection of three-letter words for combining the L with another higher-scoring consonant such as: LAW, LAY, LOW and LYE, all worth 6 points. There are also quite a few words which use X: LAX, LEX, LOX and LUX, all worth 10 points.

Two-letter words beginning with L
LA   LI   LO

Some three-letter words beginning with L

LAB	LAR	LEE	LIB
LAC	LAT	LES	LIG
LAH	LAV	LEX	LIN
LAM	LEA	LEZ	LOD

LOP	LOX	LUR	LYM
LOR	LOY	LUX	
LOS	LUG	LUZ	
LOU	LUM	LYE	

Hooks

Hooking requires a subtle change in a player's thought process, in that they must look at words already on the board without becoming distracted by their pronunciation.

Some front-hooks
Two letters to three

L-AB	L-ED	L-OP
L-AD	L-EE	L-OR
L-AG	L-ES	L-OS
L-AH	L-ET	L-OU
L-AM	L-EX	L-OW
L-AR	L-ID	L-OX
L-AS	L-IN	L-OY
L-AT	L-IS	L-UG
L-AW	L-IT	L-UM
L-AX	L-OB	L-UR
L-AY	L-OD	L-YE
L-EA	L-OO	

L

Three letters to four

L-ACE	L-EFT	L-OON
L-AID	L-END	L-OOP
L-AIN	L-ENS	L-OOT
L-AIR	L-ESS	L-OPE
L-AKE	L-EST	L-ORD
L-ALL	L-ICE	L-ORE
L-AMP	I-ICH	L-OSE
L-ANA	L-ICK	L-OUD
L-AND	L-IMP	L-OUP
L-ANE	L-INK	L-OUR
L-ARD	L-ION	L-OUT
L-ARK	L-OAF	L-OWE
L-ASH	L-OBE	L-OWN
L-ASS	L-OBO	L-OWT
L-ATE	L-OCH	L-UDO
L-AVA	L-ODE	L-UKE
L-AWN	L-OFT	L-UMP
L-EAN	L-ONE	L-URE
L-EAR	L-OOF	L-UTE
L-EEK	L-OOM	

Four letters to five

L-ACED	L-AWED	L-EAVE
L-ACER	L-AWNY	L-EDGE
L-AGER	L-AYIN	L-FDGY
L-AIRY	L-EACH	L-EECH
L-AKED	L-EARN	L-EERY
L-ANCE	L-EASE	L-EGAL
L-APSE	L-EAST	L-EGGY

185

L-EISH   L-LAMA   L-OWED
L-ETCH   L-OATH   L-OWER
L-EVER   L-ONER   L-OWLY
L-INCH   L-OOSE   L-OWSE
L-INGO   L-OPED   L-UMPY
L-INKY   L-OTTO   L-USER
L-ISLE   L-OVER

Five letters to six

L-ACING   L-EASER   L-IZARD
L-ACKER   L-EAVED   L-OCKER
L-ADDER   L-EDGED   L-OCULI
L-AGGER   L-EDGER   L-OFTER
L-AIRED   L-EGGED   L-OLLER
L-AMBER   L-EGGER   L-ONELY
L-AMENT   L-ENDER   L-OOPED
L-AMPED   L-ETHAL   L-OPING
L-ANGER   L-ICKER   L-ORATE
L-ANKER   L-IGGED   L-OTHER
L-ARKED   L-IMBED   L-OTTER
L-ARVAL   L-IMPED   L-OUPED
L-ASHED   L-IMPLY   L-OUTED
L-ASTER   L-INKED   L-OWING
L-AWFUL   L-INKER   L-OWNED
L-AWING   L-INTEL   L-UGGED
L-EANED   L-INTER   L-UMBER
L-EARED   L-IRKED   L-UMPED
L-EASED   L-ITHER   L-USHER

L

Six letters to seven

L-AIDING	L-EDGIER	L-IONIZE
L-AIRIER	L-EECHED	L-IRKING
L-AIRING	L-EERIER	L-OCULAR
L-AMPING	L-EERILY	L-OOPING
L-ARKING	L-EFTEST	L-OUPING
L-ASHING	L-EGALLY	L-OUTING
L-AUDING	L-EGGIER	L-OVERED
L-AWLESS	L-EGGING	L-OVERLY
L-AWNIER	L-ENDING	L-OWLIER
L-EANING	L-ETCHED	L-OWNING
L-EARING	L-IGGING	L-OXYGEN
L-EARNED	L-IGNIFY	L-UGGING
L-EARNER	L-IMPING	L-ULLING
L-EASING	L-INKING	L-UMPING
L-EAVING	L-INNING	
L-ECHING	L-IONISE	

Seven letters to eight

L-ABILITY	L-EDGIEST	L-IONISER
L-ACERATE	L-EECHING	L-IONIZED
L-AIRIEST	L-EERIEST	L-IONIZER
L-AMBLING	L-EGALITY	L-ITERATE
L-ANGERED	L-EGGIEST	L-OCULATE
L-ANGUISH	L-ETCHING	L-OMENTUM
L-AUREATE	L-EVITATE	L-ONENESS
L-AWFULLY	L-IGNEOUS	L-OURIEST
L-AWNIEST	L-INCHPIN	L-OWLIEST
L-EARNING	L-IONISED	L-UMBERED

Some end-hooks
Two letters to three

AA-L	EE-L	OW-L
AI-L	EL-L	PA-L
AL-L	GU-L	PO-L
AW-L	JO-L	SO-L
BA-L	MA-L	TE-L
BE-L	ME-L	TI-L
DA-L	MI-L	ZO-L
DE-L	MO-L	
DO-L	OI-L	

Three letters to four

AXE-L	GAL-L	POL-L
BAL-L	GOA-L	PUL-L
BOW-L	HOW-L	PUR-L
CEL-L	JAI-L	SEA-L
COO-L	JOW-L	SOU-L
COW-L	MAL-L	TAI-L
CUR-L	MEL-L	TEA-L
DAH-L	MEW-L	TEL-L
DOL-L	MIL-L	TIL-L
DOW-L	MOL-L	TOO-L
DUE-L	NIL-L	VIA-L
EAR-L	ORA-L	WAI-L
FEE-L	OVA-L	WOO-L
FOU-L	PAL-L	YOW-L
FUR-L	PEA-L	ZEA-L

L

Four letters to five

ALKY-L
ALLY-L
ANNA-L
AURA-L
BABE-L
BRAW-L
CABA-L
CAME-L
CRAW-L
CREE-L
CRUE-L
DRAW-L
DURA-L
EASE-L
FAVE-L
FETA-L
GAVE-L
GNAR-L
GROW-L
GRUE-L

HAZE-L
HOTE-L
HOVE-L
IDEA-L
IDYL-L
KNEE-L
LEVE-L
LOCA-L
META-L
MODE-L
MORA-L
MOTE-L
MURA-L
NAVE-L
OCTA-L
PANE-L
PEAR-L
PERI-L
PROW-L
PUPA-L

QUAI-L
RAVE-L
RIVA-L
ROTA-L
RUBE-L
SCOW-L
SHAW-L
SNAR-L
SPIE-L
UREA-L
VASA-L
VENA-L
VINY-L
VITA-L
WHEE-L
WHIR-L
YODE-L
YOKE-L
ZONA-L

Five letters to six

ANIMA-L
AORTA-L
APPAL-L
ATRIA-L
BARBE-L
BARRE-L
CARTE-L

CAUSA-L
COSTA-L
DERMA-L
DORSA-L
DRIVE-L
ENROL-L
EXTOL-L

FACIA-L
FAUNA-L
FLORA-L
FLOTE-L
GRAVE-L
GROVE-L
LARVA-L

189

L

MAMMA-L PORTA-L SWIVE-L
MANGE-L PRIMA-L TASSE-L
MEDIA-L RECAL-L TEASE-L
MENTA-L REDIA-L TIBIA-L
MONGO-L REGNA-L TRAVE-L
MORSE-L SCRAW-L VANDA-L
MUSSE-L SEPTA-L VESTA-L
NORMA-L SHOVE-L VISTA-L
PASTE-L SIGNA-L
PETRE-L SPINA-L

Six letters to seven

ANGINA-L DISTIL-L MIASMA-L
BARBEL-L EPOCHA-L MINIMA-L
CAMERA-L FASCIA-L NATURA-L
CAPITA-L FEMORA-L NOMINA-L
CENTRA-L FULFIL-L OPTIMA-L
CHANCE-L GENERA-L ORBITA-L
CHROMY-L INSTAL-L RETINA-L
COLONE-L INSTIL-L SALIVA-L
CORNEA-L LATERA-L STADIA-L
CORONA-L LEXICA-L STIGMA-L
CRESTA-L LINGUA-L TRIVIA-L
CUBICA-L MAXIMA-L

Seven letters to eight

ALLUVIA-L	CRIMINA-L	MINUTIA-L
AMPHORA-L	ENTHRAL-L	PERINEA-L
ANTENNA-L	HYDROXY-L	PERSONA-L
BRACHIA-L	IMPERIA-L	RESIDUA-L
BRIMFUL-L	INERTIA-L	SPECTRA-L
CAROUSE-L	MALARIA-L	STAMINA-L
CEREBRA-L	MANDRIL-L	VISCERA-L
CORPORA-L	MARSHAL-L	

Blockers

It is useful to know which words are blockers and can't therefore be extended before or after. You may want to play a blocker that your opponent can't extend, or you may want to avoid playing a blocker because you want to keep the board open.

Some three-letter blockers beginning with L

LOX   LUZ

Some four-letter blockers beginning with L

LACY   LEVY   LEWD   LYNX

L

191

Some five-letter blockers beginning with L (except words ending in '-ED', '-J', '-S', '-X', '-Y' or '-Z')

LAXER	LEISH	LURCH
LEANT	LIVID	LURID
LEAPT	LOYAL	LYNCH
LEASH	LUCID	

Some six-letter blockers beginning with L (except words ending in '-ED', '-J', '-S', '-X', '-Y' or '-Z')

LACTIC	LAYMAN	LINEAR
LAKISH	LAYMEN	LIVEST
LAMEST	LEARNT	LOOSER
LARGER	LEFTER	LOUCHE
LARVAE	LEGMAN	LOUDER
LARVAL	LEWDER	LUBING
LAWFUL	LIMBIC	LURING
LAWMAN	LIMPID	
LAXEST	LINEAL	

Bonus words

Bonus words on your rack can be hard to spot, especially for the less experienced player. One way to help find them is by using prefixes and suffixes.

Many larger words include a common prefix or suffix – remembering these and using them where you can is a good way to discover any longer words on your rack, including any potential bonus words. The key suffixes to remember beginning with L are -LAND, -LESS, -LET, -LIKE, -LOGY and -LY.

Some words ending with -LAND

Seven-letter words

BAD-LAND	HIE-LAND	NOR-LAND
BOG-LAND	HOL-LAND	OUT-LAND
DRY LAND	LAW-LAND	SUN-LAND
FEN-LAND	LOW-LAND	WET-LAND
GAR-LAND	MID-LAND	

Eight-letter words

BACK-LAND	DUNE-LAND	HOME-LAND
BOOK-LAND	FARM-LAND	LAKE-LAND
BUSH-LAND	FLAT-LAND	MAIN-LAND
CLUB-LAND	GANG-LAND	MOOR-LAND
CROP-LAND	HEAD-LAND	OVER-LAND
DOCK-LAND	HIGH-LAND	PARK-LAND

L

PEAT-LAND	SHET-LAND	WILD-LAND
PINE-LAND	SNOW-LAND	WOOD-LAND
PORT-LAND	TIDE-LAND	YARD-LAND

Some words ending with -LESS
Seven-letter words

AGE-LESS	GOD-LESS	LEG-LESS
AIM-LESS	GUN-LESS	MAP-LESS
AIR-LESS	GUT-LESS	RIB-LESS
ARM-LESS	HAP-LESS	SEX-LESS
ART-LESS	HAT-LESS	SUN-LESS
BAG-LESS	IRE-LESS	USE-LESS
EAR-LESS	JOB-LESS	WIT-LESS
END-LESS	JOY-LESS	ZIP-LESS
EYE-LESS	LAW-LESS	

Eight-letter words

BACK-LESS	GAIN-LESS	PEER-LESS
BONE-LESS	GOAL-LESS	REST-LESS
CARE-LESS	HAIR-LESS	RUTH-LESS
CASH-LESS	HARM-LESS	SEAM-LESS
CHIN-LESS	HEAD-LESS	SEED-LESS
CLUE-LESS	HELP-LESS	SELF-LESS
CORD-LESS	LIFE-LESS	TACT-LESS
DEBT-LESS	LIST-LESS	TAIL-LESS
FACE-LESS	LOVE-LESS	TIME-LESS
FEAR-LESS	MIND-LESS	WIRE-LESS
FLAW-LESS	NAME-LESS	
FORM-LESS	PAIN-LESS	

Some words ending with -LET
Seven-letter words

BOOK-LET
COUP-LET
DOUB-LET
EPAU-LET
LAKE-LET
LEAF-LET
NECK-LET

NOTE-LET
OVER-LET
RING-LET
RIVU-LET
ROOT-LET
SCAR-LET
SERV-LET

SING-LET
SKIL-LET
STAR-LET
TART-LET
TRIO-LET

Eight-letter words

BRACE-LET
COVER-LET
FRUIT-LET
GAUNT-LET

GLOBU-LET
PAMPH-LET
PISTO-LET
PLATE-LET

UNDER-LET
VALVE-LET

Some words ending with -LIKE
Seven-letter words

APE-LIKE
BAT-LIKE
CAT-LIKE
DIS-LIKE
DOG-LIKE
FAN-LIKE

GOD-LIKE
HOG-LIKE
MAN-LIKE
MIS-LIKE
POD-LIKE
SKY-LIKE

TOY-LIKE
WAR-LIKE
WAX-LIKE
WIG-LIKE

L

Eight-letter words

AUNT-LIKE	HAWK-LIKE	REED-LIKE
BEAR-LIKE	HERD-LIKE	ROCK-LIKE
BIRD-LIKE	KING-LIKE	SILK-LIKE
CLAW-LIKE	LADY-LIKE	SWAN-LIKE
DOME-LIKE	LIFE-LIKE	TWIG-LIKE
FISH-LIKE	LORD-LIKE	VICE-LIKE
GAME-LIKE	MAZE-LIKE	WHIP-LIKE
GERM-LIKE	OVEN-LIKE	WOLF-LIKE

Some words ending with -LOGY
Seven-letter words

ANA-LOGY	GEO-LOGY	URO-LOGY
APO-LOGY	NEO-LOGY	ZOO-LOGY
BIO-LOGY	TRI-LOGY	
ECO-LOGY	UFO-LOGY	

Eight-letter words

AERO-LOGY	ONTO-LOGY	TYPO-LOGY
AUTO-LOGY	PYRO-LOGY	VENO-LOGY
HOMO-LOGY	SINO-LOGY	VIRO-LOGY
IDEO-LOGY	THEO-LOGY	
ONCO-LOGY	TOPO-LOGY	

L

Some words ending with -LY
Seven-letter words

ACUTE-LY
AGILE-LY
AWFUL-LY
BEAST-LY
BLACK-LY
BLANK-LY
BLUNT-LY
BRAVE-LY
BROAD-LY
CHEAP-LY
CHIEF-LY
CLEAR-LY
CRACK-LY
DAZED-LY
DEATH-LY
EAGER-LY
ELDER-LY
FAINT-LY
FALSE-LY
FLUID-LY
FRESH-LY

GHOST-LY
GREAT-LY
GROSS-LY
HARSH-LY
IDEAL-LY
INEPT-LY
JOINT-LY
LARGE-LY
LEGAL-LY
LITHE-LY
LOCAL-LY
MISER-LY
MONTH-LY
MUTED-LY
NASAL-LY
NIGHT-LY
ORDER-LY
PLAIN-LY
PRICK-LY
QUICK-LY
QUIET-LY

RAPID-LY
RIGHT-LY
ROUGH-LY
SHAPE-LY
SIGHT-LY
SMART-LY
SOUND-LY
STATE-LY
STERN-LY
TACIT-LY
TENSE-LY
TOTAL-LY
TOUGH-LY
TRICK-LY
TWINK-LY
USUAL-LY
UTTER-LY
VAGUE-LY
VIRAL-LY
WEIRD-LY
WORLD-LY

L

Eight-letter words

ABRUPT-LY	GINGER-LY	PROPER-LY
ABSURD-LY	HEATED-LY	QUAINT-LY
ACTIVE-LY	HEAVEN-LY	RECENT-LY
AUGUST-LY	INSANE-LY	REMOTE-LY
BENIGN-LY	JOYFUL-LY	SCARCE-LY
BOYISH-LY	KNIGHT-LY	SECOND-LY
BRUTAL-LY	LAWFUL-LY	SECURE-LY
CANDID-LY	MANFUL-LY	SOLEMN-LY
CASUAL-LY	MANNER-LY	TRIBAL-LY
DEMURE-LY	MANUAL-LY	TURGID-LY
DIRECT-LY	MENTAL-LY	UNEVEN-LY
ENTIRE-LY	MINUTE-LY	UNFAIR-LY
EXPERT-LY	NATIVE-LY	VERBAL-LY
FACIAL-LY	ONWARD-LY	WESTER-LY
FORMAL-LY	PATENT-LY	WINTER-LY
FRIEND-LY	PRIMAL-LY	WOODEN-LY

Unusual letter combinations

If you have an unusual combination of letters on your rack, or want to impress your opponent with an unusual word, a few words from World English can come in handy.

Australian words

LOPPY	man employed to do maintenance work on a ranch
LOWAN	ground-dwelling bird

Canadian words

LOGAN   backwater
LOONIE   Canadian dollar coin with loon bird on
              one face

Hindi words

LAKH   100,000
LANGUR   arboreal monkey
LASSI   yoghurt drink
LATHI   long heavy stick used as a weapon
LUNGI   long piece of cloth worn as loincloth
              or turban

South African words

LEGUAAN   large monitor lizard

Urdu words

LASCAR   sailor from the East Indies

L

Handy Hint: Do Your Homework

A game of Scrabble can go either way and a less
prepared player will always be at a disadvantage.
A few simple steps can improve your chances before
even starting the game, for example:

• Learn two and three-letter words, especially those
with a tile worth 4 or more points (FHJKQVWXYZ),
for scoring well in tight situations and milking the
premium squares

• Don't forget using all your letters at once gets you
a 50-point bonus

199

M is a good letter for forming short words as it begins a two-letter word with every vowel, as well as with Y and with another M. M combines well with power tiles X and Z: MAX, MIX and MUX (an old American word meaning to make a mess of something) are all worth 12 points and MIZ (informal short form of misery) is worth 14. It is also worth remembering the three-letter words ending in W: MAW, MEW and MOW (8 points each).

Two-letter words beginning with M

MA	MI	MO	MY
ME	MM	MU	

Some three-letter words beginning with M

MAA	MED	MIC	MOC	MOT
MAC	MEE	MID	MOD	MOU
MAE	MEG	MIG	MOE	MOY
MAG	MEL	MIL	MOG	MOZ
MAK	MEM	MIM	MOI	MUN
MAL	MEU	MIR	MOL	MUT
MAM	MEW	MIZ	MOM	MUX
MAW	MHO	MNA	MON	MYC
MAX	MIB	MOA	MOR	

Hooks

Hooking requires a subtle change in a player's thought process, in that they must look at words already on the board without becoming distracted by their pronunciation.

Some front-hooks
Two letters to three

M-AA	M-EE	M-OM
M-AD	M-EL	M-ON
M-AE	M-EM	M-OO
M-AG	M-EN	M-OP
M-AL	M-ES	M-OR
M-AM	M-ET	M-OS
M-AN	M-HO	M-OU
M-AR	M-ID	M-OW
M-AS	M-IS	M-OY
M-AT	M-NA	M-UG
M-AW	M-OB	M-UM
M-AX	M-OD	M-UN
M-AY	M-OE	M-US
M-ED	M-OI	M-UT

Three letters to four

M-ACE	M-AIN	M-AMA
M-ACH	M-AIR	M-ANE
M-AGE	M-AKE	M-ANY
M-AID	M-ALE	M-ARE
M-AIL	M-ALL	M-ARK
M-AIM	M-ALT	M-ART

M-ARY	M-ESS	M-OLE
M-ASH	M-ETA	M-ONO
M-ASK	M-ETH	M-OON
M-ASS	M-ICE	M-OOR
M-ATE	M-IFF	M-OOT
M-EAN	M-ILK	M-OPE
M-EAT	M-ILL	M-ORE
M-EEK	M-INK	M-ORT
M-ELD	M-IRE	M-OWN
M-ELL	M-IRK	M-ULE
M-ELT	M-ISO	M-UMP
M-EME	M-OAT	M-UMU
M-EMO	M-ODE	M-USE
M-END	M-OKE	M-UTE
M-ERE	M-OLD	

M

Four letters to five

M-ACED	M-AXIS	M-ORAL
M-ACER	M-ETIC	M-OSES
M-ACHE	M-IFFY	M-OTTO
M-AGMA	M-IRED	M-OUCH
M-AMBO	M-ITCH	M-OULD
M-ANGA	M-ODAL	M-OURN
M-ANNA	M-OLDY	M-OUST
M-ANTA	M-OLLA	M-OVER
M-ARCH	M-ONER	M-OWED
M-ASHY	M-ONIE	M-OWER
M-AWED	M-OOSE	M-USED
M-AXED	M-OPED	M-USER
M-AXES	M-OPUS	

Five letters to six

M-ACERS	M-ASKED	M-ISLED
M-ACING	M-ASKER	M-ITHER
M-ADDED	M-ASTER	M-OCKER
M-ADDER	M-AWING	M-OILED
M-ADMAN	M-AXING	M-OILER
M-ADMEN	M-EAGER	M-OLDER
M-AGISM	M-EAGRE	M-OLLIE
M-AIDED	M-EANED	M-OPING
M-AILED	M-EASED	M-ORGAN
M-AIMED	M-EASLE	M-ORGUE
M-AIMER	M-ELDER	M-ORRIS
M-AKING	M-EMBER	M-OTHER
M-ALIGN	M-ENDED	M-OUGHT
M-ALLOW	M-ENDER	M-OUPED
M-AMMON	M-ERING	M-OUTER
M-ANGEL	M-ESSES	M-OWING
M-ANGER	M-ESTER	M-OZZIE
M-ANGLE	M-ETHOS	M-UDDER
M-ANTIC	M-ETHYL	M-UGGED
M-ANTIS	M-ETTLE	M-UMBLE
M-ANTRA	M-ICKLE	M-UMPED
M-ARKED	M-ILLER	M-UNIFY
M-ARROW	M-INGLE	M-UNITE
M-ASCOT	M-INION	M-USHER
M-ASHED	M-INTER	M-USING
M-ASHES	M-IRING	M-UTTER

M

M

Six letters to seven

M-ADDING
M-AGNATE
M-AIDING
M-AILING
M-AIMING
M-ANGLED
M-ANGLER
M-ARCHED
M-ARCHER
M-ARCHES
M-ARGENT
M-ARKING
M-ARROWY
M-ASHIER
M-ASHING

M-ASKING
M-EANING
M-EARING
M-EASING
M-ELDING
M-ENDING
M-ETHANE
M-ETHOXY
M-ETTLED
M-ICKLER
M-IFFIER
M-ITCHED
M-OILING
M-OMENTA
M-ONEYER

M-OPUSES
M-ORALLY
M-ORPHIC
M-OUCHED
M-OUCHES
M-OULDER
M-OUPING
M-OUSTED
M-OUTHER
M-OZZIES
M-UGGING
M-ULLING
M-UMPING
M-UNITED
M-USEFUL

Seven letters to eight

M-ACERATE
M-ADWOMAN
M-ADWOMEN
M-AGISTER
M-AIDLESS
M-ALIGNED
M-ALIGNER
M-ANGLING
M-ARCHING
M-ARRIAGE
M-ARROWED
M-ASHIEST

M-EAGERLY
M-ENOLOGY
M-ERISTIC
M-ETHANOL
M-ETHOXYL
M-ETHYLIC
M-ICKLEST
M-IFFIEST
M-ISOGAMY
M-ITCHING
M-OATLIKE
M-OMENTUM

M-OORIEST
M-ORALISM
M-ORALIST
M-ORALITY
M-ORATORY
M-UNIFIED
M-UNITING
M-UNITION
M-UTTERED
M-UTTERER

Some end-hooks
Two letters to three

AI-M	HE-M	MI-M	SI-M
AR-M	HI-M	MO-M	SO-M
BA-M	HM-M	MU-M	TA-M
DA-M	HO-M	NA-M	TO-M
DI-M	IS-M	NO-M	UM-M
DO-M	JA-M	OH-M	WE-M
EL-M	KA-M	OO-M	YA-M
FE-M	LA-M	PA-M	YO-M
GU-M	MA-M	PO-M	YU-M
HA-M	ME-M	RE-M	

Three letters to four

BAL-M	FIR-M	MUM-M	SOW-M
BAR-M	FOR-M	NEE-M	SPA-M
BOO-M	FRO-M	NOR-M	TEA-M
BOR-M	GAU-M	PAL-M	TEE-M
CHA-M	GOR-M	PER-M	THE-M
COO-M	HAE-M	PLU-M	TOO-M
COR-M	HAW-M	PRE-M	WAR-M
DEE-M	HER-M	PRO-M	WAS-M
DOO-M	IDE-M	ROO-M	WEE-M
DOR-M	LEA-M	SEA-M	WHA-M
FAR-M	LOO-M	SEE-M	WHO-M
FER-M	MAL-M	SHA-M	ZOO-M
FIL-M	MAR-M	SKI-M	

M

Four letters to five

ABRI-M	FLAM-M	MAXI-M	SATE-M
ABYS-M	FLEA-M	MINI-M	SEIS-M
ALAR-M	FORA-M	MODE-M	SHAW-M
BREE-M	GOLE-M	PASH-M	SPAS-M
BROO-M	HAKA-M	PURI-M	STUM-M
CHAR-M	HARE-M	REAL-M	THAR-M
CHAS-M	HAUL-M	REAR-M	THRU-M
DENI-M	MALA-M	RETE-M	TOTE-M

Five letters to six

BALSA-M	DODGE-M	MURRA-M	SHTUM-M
BESEE-M	LINGA-M	MUTIS-M	SPIRE-M
CENTU-M	MALIS-M	PARTI-M	TELES-M
CHIAS-M	MERIS-M	PURIS-M	YOGIS-M
CONDO-M	MESTO-M	SADIS-M	
COPAL-M	MONTE-M	SCRAW-M	

Six letters to seven

ANIMIS-M	GOPURA-M	MISTER-M
BUCKRA-M	MANTRA-M	PREWAR-M
FASCIS-M	MISSEE-M	SENSIS-M

Seven letters to eight

CLASSIS-M	FINALIS-M	JIHADIS-M
CYMBALO-M	JEHADIS-M	TITANIS-M

M

Blockers

It is useful to know which words are blockers and can't therefore be extended before or after. You may want to play a blocker that your opponent can't extend, or you may want to avoid playing a blocker because you want to keep the board open.

Three-letter blocker beginning with M
MUX

Some four-letter blockers beginning with M

MADE	MAZY	MONY	MOZZ
MANY	MINX	MOPY	
MARY	MIXY	MOSH	
MATY	MOBY	MOWN	

Some five-letter blockers beginning with M (except words ending in '-ED', '-J', '-S', '-X', '-Y' or '-Z')

MACHI	MENSH	MUCHO
MARCH	MERCH	MULCH
MARIA	MICRA	MULSH
MAYAN	MITCH	MUNCH
MEANT	MOOSE	MUTER

M

Some six-letter blockers beginning with M (except words ending in '-ED', '-J', '-S', '-X', '-Y' or '-Z')

MACING	MEEKER	MIXING
MADMAN	MEIKLE	MODISH
MADMEN	MEREST	MODULI
MAGYAR	MERMAN	MONACT
MAINER	MERMEN	MOOING
MALIBU	METING	MOPIER
MANATU	MEWING	MOPING
MANFUL	MILDER	MORBID
MANTIC	MILKEN	MORISH
MAOMAO	MIMING	MURKER
MATIER	MINIER	MUTEST
MAXING	MIRING	MUTING
MAYEST	MISDID	MYSELF
MAYHAP	MISLIT	MYTHIC
MAZIER	MITRAL	
MEAGER	MIXIER	

M is for Mnemonic

You may find it useful to use memory aids when trying to remember long lists of Scrabble words. Some more experienced players prefer to remember words in their entirety, but for beginners a mnemonic or two can be a great help. Eg, the initial letters of the words in the mnemonic: Please Don't Holler So, Be Nice For Once gives the front hooks for the two-letter word OH.

Bonus words

Bonus words on your rack can be hard to spot, especially for the less experienced player. One way to help find them is by using prefixes and suffixes.

Many larger words include a common prefix or suffix – remembering these and using them where you can is a good way to discover any longer words on your rack, including any potential bonus words. The key prefixes to remember beginning with M are MAN- and MIS- and the key suffixes are -MAN and -MEN.

Some words beginning with MAN-

Seven-letter words

MAN-AGED	MAN-HOLE	MAN-LIKE
MAN-AGER	MAN-HOOD	MAN-MADE
MAN-DATE	MAN-HUNT	MAN-TIDS
MAN-GING	MAN-JACK	MAN-TRAP
MAN-GLED	MAN-KIER	MAN-URES
MAN-GOES	MAN-KIND	MAN-WARD
MAN-GOLD	MAN-LIER	

Eight-letter words

MAN-AGING	MAN-FULLY	MAN-SWORN
MAN-DATED	MAN-GROVE	MAN-URIAL
MAN-DRAKE	MAN-POWER	
MAN-DRILL	MAN-SHIFT	

Some words beginning with MIS-

Seven-letter words

MIS-ALLY	MIS-FITS	MIS-SILE
MIS-CALL	MIS-GIVE	MIS-SING
MIS-CAST	MIS-HAPS	MIS-STEP
MIS-CODE	MIS-HEAR	MIS-TAKE
MIS-CUED	MIS-LAID	MIS-TIME
MIS-DEED	MIS-LEAD	MIS-TING
MIS-DIAL	MIS-MARK	MIS-TOOK
MIS-DOER	MIS-NAME	MIS-USED
MIS-FILE	MIS-READ	
MIS-FIRE	MIS-RULE	

Eight-letter words

MIS-ALIGN	MIS-HEARD	MIS-SPEND
MIS-APPLY	MIS-JUDGE	MIS-SPOKE
MIS-BEGOT	MIS-MATCH	MIS-TAKEN
MIS-CARRY	MIS-PLACE	MIS-TIMED
MIS-CHIEF	MIS-PRICE	MIS-TREAT
MIS-CHOSE	MIS-PRINT	MIS-TRESS
MIS-COLOR	MIS-QUOTE	MIS-TRIAL
MIS-COUNT	MIS-RULED	MIS-TRUST
MIS-FILED	MIS-SABLE	MIS-TRUTH
MIS-FIRED	MIS-SHAPE	MIS-USAGE
MIS-GIVEN	MIS-SPEAK	MIS-USING
MIS-GUIDE	MIS-SPELL	

M

Some words ending with -MAN

Seven-letter words

AUTO-MAN	FOOT-MAN	MILK-MAN
BATS-MAN	FORE-MAN	NEWS-MAN
BIRD-MAN	FREE-MAN	OARS-MAN
BOAT-MAN	FROG-MAN	OTTO-MAN
BOND-MAN	HANG-MAN	PLOW-MAN
BUSH-MAN	HARD-MAN	POST-MAN
CAVE-MAN	HEAD-MAN	REPO-MAN
COAL-MAN	JAZZ-MAN	SAND-MAN
CREW-MAN	JURY-MAN	SHOW-MAN
DEAD-MAN	KINS-MAN	SNOW-MAN
DOOR-MAN	LENS-MAN	SWAG-MAN
DUST-MAN	LINE-MAN	WING-MAN
FIRE-MAN	MAIL-MAN	WORK-MAN

Eight-letter words

BAILS-MAN	FRESH-MAN	POINT-MAN
BLUES-MAN	FRONT-MAN	RIFLE-MAN
BOATS-MAN	GAMES-MAN	SALES-MAN
BOGEY-MAN	HANDY-MAN	SHORE-MAN
BONDS-MAN	HELMS-MAN	SOUND-MAN
BRINK-MAN	HENCH-MAN	SPACE-MAN
CHAIR-MAN	HERDS-MAN	STUNT-MAN
CLANS-MAN	HUNTS-MAN	SWORD-MAN
CLASS-MAN	KNIFE-MAN	TALIS-MAN
COACH-MAN	LANDS-MAN	TRASH-MAN
EARTH-MAN	LINES-MAN	WATCH-MAN
EVERY-MAN	MARKS-MAN	WHEEL-MAN
FERRY-MAN	NOBLE-MAN	WOODS-MAN

M

Some words ending with -MEN
Seven-letter words

ABDO-MEN	DOOR-MEN	LENS-MEN
ALBU-MEN	DUST-MEN	LINE-MEN
BATS-MEN	FOOT-MEN	RAIL-MEN
BIRD-MEN	FORE-MEN	REGI-MEN
BITU-MEN	FREE-MEN	REPO-MEN
BOAT-MEN	FROG-MEN	SHIP-MEN
BOOK-MEN	HANG-MEN	SHOW-MEN
BUSH-MEN	HARD-MEN	SNOW-MEN
CAVE-MEN	HEAD-MEN	SWAG-MEN
COAL-MEN	HILL-MEN	WING-MEN
CREW-MEN	JAZZ-MEN	WORK-MEN
DEAD-MEN	KINS-MEN	

Eight-letter words

BAILS-MEN	GAMES-MEN	RIFLE-MEN
BARGE-MEN	HANDY-MEN	ROADS-MEN
BLUES-MEN	HELMS-MEN	SALES-MEN
BOATS-MEN	HENCH-MEN	SHORE-MEN
BONDS-MEN	HERDS-MEN	SOUND-MEN
BOOGY-MEN	HORSE-MEN	SPACE-MEN
BRINK-MEN	HUNTS-MEN	STUNT-MEN
CHAIR-MEN	KNIFE-MEN	SUPER-MEN
CLANS-MEN	LINES-MEN	WATCH-MEN
COACH-MEN	MARKS-MEN	WHEEL-MEN
DOORS-MEN	MERRY-MEN	WOODS-MEN
EVERY-MEN	NOBLE-MEN	
FERRY-MEN	POINT-MEN	
FREED-MEN	RANCH-MEN	

M

Unusual letter combinations

If you have an unusual combination of letters on your rack, or want to impress your opponent with an unusual word, a few words from World English can come in handy.

Australian words

MALLEE	low shrubby eucalyptus tree
MARRI	type of eucalyptus
MIDDY	middle-sized glass of beer
MILKO	milkman
MOLOCH	spiny lizard
MOPOKE	small spotted owl
MOZ	hoodoo or hex
MUGGA	eucalyptus tree with pink flowers
MULGA	acacia shrub
MULLOCK	waste material from a mine
MUSO	musician
MYALL	acacia with hard scented wood
MYXO	myxomatosis

Canadian words

MUCKAMUCK	food
MUKTUK	beluga skin used as food

Hindi words

MACHAN	platform used in tiger hunting
MAHOUT	elephant driver
MAHSEER	large freshwater fish
MANDI	big market
MANDIR	Hindu or Jain temple

MAUND	unit of weight
MELA	cultural or religious festival
MOHUR	old gold coin
MONAL	Asian pheasant
MORCHA	hostile demonstration
MRIDANG	drum used in Indian music
MYNAH	tropical starling

New Zealand words

MANUKA	myrtaceous tree
MATAI	evergreen tree
MIHI	ceremonial greeting
MOA	extinct large flightless bird
MOKI	edible sea fish
MOKO	Maori tattoo or tattoo pattern
MOOLOO	person from Waikato
MOPOKE	small spotted owl
MUNGA	army canteen

South African words

MEERKAT	sociable mongoose
MENEER	Mr or Sir
MEVROU	Mrs or Madam
MOOI	pleasing
MUTI	herbal medicine

Urdu words

MAIDAN	open space used for meetings and sports
MASALA	mixed spices ground into a paste
MOOLVI	Muslim doctor of the law

Essential info
Value: 1 points
Number in set: 6

There are six **N** tiles in the Scrabble set, making it one of the most common consonants. N is very useful for short words to facilitate parallel plays as it begins a two-letter word with every vowel except I. While three-letter words beginning with N are common, there are fewer high-scoring ones than you might think. These include NAB (5 points) and NAY, NEW and NOW (all 6 points). N is one of the letters of the RETAIN set and is therefore a good letter to keep if trying to get a bonus word.

Two-letter words beginning with N
| NA | NE | NO | NU | NY |

Some three-letter words beginning with N
NAE	NED	NIS	NON	NUR
NAH	NEE	NIT	NOO	NYE
NAM	NEF	NIX	NOR	NYS
NAT	NEG	NOB	NOT	
NAW	NEK	NOG	NOX	
NAY	NEP	NOH	NOY	
NEB	NID	NOM	NUB	

Hooks
Hooking requires a subtle change in a player's
thought process, in that they must look at words
already on the board without becoming distracted
by their pronunciation.

Some front-hooks
Two letters to three

N-AB	N-AT	N-ID	N-ON	N-UN
N-AE	N-AW	N-IS	N-OO	N-UR
N-AG	N-AY	N-IT	N-OR	N-US
N-AH	N-ED	N-OB	N-OS	N-UT
N-AM	N-EE	N-OD	N-OW	N-YE
N-AN	N-EF	N-OH	N-OX	
N-AS	N-ET	N-OM	N-OY	

Three letters to four

N-AFF	N-EAT	N-ODE
N-AGA	N-EON	N-ONE
N-AIL	N-ERK	N-OON
N-ANA	N-ESS	N-OPE
N-ANE	N-EST	N-OSE
N-APE	N-EUK	N-OUS
N-ARC	N-EWT	N-OUT
N-ARE	N-ICE	N-OVA
N-ARK	N-ICK	N-OWL
N-ARY	N-ILL	N-OWN
N-AVE	N-ISH	N-OWT
N-EAR	N-ITS	N-UKE

Four letters to five

N-ACHE	N-EMPT	N-ONCE
N-AILS	N-EVER	N-ONES
N-AKED	N-EWER	N-OOSE
N-APED	N-ICER	N-OPAL
N-ARCO	N-ICKY	N-OULD
N-AUNT	N-IFFY	N-OUPS
N-AVAL	N-ODAL	N-OVEL
N-AVEL	N-OILY	N-OVUM
N-EATH	N-OINT	N-OWED
N-EDDY	N-OMEN	

Five letters to six

N-ABBED	N-EATER	N-ODDER
N-AGGER	N-EBBED	N-OGGIN
N-AILED	N-ESSES	N-OSIER
N-APERY	N-ESTER	N-OTARY
N-APING	N-ETHER	N-OTHER
N-APRON	N-ETTLE	N-OUGHT
N-ARKED	N-EWEST	N-UMBER
N-ARROW	N-ICHED	N-UMPTY
N-AUGHT	N-ICKER	N-UNCLE
N-EARED	N-ICKLE	N-UTTER
N-EARLY	N-IMBED	
N-EATEN	N-ITHER	

N

Six letters to seven

N-AILING	N-EMESES	N-OVATED
N-APHTHA	N-EMESIS	N-OYESES
N-ARKING	N-EOLITH	N-ULLING
N-ASCENT	N-ETTLED	N-UNDINE
N-ATRIUM	N-ICHING	N-UNHOOD
N-EARING	N-IFFIER	N-UNLIKE
N-EBBING	N-OINTED	N-UNSHIP
N-EDDISH	N-ONUSES	
N-EITHER	N-OOLOGY	

Seven letters to eight

N-AINSELL	N-EARLIER	N-OVATION
N-APERIES	N-ETTLING	N-ULLINGS
N-ARRASES	N-IFFIEST	N-UMBERED
N-ARROWED	N-OINTING	N-YAFFING
N-ATRIUMS	N-OTARIES	

Some end-hooks
Two letters to three

AI-N	DO-N	HE-N	MO-N
AN-N	EA-N	HI-N	MU-N
AW-N	EE-N	HO-N	NA-N
BA-N	ER-N	IN-N	NO-N
BE-N	FA-N	IO-N	NU-N
BI-N	FE-N	KI-N	OO-N
BO-N	GI-N	KO-N	OW-N
DA-N	GO-N	LI-N	PA-N
DE-N	GU-N	MA-N	PE-N
DI-N	HA-N	ME-N	PI-N

RE-N	TA-N	TO-N	WO-N
SI-N	TE-N	UR-N	YE-N
SO-N	TI-N	WE-N	YO-N

Three letters to four

BAR-N	GOO-N	RAI-N
BEE-N	GUR-N	SAW-N
BOO-N	HEW-N	SEE-N
BOR-N	HOO-N	SEW-N
BRA-N	JIN-N	SKI-N
BUR-N	LAW-N	SOW-N
CHI-N	LEA-N	SPA-N
COR-N	LIE-N	TEE-N
DAW-N	LOO-N	THE-N
DEE-N	MOA-N	TOO-N
DOO-N	MOO-N	TOR-N
DOW-N	MOR-N	TOW-N
EAR-N	MOW-N	UPO-N
EVE-N	NOO-N	YAR-N
FAW-N	OPE-N	YAW-N
FER-N	PAW-N	

Handy Hint

Use a dictionary when playing Scrabble to check the validity of words when a play is challenged (and to avoid any arguments!). We recommend Collins Official Scrabble Dictionary, where you will find the meanings for all the words listed in this book.

Four letters to five

BLOW-N	GROW-N	SARI-N
BRAW-N	HALO-N	SATI-N
BROW-N	HERO-N	SHAW-N
CHAI-N	HOSE-N	SHOW-N
CLOW-N	HUMA-N	SIRE-N
COVE-N	KNOW-N	SPAW-N
CROW-N	LADE-N	SPUR-N
DEMO-N	LEAR-N	STOW-N
DJIN-N	LIKE-N	TAKE-N
DOVE-N	LINE-N	TOKE-N
DOZE-N	LOGO-N	TWEE-N
DRAW-N	MAYA-N	VEGA-N
FLOW-N	RAVE-N	WAKE-N
FROW-N	RIPE-N	WIDE-N
GIVE-N	RISE-N	WOKE-N
GNAW-N	RIVE-N	WOVE-N
GREE-N	ROMA-N	YEAR-N

Five letters to six

ALTER-N	CARBO-N	GRAVE-N
ARISE-N	CARVE-N	HASTE-N
ASTER-N	CAVER-N	HEAVE-N
AWAKE-N	CHOSE-N	HOOVE-N
AWOKE-N	CLOVE-N	INTER-N
BABOO-N	COMMO-N	LARGE-N
BARRE-N	CRAVE-N	LEAVE-N
BITTE-N	DRIVE-N	LOOSE-N
BRAZE-N	FROZE-N	MACRO-N
BROKE-N	GLUTE-N	MEDIA-N

220

MICRO-N	ROTTE-N	STRAW-N
MODER-N	SCREE-N	STREW-N
NORMA-N	SHAKE-N	STROW-N
PHOTO-N	SHAMA-N	SYLVA-N
PROVE-N	SHAPE-N	THRAW-N
RATIO-N	SHAVE-N	THROW-N
RESEE-N	SPOKE-N	WHITE-N
RESEW-N	STOLE-N	WICCA-N
RESOW-N	STONE-N	

Six letters to seven

ACKNOW-N	PATTER-N	SMIDGE-N
ALKALI-N	POSTER-N	STONER-N
BRONZE-N	PREWAR-N	STRIVE-N
CAPITA-N	PROTEA-N	STROKE-N
CHASTE-N	PROTEI-N	TERTIA-N
COARSE-N	REDRAW-N	THRIVE-N
EASTER-N	REFLOW-N	TRUDGE-N
EMBRYO-N	REGIME-N	UNDRAW-N
ENVIRO-N	REGIVE-N	UNWOVE-N
GELATI-N	REGROW-N	UPGROW-N
HOARSE-N	RERISE-N	UPRISE-N
JIGSAW-N	RESHOW-N	UPTAKE-N
MEDUSA-N	RETAKE-N	URANIA-N
NUCLEI-N	REWAKE-N	UTOPIA-N
OUTSEE-N	REWOVE-N	WESTER-N
PAPAYA-N	RIPSAW-N	WRITHE-N
PASTER-N	SIERRA-N	ZITHER-N

Seven letters to eight

AQUARIA-N	FORGIVE-N	OVERSEE-N
ARCADIA-N	FORSAKE-N	PANACEA-N
AURELIA-N	HACKSAW-N	PARAZOA-N
BEREAVE-N	LEATHER-N	PARTAKE-N
BESPOKE-N	MAGNETO-N	PRESHOW-N
BESTREW-N	MALARIA-N	QUARTER-N
BOHEMIA-N	MISDRAW-N	REAWAKE-N
CODRIVE-N	MISGIVE-N	REFROZE-N
COLLAGE-N	MISGROW-N	REGALIA-N
DEFROZE-N	MISKNOW-N	RESHAVE-N
DILUVIA-N	MISTAKE-N	ROSARIA-N
DISLIKE-N	NORTHER-N	RUBELLA-N
ELECTRO-N	OUTDRAW-N	SLATTER-N
ENGRAVE-N	OUTFLOW-N	SOUTHER-N
ENLARGE-N	OUTGIVE-N	UNBROKE-N
FLYBLOW-N	OUTGROW-N	UNFROZE-N
FORESEE-N	OUTTAKE-N	UNSPOKE-N

Blockers

It is useful to know which words are blockers and can't therefore be extended before or after. You may want to play a blocker that your opponent can't extend, or you may want to avoid playing a blocker because you want to keep the board open.

Some three-letter blockers beginning with N

NAE	NOH	NTH
NAH	NOX	

Some four-letter blockers beginning with N

NAVY	NOPE	NOUS
NESS	NOSH	
NIXY	NOSY	

Some five-letter blockers beginning with N
(except words ending in '-ED', '-J', '-S', '-X', '-Y' or '-Z')

NATAL	NEWER	NOMEN
NAVAL	NICER	NUTSO
NEVER	NOHOW	

Some six-letter blockers beginning with N
(except words ending in '-ED', '-J', '-S', '-X', '-Y' or '-Z')

NAFFER	NEWEST	NONMEN
NAIFER	NEWISH	NONPAR
NAIVER	NICEST	NORDIC
NAPING	NICISH	NOSIER
NEARER	NIGHER	NOSTRO
NEATER	NITRIC	NOTING
NEBISH	NIXING	NOTOUR
NERVAL	NOBLER	NOUNAL
NETHER	NONFAT	NOWISE
NEURAL	NONMAN	NUKING

N

Bonus words

Bonus words on your rack can be hard to spot, especially for the less experienced player. One way to help find them is by using prefixes and suffixes.

Many larger words include a common prefix or suffix – remembering these and using them where you can is a good way to discover any longer words on your rack, including any potential bonus words. The key suffix to remember beginning with N is -NESS.

Some words ending with -NESS
Seven-letter words

APT-NESS	HIP-NESS	ONE-NESS
BAD-NESS	HOT-NESS	RAW-NESS
BIG-NESS	ICI-NESS	RED-NESS
COY-NESS	ILL-NESS	SAD-NESS
DIM-NESS	LIO-NESS	SHY-NESS
DRY-NESS	LOW-NESS	WET-NESS
FAT-NESS	MAD-NESS	WIT-NESS
FIT-NESS	NEW-NESS	WRY-NESS
FUL-NESS	ODD-NESS	
HAR-NESS	OLD-NESS	

Eight-letter words

AGED-NESS	FOND-NESS	POSH-NESS
ARCH-NESS	GLAD-NESS	PURE-NESS
BALD-NESS	GOOD-NESS	RARE-NESS
BARE-NESS	GREY-NESS	RIPE-NESS
BOLD-NESS	HARD-NESS	SAME-NESS
BUSI-NESS	HIGH-NESS	SICK-NESS
CALM-NESS	HUGE-NESS	SLOW-NESS
COLD-NESS	IDLE-NESS	SURE-NESS
COSI-NESS	KIND-NESS	TALL-NESS
CURT-NESS	LATE-NESS	TAME-NESS
DAMP-NESS	LIKE-NESS	TAUT-NESS
DARK-NESS	MEAN-NESS	VAST-NESS
DEAF-NESS	MILD-NESS	WARM-NESS
DEFT-NESS	MUCH-NESS	WEAK-NESS
DEMO-NESS	NEAT-NESS	WELL-NESS
EVIL-NESS	NUMB-NESS	WILD-NESS
FAIR-NESS	OPEN-NESS	
FIRM-NESS	PALE-NESS	

Unusual letter combinations

If you have an unusual combination of letters on your rack, or want to impress your opponent with an unusual word, a few words from World English can come in handy.

Australian words

NARDOO	cloverlike fern
NEDDY	horse
NOAH	shark

| NONG | stupid or incompetent person |
| NUMBAT | small marsupial with long snout |

Canadian words

| NANOOK | polar bear |

Hindi words

NAUCH	intricate Indian dance
NAWAB	Muslim prince in India
NEEM	large tree
NILGAI	large Indian antelope
NULLAH	stream or drain
NUMDAH	coarse felt

New Zealand words

NGAIO	small tree
NGATI	tribe or clan
NIKAU	palm tree

South African words

NAARTJIE	tangerine
NEK	mountain pass
NKOSI	master or chief

N

Essential info
Value: 1 point
Number in set: 8

O is a common letter in Scrabble, with eight tiles in the set. It forms a two-letter word with every other vowel except for A, and is useful when it comes to forming short words in order to score in two directions at once using premium squares, or in tight corners, or for parallel plays, for example OB, OM and OP (4 points each) and OF, OH, OW (5 points each). O also combines well with X to form short words such as OXO (10 points) and OXY (13 points)

Two-letter words beginning with O

OB	OH	OO	OU
OD	OI	OP	OW
OE	OM	OR	OX
OF	ON	OS	OY

Some three-letter words beginning with O

OBA	OHM	OOM	ORC	OUS
OBE	OHO	OON·	ORD	OWT
OBI	OIK	OOP	ORF	OXO
OBO	OKA	OOR	ORT	OXY
OCH	ONO	OOT	OSE	OYE
ODA	ONY	OPE	OUD	
OFF	OOF	ORA	OUK	
OFT	OOH	ORB	OUP	

O

227

Some front-hooks
Two letters to three

O-AR	O-DE	O-OF	O-RE
O-AT	O-ES	O-OH	O-UP
O-BA	O-HM	O-OM	O-UR
O-BE	O-HO	O-ON	O-US
O-BI	O-KA	O-OP	O-UT
O-BO	O-NE	O-OR	O-WE
O-CH	O-NO	O-OS	O-YE
O-DA	O-NY	O-PE	

Three letters to four

O-ARY	O-GEE	O-PEN
O-BEY	O-INK	O-PUS
O-BIT	O-KAY	O-RAD
O-CHE	O-LEA	O-RES
O-DAH	O-LES	O-SAR
O-DAL	O-LID	O-TIC
O-DOR	O-MEN	O-URN
O-DSO	O-OSE	O-VUM
O-FAY	O-PAL	O-WED
O-GAM	O-PED	O-YES

Four letters to five

O-AKED	O-MEGA	O-READ
O-ARED	O-OBIT	O-RIEL
O-AVES	O-OHED	O-SCAR
O-BANG	O-OPED	O-UNCE
O-BOLE	O-OSES	O-UNDY
O-CHER	O-PINE	O-VARY
O-DOUR	O-PING	O-VERT
O-FLAG	O-PIUM	O-VINE
O-GIVE	O-RACH	O-VOID
O-GLED	O-RACY	O-WING
O-HING	O-RANG	O-ZONE
O-LIVE	O-RANT	
O-LOGY	O-RATE	

Five letters to six

O-BITER	O-MENED	O-RALLY
O-BLAST	O-MENTA	O-RANGE
O-BLATE	O-OHING	O-RANGY
O-BOLUS	O-OLOGY	O-RATED
O-CELLI	O-OPING	O-STEAL
O-EDEMA	O-OSIER	O-STENT
O-GAMIC	O-PALED	O-TITIS
O-GIVES	O-PENED	O-UNCES
O-INKED	O-PINED	O-WRIER
O-LINGO	O-PUSES	O-YESES
O-LIVER	O-RACHE	

O

Six letters to seven

O-CARINA	O-MENTAL	O-ROTUND
O-CELLAR	O-MENTUM	O-STRICH
O-CREATE	O-MICRON	O-UGLIED
O-DONATE	O-MIKRON	O-UGLIES
O-DORISE	O-PACIFY	O-UTMOST
O-DORIZE	O-PENING	O-VARIES
O-ESTRAL	O-PINING	O-VERBID
O-ESTRUM	O-PINION	O-VERSET
O-INKING	O-POSSUM	O-WRIEST
O-KIMONO	O-RANGER	O-YESSES
O-LOGIES	O-RATING	O-ZONATE
O-MENING	O-RATION	

Seven letters to eight

O-DORISED	O-ESTRONE	O-RANGIER
O-DORIZED	O-ESTROUS	O-STOMATE
O-ECOLOGY	O-MISSION	O-UROLOGY
O-EDEMATA	O-MISSIVE	O-VARIOLE
O-ENOLOGY	O-OLOGIES	O-VARIOUS
O-ESTRIOL	O-OLOGIST	O-ZONATED

O

Some end-hooks
Two letters to three

AB-O	EX-O	MO-O	RE-O
AD-O	GI-O	NO-O	TA-O
AG-O	GO-O	OB-O	TO-O
BI-O	HA-O	OH-O	UP-O
BO-O	HO-O	ON-O	WO-O
DO-O	IS-O	OX-O	ZO-O
EM-O	LO-O	PO-O	

Three letters to four

ALS-O	FIN-O	MON-O
ALT-O	HER-O	MUS-O
ANN-O	HOB-O	PES-O
BIT-O	HYP-O	PIS-O
BOH-O	JUD-O	POL-O
BOY-O	KAY-O	RED-O
BUB-O	KIN-O	REG-O
BUD-O	LID-O	REP-O
CAM-O	LIN-O	ROT-O
CAP-O	LIP-O	SAD-O
CIT-O	LOB-O	SAG-O
DAD-O	LOG-O	SOH-O
DIN-O	LOT-O	SOL-O
DOC-O	LUD-O	SUM-O
DOD-O	MAK-O	TAR-O
ECH-O	MAN-O	TOP-O
ERG-O	MAY-O	TOR-O
FAR-O	MEM-O	VEG-O
FID-O	MIC-O	VET-O
FIG-O	MIL-O	VIN-O
FIL-O	MIS-O	WIN-O

O

Four letters to five

AMIN-O	CRED-O	MACH-O
BANC-O	CUFF-O	MANG-O
BARD-O	DECK-O	MENT-O
BASH-O	DING-O	METH-O
BEAN-O	DIPS-O	MEZZ-O
BENT-O	DISC-O	MILK-O
BERK-O	DITT-O	MIME-O
BIFF-O	DRAC-O	MOTT-O
BING-O	DUMB-O	MUCH-O
BOFF-O	FANG-O	NACH-O
BOMB-O	FATS-O	NARC-O
BONG-O	FUNG-O	NUTS-O
BUCK-O	GAMB-O	PANT-O
BUFF-O	GECK-O	PEST-O
BUNK-O	GISM-O	PHON-O
BURR-O	GUAN-O	PHOT-O
CACA-O	GUST-O	PIAN-O
CAME-O	HALL-O	PINK-O
CARB-O	HELL-O	PINT-O
CELL-O	HILL-O	PONG-O
CHIA-O	HOWS-O	POSH-O
CHIC-O	HULL-O	POTT-O
CHIN-O	JELL-O	PRIM-O
CHOC-O	JOCK-O	PROM-O
COMB-O	KEEN-O	PROS-O
COMM-O	LASS-O	PULA-O
COMP-O	LENT-O	PUNT-O
COND-O	LIMB-O	RODE-O
CORN-O	LING-O	RUMP-O

232

SANT-O	TANG-O	VIDE-O
SICK-O	TEMP-O	WACK-O
SOCK-O	TORS-O	WALD-O
STEN-O	VERS-O	WHAM-O

Five letters to six

AMMON-O	FRANC-O	REECH-O
BILLY-O	HALLO-O	RIGHT-O
BRILL-O	HOLLO-O	ROMAN-O
BRONC-O	HULLO-O	SHACK-O
CARDI-O	LIBER-O	SHEEP-O
CHARR-O	LIVED-O	SOLAN-O
CHEAP-O	MEDIC-O	SPEED-O
CHEER-O	MORPH-O	STERE-O
CHOCK-O	NYMPH-O	STINK-O
CHURR-O	PEDAL-O	THICK-O
CONCH-O	PLONK-O	TOLED-O
CRYPT-O	PREST-O	TRILL-O
DINER-O	PSEUD-O	VIGOR-O
DORAD-O	PSYCH-O	WEIRD-O
DUETT-O	QUART-O	WHACK-O
ERING-O	RABAT-O	WHATS-O
FASCI-O	RANCH-O	

O

Six letters to seven

BANDIT-O	MOMENT-O	RABBIT-O
BATTER-O	NITROS-O	REVERS-O
BRACER-O	PAESAN-O	SECOND-O
BUDGER-O	PAISAN-O	SERRAN-O
CANTIC-O	PAMPER-O	TAMARA-O
CYMBAL-O	PIMENT-O	TYMPAN-O
GRADIN-O	PRIMER-O	VERISM-O
MAGNET-O	PUMMEL-O	WHERES-O

Seven letters to eight

ARMIGER-O	FASCISM-O	PRELUDI-O
CAPITAN-O	FLAMING-O	RANCHER-O
CLASSIC-O	INTAGLI-O	SESTETT-O
COMMAND-O	LEGGIER-O	SOMBRER-O
CONCERT-O	MONTANT-O	STAMPED-O
CORNETT-O	PEEKABO-O	VIGOROS-O
COURANT-O	PERFECT-O	ZECCHIN-O
EXPRESS-O	POLITIC-O	

O

Blockers

It is useful to know which words are blockers and can't therefore be extended before or after. You may want to play a blocker that your opponent can't extend, or you may want to avoid playing a blocker because you want to keep the board open.

Three-letter blocker beginning with O

OXO

Some four-letter blockers beginning with O

OAKY	ONYX	OYEZ
OCCY	ORYX	

Some five-letter blockers beginning with O (except words ending in '-ED', '-J', '-S', '-X', '-Y' or '-Z')

OATEN	ORGIC	OUTDO
OLEIC	OSSIA	OUTGO

O

Some six-letter blockers beginning with O (except words ending in '-ED', '-J', '-S', '-X', '-Y' or '-Z')

OAFISH	OILMEN	OUTBYE
OAKIER	OMIGOD	OUTDID
OBESER	ONRUSH	OUTSAT
OBITER	OPTING	OUTSAW
OBTECT	ORBIER	OUTWON
OCTOPI	ORGANA	OWLISH
ODDEST	ORGIAC	OXIDIC
ODDISH	OSTEAL	OZONIC
OGRISH	OSTIAL	
OILMAN	OSTIUM	

Bonus words

Bonus words on your rack can be hard to spot, especially for the less experienced player. One way to help find them is by using prefixes and suffixes.

Many larger words include a common prefix or suffix – remembering these and using them where you can is a good way to discover any longer words on your rack, including any potential bonus words. The key prefixes to remember beginning with O are OUT- and OVER- and the key suffixes are -OID, -OR, -OUS and -OUT.

O

Some words beginning with OUT-
Seven-letter words

OUT-ACTS	OUT-GROW	OUT-RANK
OUT-AGES	OUT-GUNS	OUT-RIDE
OUT-BACK	OUT-GUSH	OUT-RUNS
OUT-BIDS	OUT-KEEP	OUT-SELL
OUT-CAST	OUT-LAID	OUT-SIDE
OUT-COME	OUT-LAND	OUT-SING
OUT-CROP	OUT-LAST	OUT-SIZE
OUT-DOER	OUT-LAWS	OUT-SOLD
OUT-DONE	OUT-LAYS	OUT-SPAN
OUT-DOOR	OUT-LETS	OUT-STAY
OUT-DRAW	OUT-LIES	OUT-TAKE
OUT-EARN	OUT-LIVE	OUT-TALK
OUT-FALL	OUT-LOOK	OUT-VOTE
OUT-FISH	OUT-MODE	OUT-WAIT
OUT-FITS	OUT-PACE	OUT-WARD
OUT-FLOW	OUT-PLAY	OUT-WITH
OUT-FOOT	OUT-POST	OUT-WITS
OUT-GAVE	OUT-PUTS	
OUT-GOER	OUT-RAGE	

O

237

Eight-letter words

OUT-ACTED	OUT-FENCE	OUT-RIDER
OUT-ARGUE	OUT-FIELD	OUT-SCORE
OUT-BOARD	OUT-FLANK	OUT-SIDER
OUT-BOUND	OUT-FOXED	OUT-SIZED
OUT-BREAK	OUT-GOING	OUT-SPEAK
OUT-CHARM	OUT-GROWN	OUT-SPOKE
OUT-CLASS	OUT-LAWED	OUT-STAND
OUT-CRIES	OUT-LINED	OUT-STARE
OUT-DANCE	OUT-MATCH	OUT-SWEPT
OUT-DATED	OUT-PACED	OUT-THINK
OUT-DOING	OUT-PRICE	OUT-VOICE
OUT-DRINK	OUT-RAGED	OUT-WEIGH
OUT-FACED	OUT-REACH	

Some words beginning with OVER-
Seven-letter words

OVER-ACT	OVER-DUB	OVER-LAY
OVER-AGE	OVER-DUE	OVER-PAY
OVER-ALL	OVER-EAT	OVER-RAN
OVER-ATE	OVER-EGG	OVER-SAW
OVER-AWE	OVER-FED	OVER-SEE
OVER-CUT	OVER-JOY	OVER-TAX
OVER-DID	OVER-LAP	OVER-USE

Eight-letter words

OVER-ARCH	OVER-GROW	OVER-PAGE
OVER-AWED	OVER-HAND	OVER-PAID
OVER-BEAR	OVER-HANG	OVER-PLAY
OVER-BITE	OVER-HAUL	OVER-RATE
OVER-BRED	OVER-HEAR	OVER-RODE
OVER-BUSY	OVER-HEAT	OVER-RULE
OVER-CAME	OVER-HYPE	OVER-SEEN
OVER-CAST	OVER-IDLE	OVER-SELL
OVER-COAT	OVER-KEEN	OVER-SHOT
OVER-COME	OVER-KILL	OVER-SIZE
OVER-COOK	OVER-LAID	OVER-STAY
OVER-DOES	OVER-LAND	OVER-STEP
OVER-DONE	OVER-LEAF	OVER-TAKE
OVER-DOSE	OVER-LOAD	OVER-TIME
OVER-EASY	OVER-LONG	OVER-TONE
OVER-FEED	OVER-LOOK	OVER-TOOK
OVER-FILL	OVER-LORD	OVER-TURN
OVER-GOES	OVER-PACK	OVER-WORK

O

Some words ending with -OID
Seven-letter words

ADEN-OID
ANDR-OID
COSM-OID
CYST-OID
DELT-OID
DISC-OID

FACT-OID
FUNG-OID
GLOB-OID
HYDR-OID
NEUR-OID
SAUR-OID

SPOR-OID
STER-OID
TABL-OID
THYR-OID
TYPH-OID

Eight-letter words

ALKAL-OID
AMOEB-OID
BLAST-OID
CAMEL-OID
CENTR-OID
DENDR-OID
GROUP-OID
HEMAT-OID
HUMAN-OID
LEMUR-OID

LYMPH-OID
MANAT-OID
MEDUS-OID
MELAN-OID
NEMAT-OID
NUCLE-OID
PARAN-OID
PLASM-OID
POLYP-OID
PSYCH-OID

RESIN-OID
RETIN-OID
RHOMB-OID
SCHIZ-OID
SLEAZ-OID
SPHER-OID
TETAN-OID
VARIC-OID
VIRUS-OID

Some words ending with -OR
Seven-letter words

ADAPT-OR
ADVIS-OR
AUDIT-OR
AVIAT-OR
BICOL-OR
CREAT-OR
CURAT-OR
DEBIT-OR
DILUT-OR
EJECT-OR
ELECT-OR

EMPER-OR
ENACT-OR
EQUAT-OR
EXCIT-OR
GRANT-OR
IGNIT-OR
JANIT-OR
NEGAT-OR
OFFER-OR
QUEST-OR
REACT-OR

ROTAT-OR
SCISS-OR
SENAT-OR
SETTL-OR
SPONS-OR
SQUAL-OR
TRACT-OR
TRAIT-OR
TRUST-OR
VISIT-OR

Eight-letter words

ABDUCT-OR
ACCENT-OR
ACCEPT-OR
ADJUST-OR
AGITAT-OR
ANIMAT-OR
ASSESS-OR
ASSIGN-OR
BEHAVI-OR
BISECT-OR
CAVEAT-OR
CODEBT-OR
CONVEN-OR
CONVEY-OR
CORRID-OR

CREDIT-OR
DEFECT-OR
DEPICT-OR
DETECT-OR
DICTAT-OR
DIRECT-OR
EFFECT-OR
ELEVAT-OR
ENDEAV-OR
EXECUT-OR
GOVERN-OR
IMITAT-OR
IMPOST-OR
INFECT-OR
INJECT-OR

INVENT-OR
INVEST-OR
ISOLAT-OR
METAPH-OR
NARRAT-OR
NEIGHB-OR
OBJECT-OR
OBSESS-OR
PREDAT-OR
PROVID-OR
PURVEY-OR
RADIAT-OR
REDUCT-OR
REJECT-OR
RESIST-OR

241

SCULPT-OR	STRESS-OR	VIOLAT-OR
SECRET-OR	SURVEY-OR	
SELECT-OR	TESTAT-OR	

Some words ending with -OUS
Seven-letter words

AMOR-OUS	GIBB-OUS	POMP-OUS
ARDU-OUS	GLOB-OUS	RAUC-OUS
BILI-OUS	HEIN-OUS	RIOT-OUS
BULB-OUS	HIDE-OUS	RUIN-OUS
CALL-OUS	IGNE-OUS	TEDI-OUS
CURI-OUS	JEAL-OUS	TENU-OUS
DEVI-OUS	NITR-OUS	TIME-OUS
DUBI-OUS	NOXI-OUS	VACU-OUS
ENVI-OUS	OBVI-OUS	VARI-OUS
FATU-OUS	ODOR-OUS	VICI-OUS
FERR-OUS	OMIN-OUS	ZEAL-OUS
FIBR-OUS	ONER-OUS	
FURI-OUS	PITE-OUS	

Tile Tracking

This means being aware of what tiles have already been played and therefore what might remain in the bag or on your opponent's rack. Tile tracking can be useful to manage your expectations of what common vowels or consonants you are likely to pick from the bag, and whether there are any goodies (blanks Ss JQXZ) left. At the end of a game it could even enable you to know what your opponent is holding. This practice is more common at club and tournament level.

Eight-letter words

ARSON-OUS	GRACI-OUS	RIGOR-OUS
BIBUL-OUS	GRIEV-OUS	SENSU-OUS
CHROM-OUS	LIBEL-OUS	SQUAM-OUS
COUSC-OUS	LUMIN-OUS	STUDI-OUS
COVET-OUS	LUSCI-OUS	TIMOR-OUS
DECOR-OUS	LUSTR-OUS	TORTU-OUS
DESIR-OUS	MUTIN-OUS	ULCER-OUS
DEXTR-OUS	NITRE-OUS	UNCTU-OUS
ENORM-OUS	NUMER-OUS	VAPOR-OUS
FABUL-OUS	ORDUR-OUS	VENOM-OUS
FACTI-OUS	PERIL-OUS	VIGOR-OUS
FEVER-OUS	POPUL-OUS	VIRTU-OUS
GENER-OUS	PRECI-OUS	WONDR-OUS
GORGE-OUS	PREVI-OUS	

Some words ending with -OUT
Seven-letter words

BACK-OUT	HAND-OUT	SHUT-OUT
BAIL-OUT	HANG-OUT	SPIN-OUT
BESP-OUT	HIDE-OUT	TAKE-OUT
BLOW-OUT	LOCK-OUT	TIME-OUT
BURN-OUT	LOOK-OUT	TURN-OUT
CAMP-OUT	MISS-OUT	WALK-OUT
COOK-OUT	PASS-OUT	WASH-OUT
DROP-OUT	PULL-OUT	WITH-OUT
FADE-OUT	READ-OUT	WORK-OUT
FALL-OUT	ROLL-OUT	
FOLD-OUT	SELL-OUT	

Eight-letter words

BLACK-OUT	OUTSH-OUT	SPEAK-OUT
BREAK-OUT	PHASE-OUT	STAKE-OUT
CARRY-OUT	PRINT-OUT	STAND-OUT
CHECK-OUT	RUNAB-OUT	STICK-OUT
FLAME-OUT	SEASC-OUT	THERE-OUT
FREAK-OUT	SEATR-OUT	UNDEV-OUT
INDEV-OUT	SHAKE-OUT	WATCH-OUT
KNOCK-OUT	SHOOT-OUT	WHITE-OUT
LAYAB-OUT	SLEEP-OUT	

Unusual letter combinations

If you have an unusual combination of letters on your rack, or want to impress your opponent with an unusual word, a few words from World English can come in handy.

O

Australian words

OCKER   uncultivated or boorish Australian

Hindi words

OONT   camel

South African words

OKE   man
OOM   title of respect

P
3

Essential info
Value: 3 points
Number in set: 2

There are two-letter words beginning with **P** for each vowel except U which, combined with OP and UP, make it very flexible for short words such as PE (the 17th letter in the Hebrew alphabet, 4 points) and PO (an informal word for chamber pot, also 4 points). P also combines well with X, forming three-letter words PAX, PIX and POX (12 points each) and also Z, for example the three-letter POZ (an old-fashioned short form of positive, 14 points).

Two-letter words beginning with P

PA	PE	PI	PO

Some three-letter words beginning with P

PAC	PEP	PIX	PSI
PAH	PER	POA	PST
PAM	PEW	POH	PUG
PAP	PHI	POI	PUH
PAR	PHO	POL	PUR
PAV	PHT	POM	PUS
PAX	PIA	POW	PUY
PEC	PIC	POX	PYA
PED	PIR	POZ	PYE
PEH	PIU	PRE	PYX

245

Hooks

Hooking requires a subtle change in a player's thought process, in that they must look at words already on the board without becoming distracted by their pronunciation.

Some front-hooks
Two letters to three

P-AD	P-AX	P-ET	P-OM	P-UG
P-AH	P-AY	P-HI	P-OO	P-UH
P-AL	P-EA	P-HO	P-OP	P-UN
P-AM	P-ED	P-IN	P-OS	P-UP
P-AN	P-EE	P-IS	P-OW	P-UR
P-AR	P-EH	P-IT	P-OX	P-US
P-AS	P-EN	P-OD	P-RE	P-UT
P-AT	P-ER	P-OH	P-SI	P-YA
P-AW	P-ES	P-OI	P-ST	P-YE

Three letters to four

P-ACE	P-AND	P-EAR
P-ACT	P-ANE	P-EAT
P-AGE	P-ANT	P-EEK
P-AID	P-ARE	P-EEL
P-AIL	P-ARK	P-EEN
P-AIN	P-ART	P-ELT
P-AIR	P-ASH	P-END
P-AIS	P-ASS	P-EON
P-ALE	P-ATE	P-ERE
P-ALL	P-AVE	P-ERK
P-ALP	P-AWN	P-EST

P-HAT	P-LOP	P-OUT
P-HEW	P-LOT	P-OXY
P-HUT	P-LOW	P-RAM
P-ICK	P-LOY	P-RAT
P-ILL	P-LUG	P-RAY
P-IMP	P-LUM	P-REP
P-INK	P-OKE	P-REZ
P-ION	P-OLE	P-RIG
P-ITA	P-ONE	P-RIM
P-LAT	P-ONY	P-ROB
P-LAY	P-OOR	P-ROD
P-LEA	P-OPE	P-ROM
P-LED	P-ORE	P-ROW
P-LEX	P-ORT	P-UKE
P-LIE	P-OSE	P-UMP
P-LOD	P-OUR	P-URE

Four letters to five

P-ACED	P-AVER	P-ITCH
P-ACER	P-AWED	P-LACE
P-AEON	P-EACH	P-LACK
P-AGED	P-EARL	P-LAID
P-AGER	P-EASE	P-LAIN
P-ALAS	P-EGGY	P-LANE
P-ALLY	P-ESKY	P-LANK
P-APER	P-HONE	P-LANT
P-ARCH	P-ICKY	P-LAST
P-ARED	P-INCH	P-LATE
P-ARIS	P-INKY	P-LEAD
P-ARTY	P-INTO	P-LEAT

P

P-LIED	P-RANK	P-ROLL
P-LIER	P-RAWN	P-RONG
P-LINK	P-REEN	P-ROOF
P-LUCK	P-RICE	P-ROSE
P-LUMP	P-RICY	P-ROVE
P-LUSH	P-RIDE	P-RUDE
P-OINT	P-RIMA	P-RUNE
P-OLIO	P-RIME	P-SHAW
P-OUCH	P-RISE	P-UNTO
P-OWER	P-ROBE	P-URGE
P-RANG	P-ROLE	

Five letters to six

P-ACING	P-AWNED	P-INKER
P-ACKER	P-AWNER	P-INNED
P-ADDED	P-EASED	P-INNER
P-ADDER	P-EGGED	P-IRATE
P-ADDLE	P-ELVES	P-ITCHY
P-AGING	P-ENDED	P-LACED
P-AIRED	P-ESTER	P-LACER
P-AIRER	P-HONED	P-LATED
P-ALATE	P-HONER	P-LATER
P-ANTED	P-HONEY	P-LAYED
P-ARISH	P-HOOEY	P-LAYER
P-ARKED	P-ICKER	P-LEASE
P-ARLED	P-ICKLE	P-LEDGE
P-ARSON	P-IGGED	P-LODGE
P-ASHED	P-IMPLY	P-LOUGH
P-ASTER	P-INION	P-LOVER
P-AWING	P-INKED	P-LOWED

248

P-LOWER	P-REACH	P-RIVET
P-LUCKY	P-REACT	P-ROBED
P-LUMMY	P-REBUY	P-ROPER
P-LUMPY	P-RECUT	P-ROSED
P-LUNGE	P-REFER	P-ROTON
P-LYING	P-REFIX	P-ROVED
P-ODIUM	P-REMIX	P-ROVEN
P-OLDER	P-REPAY	P-ROVER
P-OSIER	P-RESET	P-ROWER
P-OTTER	P-RETAX	P-RUNED
P-OUNCE	P-REVUE	P-UMPED
P-OUPED	P-RICED	P-UPPED
P-OUTED	P-RICER	P-URGED
P-OUTER	P-RIEVE	P-URGER
P-RAISE	P-RIMED	P-USHER
P-RANCE	P-RIMER	P-UTTER
P-RAYED	P-RISER	

Six letters to seven

P-ADDING	P-ASHING	P-ICKIER
P-ADDLED	P-AWNING	P-ICKILY
P-AIRING	P-EANING	P-ICKLER
P-ANTHER	P-EASING	P-INCASE
P-ANTING	P-EERIER	P-INCHED
P-ANTLER	P-EGGING	P-INCHER
P-ARABLE	P-ENDING	P-INKING
P-ARCHED	P-ENFOLD	P-INNING
P-ARKING	P-HATTER	P-ITCHED
P-ARLING	P-HONIED	P-LACING
P-ARTIER	P-HONING	P-LAIDED

P

P-LANKED	P-OINTED	P-REPACK
P-LANNER	P-OODLES	P-REPAID
P-LASTER	P-ORCINE	P-REPONE
P-LATINA	P-OUCHED	P-RESALE
P-LATTER	P-OUTING	P-RESELL
P-LAYING	P-RAISED	P-RESENT
P-LAYOFF	P-RAISER	P-RESHIP
P-LEADED	P-RANCED	P-RESIDE
P-LEADER	P-RANGED	P-RESOLD
P-LEASED	P-RANKED	P-RESUME
P-LEASER	P-RANKLE	P-RETELL
P-LEDGED	P-RATTED	P-RETOLD
P-LEDGER	P-RATTLE	P-REVERB
P-LIABLE	P-RAYING	P-REVIEW
P-LODGED	P-REAVER	P-REWASH
P-LOTTED	P-REBILL	P-REWORN
P-LOTTER	P-REBOOK	P-RICIER
P-LOWING	P-RECAST	P-RICKLE
P-LUCKED	P-RECEDE	P-RICKLY
P-LUGGED	P-RECEPT	P-RIDING
P-LUGGER	P-RECOOK	P-RISING
P-LUMBER	P-REDATE	P-ROBING
P-LUMPED	P-REDIAL	P-RODDED
P-LUMPEN	P-REFACE	P-ROOFED
P-LUMPER	P-REFECT	P-ROOFER
P-LUNGED	P-REHEAT	P-ROSILY
P-LUNGER	P-REMADE	P-ROVING
P-LUNKER	P-REMISE	P-RUDISH
P-LUSHER	P-REMOVE	P-UPPING
P-LUSHLY	P-RENAME	P-URGING

Seven letters to eight

P-ADDLING
P-ALIMONY
P-ALTERED
P-ARCHING
P-ARTICLE
P-ARTISAN
P-ARTWORK
P-EARLIER
P-ENCHANT
P-ENLIGHT
P-ENOLOGY
P-ENTICED
P-HARMING
P-HISHING
P-HONEYED
P-ICKIEST
P-INCHING
P-INKIEST
P-ITCHIER
P-ITCHILY
P-ITCHING
P-LAIDING
P-LANKING
P-LAYBACK
P-LAYTIME
P-LEADING
P-LEASING
P-LEASURE
P-LIGHTED

P-LIGHTER
P-LOTTING
P-LUCKILY
P-LUCKING
P-LUGGING
P-LUGHOLE
P-LUMPING
P-LUMPISH
P-LUNGING
P-LUSHEST
P-LUSHIER
P-OTTERED
P-OUCHING
P-RAISING
P-RANCING
P-RANGING
P-RANKING
P-RANKISH
P-RATTLED
P-RATTLER
P-REACHED
P-REACHER
P-READAPT
P-READMIT
P-REAPPLY
P-REARMED
P-REBIRTH
P-REBOUND
P-REBUILD

P-REBUILT
P-RECEDED
P-RECITED
P-RECLEAN
P-RECURED
P-REDATED
P-REDRAFT
P-REFLECT
P-REFACED
P-REFIXED
P-REGNANT
P-REJUDGE
P-REMIXED
P-REMORSE
P-REMOVED
P-REORDER
P-REPAVED
P-REPLACE
P-REPOSED
P-REPRICE
P-REPRINT
P-RESERVE
P-RESHOWN
P-RESIDED
P-RESIDER
P-RESUMED
P-RESUMER
P-RETRAIN
P-RETRIAL

P

P-RETYPED	P-REWEIGH	P-ROOFING	
P-REUNION	P-REWIRED	P-ROSIEST	
P-REUNITE	P-RICIEST	P-UNITIVE	
P-REVALUE	P-RIGGISH	P-UTTERED	
P-REVISED	P-RILLING	P-UTTERER	
P-REVISIT	P-RODDING		

Some end-hooks
Two letters to three

AL-P	HE-P	NE-P	TO-P
AM-P	HI-P	OO-P	UM-P
AS-P	HO-P	OU-P	UR-P
BA-P	JA-P	PA-P	WO-P
BO-P	KI-P	PE-P	YA-P
DA-P	KO-P	PI-P	YE-P
DI-P	LA-P	PO-P	YU-P
DO-P	LI-P	RE-P	ZA-P
FA-P	LO-P	SI-P	
GI-P	MA-P	SO-P	
GU-P	MO-P	TA-P	
HA-P	NA-P	TI-P	

P

Celebrity Scrabble Players

include Mel Gibson, Nicole Kidman, Chris Martin, Madonna and Sting.

Three letters to four

BEE-P	HAS-P	PER-P
BUM-P	HEM-P	POM-P
BUR-P	HOO-P	PRE-P
CAM-P	HUM-P	PRO-P
CAR-P	JEE-P	PUL-P
CHA-P	LAM-P	RAM-P
CHI-P	LEA-P	RAS-P
COO-P	LEE-P	ROM-P
COW-P	LIS-P	RUM-P
DAM-P	LOO-P	SEE-P
DEE-P	LOU-P	SKI-P
FRA-P	LOW-P	SUM-P
GAS-P	LUM-P	TAR-P
GOO-P	MUM-P	WAR-P
GUL-P	PAR-P	WAS-P
GUM-P	PEE-P	WIS-P

Four letters to five

BICE-P	GRAM-P	SLEE-P
BLEE-P	GRUM-P	SLUM-P
CHAM-P	PLUM-P	SLUR-P
CHUM-P	POLY-P	STUM-P
CLAM-P	PRIM-P	SWAM-P
CRAM-P	SCAM-P	SWEE-P
CREE-P	SCAR-P	TRAM-P
CRIM-P	SCUL-P	WHOM-P
CRIS-P	SKIM-P	

P

253

Five letters to six

ESCAR-P	SCRUM-P	TRICE-P
SCRAW-P	SHLEP-P	
SCRIM-P	THREE-P	

Six letters to seven

BEDLAM-P	MANTRA-P	SCHLEP-P

Seven letters to eight

AUTOCAR-P	MINICAM-P

Blockers

It is useful to know which words are blockers and can't therefore be extended before or after. You may want to play a blocker that your opponent can't extend, or you may want to avoid playing a blocker because you want to keep the board open.

P

Some three-letter blockers beginning with P

PAX	PLY	PST
PHT	POH	PYX

Some four-letter blockers beginning with P

PFFT	PLEX	PREZ
PHAT	POCO	PSST
PHEW	POKY	PUKA
PHIZ	PONY	PUNY
PITY	POSY	

Some five-letter blockers beginning with P (except words ending in '-ED', '-J', '-S', '-X', '-Y' or '-Z')

PACTA	PILAR	PUKKA
PADRI	PILCH	PULMO
PAISE	PINCH	PUPAE
PAI ER	POOCH	PUPAL
PAOLO	PORCH	PURER
PAPAL	PROST	PUTID
PENAL	PROUD	PYRAL
PERCH	PUBIC	PYRIC

P

Some six-letter blockers begining with P (except words ending in '-ED', '-J', '-S', '-X', '-Y' or '-Z')

PACTUM	PHONAL	POTMAN
PAIRER	PHYLUM	POTMEN
PALEAL	PIEING	POXIER
PALEST	PIEMAN	POXING
PALISH	PIEMEN	PRELAW
PALLID	PIPIER	PRIMAL
PANINI	PITMEN	PROGUN
PARISH	PLACID	PRONER
PARTIM	PLANAR	PRONTO
PASSEE	PLIANT	PROWAR
PASSIM	POKIER	PROWER
PAUSAL	POLISH	PULPAL
PAWING	POLYPI	PUNIER
PENMAN	POSHER	PUNISH
PENMEN	POSIER	PUREST
PEPFUL	POTASH	PURING
PERISH	POTATO	PUTRID
PERTER	POTING	

Bonus words

Bonus words on your rack can be hard to spot, especially for the less experienced player. One way to help find them is by using prefixes and suffixes.

Many larger words include a common prefix or suffix – remembering these and using them where you can is a good way to discover any longer words on your rack, including any potential bonus words. The key prefixes to remember beginning with P are PER-, PRE- and PRO-.

Some words beginning with PER-

Seven-letter words

PER-CENT	PER-JURY	PER-TAKE
PER-CHER	PER-KING	PER-USED
PER-CUSS	PER-MING	PER-USER
PER-FORM	PER-PLEX	PER-VADE
PER-FUME	PER-SIST	PER-VERT
PER-HAPS	PER-SONS	
PER-JURE	PER-TAIN	

Eight-letter words

PER-FUMED	PER-SPIRE	PER-VADED
PER-ISHES	PER-SUING	PER-VERSE
PER-MUTED	PER-TAKEN	
PER-OXIDE	PER-USING	

P

Some words beginning with PRE-

Seven-letter words

PRE-ACHY	PRE-FACE	PRE-SENT
PRE-BOIL	PRE-LATE	PRE-SHOW
PRE-BOOK	PRE-LOAD	PRE-SIDE
PRE-CAST	PRE-LUDE	PRE-TEEN
PRE-CEDE	PRE-MADE	PRE-TEND
PRE-CODE	PRE-MISE	PRE-TERM
PRE-COOK	PRE-PACK	PRE-TEXT
PRE-DATE	PRE-PAID	PRE-VAIL
PRE-DAWN	PRE-PARE	PRE-VIEW
PRE-DIAL	PRE-PLAN	PRE-WARN
PRE-DICT	PRE-SAGE	PRE-WASH
PRE-EMPT	PRE-SALE	PRE-WORN

Eight-letter words

PRE-ADAPT	PRE-JUDGE	PRE-SIDED
PRE-AMBLE	PRE-MOLAR	PRE-SLEEP
PRE-BIRTH	PRE-ORDER	PRE-SOLVE
PRE-BUILT	PRE-OWNED	PRE-STORE
PRE-CEDED	PRE-PARED	PRE-TASTE
PRE-CITED	PRE-PLANT	PRE-TENSE
PRE-CURED	PRE-POSED	PRE-TRIAL
PRE-DATED	PRE-PRESS	PRE-TYPED
PRE-ELECT	PRE-PRINT	PRE-VALUE
PRE-EXIST	PRE-SAGER	PRE-VISED
PRE-FACED	PRE-SERVE	
PRE-FIXED	PRE-SHAPE	

P

Some words beginning with PRO-
Seven-letter words

PRO-BALL
PRO-BATE
PRO-BING
PRO-CESS
PRO-CURE
PRO-DRUG
PRO-DUCE
PRO-DUCT
PRO-FANE

PRO-FESS
PRO-FILE
PRO-FUSE
PRO-GRAM
PRO-LONG
PRO-MISE
PRO-MOTE
PRO-NOUN
PRO-PANE

PRO-PONE
PRO-POSE
PRO-SING
PRO-TEST
PRO-VERB
PRO-VIDE
PRO-WEST

Eight-letter words

PRO-BATED
PRO-CLAIM
PRO-CURED
PRO-FILED
PRO-FILER
PRO-FOUND
PRO-LAPSE

PRO-MISER
PRO-MOTED
PRO-MOTOR
PRO-PHASE
PRO-POSED
PRO-POUND
PRO-RATED

PRO-STATE
PRO-STYLE
PRO-TEASE
PRO-TRACT
PRO-TRADE
PRO-UNION
PRO-VISOR

P

Unusual letter combinations

If you have an unusual combination of letters on your rack, or want to impress your opponent with an unusual word, a few words from World English can come in handy.

Australian words

PINDAN	desert region of Western Australia
PLONKO	alcoholic, especially one who drinks wine
PODDY	handfed calf or lamb
POKIE	poker machine
POSSIE	position
PRELOVED	second-hand

Canadian words

PARFLECHE	dried rawhide
PARKADE	building used as a car park
PARKETTE	small public park
PLEW	beaver skin used as a standard unit
POGEY	financial relief for the unemployed
POKELOGAN	backwater
POUTINE	chipped potatoes topped with curd cheese and tomato sauce
PUNG	horse-drawn sleigh

Hindi words

PACHISI	game resembling backgammon
PAISA	one hundredth of a rupee
PAKORA	dish of deep-fried chicken or vegetables
PANEER	soft white cheese

P

PARATHA	flat unleavened bread
PEEPUL	tree similar to the banyan
PUNKAH	fan made of palm leaves
PURDAH	custom of keeping women secluded
PURI	unleavened flaky bread
PUTTEE	strip of cloth wound around the leg

New Zealand words

PAKAHI	acid soil or land
PAKOKO	small freshwater fish
PAUA	edible abalone
PIKAU	rucksack
PIPI	shellfish
PIUPIU	leaf skirt
POI	ball of woven flax
PONGA	tall tree fern
PORAE	edible sea fish
PORANGI	crazy
PORINA	moth larva
POTAE	hat
POWHIRI	welcoming ceremony
PUGGY	sticky
PUHA	sow thistle
PUKEKO	wading bird
PURIRI	forest tree

South African words

| PADKOS | snacks for a long journey |
| PLAAS | farm |

P

Essential info
Value: 10 points
Number in set: 1
Power Tile

Along with Z, **Q** is the highest-scoring letter in the Scrabble set. However, unlike Z, Q can prove difficult to use if it is not accompanied by the letter U. The best method of getting around this is to commit to memory all the short words beginning with Q which do not require a U. This is easier than it sounds, as there is only one two-letter word beginning with Q: QI (vital energy believed to circulate around the body, 11 points). There are three three-letter words (12 points each, and only one of these uses a U): QUA (in the capacity of), QAT (evergreen shrub of Africa and Asia whose leaves have narcotic properties) and QIS (plural of QI). The fourth three-letter word containing a Q is SUQ.

Two-letter word beginning with Q
QI

Three-letter words beginning with Q
QAT   QUA

262

Three-letter word using Q
SUQ

AQUA	QUAT	QUIT
QADI	QUAY	QUIZ
QAID	QUEP	QUOD
QOPH	QUEY	QUOP
QUAD	QUID	SUQS
QUAG	QUIN	WAQF
QUAI	QUIP	

Q

Hooks

Hooking requires a subtle change in a player's thought process, in that they must look at words already on the board without becoming distracted by their pronunciation.

Some front-hooks
Two letters to three
Q-AT   Q-IS

Three letters to four
Q-AID   Q-UEY

Four letters to five
Q-AIDS   Q-UEYS

Some end-hooks
Four letters to five
TALA-Q

Q

Blockers

It is useful to know which words are blockers and can't therefore be extended before or after. You may want to play a blocker that your opponent can't extend, or you may want to avoid playing a blocker because you want to keep the board open.

Three-letter blocker beginning with Q
QIS

Four-letter blocker beginning with Q
QUEP

Some five-letter blockers beginning with Q (except words ending in '-ED', '-J', '-S', '-X', '-Y' or '-Z')

QUALE	QUAYD	QURSH
QUASI	QUOAD	

Some six-letter blockers beginning with Q (except words ending in '-ED', '-J', '-S', '-X', '-Y' or '-Z')

QUAINT	QUENCH	QUOTHA
QUALIA	QUETCH	QURUSH
QUATCH	QUINIC	
QUEINT	QUOOKE	

Bonus words
Seven-letter words

QABALAH

QAWWALI
QAWWALS

QIGONGS

QINDARS
QINTARS

QUACKED
QUACKER
QUACKLE
QUADDED
QUADRAT
QUADRIC
QUAERED
QUAERES
QUAFFED
QUAFFER
QUAGGAS
QUAICHS
QUAIGHS
QUAILED
QUAKERS
QUAKIER
QUAKILY
QUAKING
QUALIFY
QUALITY

QUAMASH
QUANGOS
QUANNET
QUANTAL
QUANTED
QUANTIC
QUANTUM
QUAREST
QUARREL
QUARTAN
QUARTER
QUARTES
QUARTET
QUARTIC
QUARTOS
QUARTZY
QUASARS
QUASHED
QUASHEE
QUASHER
QUASHES
QUASHIE
QUASSIA
QUASSIN
QUATRES
QUAVERS
QUAVERY
QUAYAGE

QUEENED
QUEENIE
QUEENLY
QUEESTS
QUELLED
QUELLER
QUEMING
QUERIDA
QUERIED
QUERIER
QUERIES
QUERIST
QUESTED
QUESTER
QUESTOR
QUETZAL
QUEUERS
QUEUING
QUIBBLE
QUICHED
QUICHES
QUICKEN
QUICKER
QUICKIE
QUICKLY
QUIDAMS
QUIDDIT

Q

266

QUIESCE
QUIETED
QUIETEN
QUIETER
QUIETLY
QUIETUS
QUIGHTS
QUILLAI
QUILLED
QUILLET
QUILLON
QUILTED
QUILTER
QUINARY
QUINATE
QUINCES
QUINCHE
QUINELA
QUINIES
QUININA
QUININE
QUININS
QUINNAT
QUINOAS

QUINOID
QUINOLS
QUINONE
QUINTAL
QUINTAN
QUINTAR
QUINTAS
QUINTES
QUINTET
QUINTIC
QUINTIN
QUINZES
QUIPPED
QUIPPER
QUIPPUS
QUIRING
QUIRKED
QUIRTED
QUITING
QUITTAL
QUITTED
QUITTER
QUITTOR
QUIVERS

QUIVERY
QUIXOTE
QUIZZED
QUIZZER
QUIZZES

QUODDED
QUODLIN
QUOHOGS
QUOIFED
QUOINED
QUOISTS
QUOITED
QUOITER
QUOKKAS
QUOMODO
QUONDAM
QUONKED
QUOPPED
QUORATE
QUORUMS
QUOTERS
QUOTING
QUOTUMS

QWERTYS

Q

Eight-letter words

QABALISM
QABALIST
QALAMDAN
QINDARKA
QUAALUDE
QUACKERY
QUACKIER
QUACKING
QUACKISH
QUACKISM
QUACKLED
QUADDING
QUADPLEX
QUADRANT
QUADRATE
QUADRIGA
QUADROON
QUAESTOR
QUAFFING
QUAGGIER
QUAGMIRE
QUAGMIRY
QUAICHES
QUAILING
QUAINTER
QUAINTLY
QUAKIEST
QUALMIER

QUALMING
QUALMISH
QUANDANG
QUANDARY
QUANDONG
QUANTIFY
QUANTILE
QUANTING
QUANTISE
QUANTITY
QUANTIZE
QUANTONG
QUARRIAN
QUARRIED
QUARRIER
QUARRIES
QUARRION
QUARTERN
QUARTETT
QUARTIER
QUARTILE
QUARTZES
QUASHIES
QUASHING
QUASSIAS
QUATCHED
QUATORZE
QUATRAIN
QUAVERED

QUAVERER
QUAYLIKE
QUAYSIDE
QUAZZIER
QUEACHES
QUEASIER
QUEASILY
QUEAZIER
QUEENITE
QUEENLET
QUELCHED
QUELCHES
QUELLING
QUENCHED
QUENCHER
QUENCHES
QUENELLE
QUERCINE
QUERYING
QUESTANT
QUESTERS
QUESTING
QUESTION
QUETCHED
QUETCHES
QUETHING
QUEUEING

Q

QUIBBLED
QUIBBLER
QUIBBLES
QUICHING
QUICKEST
QUICKIES
QUICKSET
QUIDDANY
QUIDDITY
QUIDDLED
QUIDDLER
QUIDNUNC
QUIESCED
QUIESCES
QUIETEST
QUIETING
QUIETISM
QUIETIST
QUIETIVE
QUIETUDE
QUIGHTED
QUILLAIA
QUILLAJA
QUILLING
QUILLMAN
QUILLMEN
QUILTING

QUINCHED
QUINCHES
QUINCUNX
QUINELLA
QUINIELA
QUININES
QUINOIDS
QUINOLIN
QUINONES
QUINSIED
QUINSIES
QUINTAIN
QUINTETS
QUINTETT
QUINTICS
QUINTILE
QUIPPIER
QUIPPING
QUIPPISH
QUIPSTER
QUIRKIER
QUIRKILY
QUIRKING
QUIRKISH
QUIRTING
QUISLING
QUITCHED

QUITCHES
QUITRENT
QUITTALS
QUITTERS
QUITTING
QUIVERED
QUIVERER
QUIXOTES
QUIXOTIC
QUIXOTRY
QUIZZERY
QUIZZIFY
QUIZZING

QUODDING
QUODLINS
QUOIFING
QUOINING
QUOITERS
QUOITING
QUONKING
QUOPPING
QUOTABLE
QUOTABLY
QUOTIENT

QWERTIES

Q

Unusual letter combinations

If you have an unusual combination of letters on your rack, or want to impress your opponent with an unusual word, a few words from World English can come in handy.

Australian words

QUOKKA   small wallaby
QUOLL   native cat

Urdu words

QORMA   Indian dish of meat or vegetables
          braised with yoghurt or cream

QUIZ show

If you are lucky enough to have the letters Q, U, I and Z on your rack, or with one of them in a usable place on the board, the obvious choice would be to play QUIZ, an extremely useful and high-scoring word (22 points). Should your opponent be the lucky one to play QUIZ then perhaps you can then reap the benefits of front-hooking it with an S to make SQUIZ (23 points).

Essential info
Value: 1 point
Number in set: 6

R is one of the most common consonants in Scrabble but, surprisingly, only begins one two-letter word: RE (2 points). Some useful three-letter words to remember include ROW and RAY (6 points each) and there are also more unusual words such as RAX (a Scots word for stretch or extend, 10 points) and REZ (a short informal word for reservation, 12 points) which use power tiles. R is one of the letters of the RETAIN set and is therefore a good letter to keep if trying to get a bonus word.

Two-letter word beginning with R
RE

Some three-letter words beginning with R

RAD	REE	RET	RIT
RAH	REG	REW	RIZ
RAI	REH	REX	ROM
RAJ	REI	REZ	ROO
RAS	REM	RHO	RYA
RAX	REN	RHY	
REB	REO	RIF	
REC	REP	RIN	

R

Hooks

Hooking requires a subtle change in a player's thought process, in that they must look at words already on the board without becoming distracted by their pronunciation.

Some front-hooks
Two letters to three

R-AD	R-EF	R-OD
R-AG	R-EH	R-OE
R-AH	R-EM	R-OM
R-AI	R-EN	R-OO
R-AM	R-ES	R-OW
R-AN	R-ET	R-UG
R-AS	R-EX	R-UM
R-AT	R-HO	R-UN
R-AW	R-ID	R-UT
R-AX	R-IF	R-YA
R-AY	R-IN	R-YE
R-ED	R-IT	
R-EE	R-OB	

Three letters to four

R-ACE	R-ALE	R-ATE
R-AFF	R-AMP	R-AVE
R-AFT	R-AND	R-AWN
R-AGE	R-ANT	R-EAR
R-AID	R-APT	R-EEK
R-AIL	R-ARE	R-EEL
R-AIN	R-ASH	R-EFT
R-AKE	R-ASP	R-END

R

R-EST	R-INK	R-OOT
R-ICE	R-OAR	R-OPE
R-ICH	R-OBE	R-OSE
R-ICK	R-ODE	R-OUT
R-ICY	R-OIL	R-ULE
R-IDE	R-OLE	R-UMP
R-IFF	R-OOF	R-USE
R-IGG	R-OOM	R-YES

Four letters to five

R-ABID	R-AVER	R-OAST
R-ACED	R-EACH	R-OILY
R-ACER	R-EAVE	R-OPED
R-AGED	R-EDDY	R-OUST
R-AGER	R-EGAL	R-OVEN
R-AKED	R-EMIT	R-OVER
R-ALLY	R-ENEW	R-OWED
R-AMEN	R-ETCH	R-OWER
R-ARED	R-ICED	
R-AVEL	R-OARY	

R

Five letters to six

R-ABIES	R-AVINE	R-ICKLE
R-ACING	R-AZURE	R-ICTAL
R-ADDER	R-EARED	R-ICTUS
R-ADIOS	R-EAVED	R-IGGED
R-AFTER	R-EBOOK	R-INKED
R-AGING	R-EDUCE	R-OARED
R-AIDED	R-EFFED	R-OCKER
R-AIDER	R-EGRET	R-OILED
R-AILED	R-EJECT	R-OLLER
R-AKING	R-ELATE	R-OPING
R-AMBLE	R-EMAIL	R-OSIER
R-AMPED	R-EMOTE	R-OTARY
R-ANGER	R-EMOVE	R-OTTER
R-ANKER	R-ENDED	R-OUGHT
R-ANKLE	R-ENTER	R-OUNCE
R-ANTED	R-ESTER	R-OUPED
R-APPEL	R-ETAPE	R-OUTED
R-APTLY	R-EVERT	R-OUTER
R-AREFY	R-EVERY	R-OWING
R-ASHED	R-EVOKE	R-UDDER
R-ASPER	R-ICIER	R-USHER
R-AUGHT	R-ICING	R-UTTER

R

Six letters to seven

R-ABIDER	R-EFFING	R-EVOKED
R-ADDLED	R-EGALLY	R-EVOKER
R-AIDING	R-EGENCE	R-EVOLVE
R-AILING	R-EGENCY	R-ICHING
R-ALLIED	R-EGRESS	R-ICIEST
R-AMBLED	R-ELAPSE	R-IGGING
R-AMBLER	R-ELATED	R-INKING
R-AMPING	R-ELATER	R OARING
R-ANKLED	R-EMERGE	R-OILING
R-ANTING	R-EMOTER	R-OUGHLY
R-APPORT	R-EMOVED	R-OUSTED
R-ASHING	R-ENDING	R-OUSTER
R-ASPISH	R-ENEWED	R-OUTING
R-EARING	R-EPRISE	R-OYSTER
R-EAVING	R-ESTATE	R-UGGING
R-EDDISH	R-ETCHED	R-UNLESS
R-EDUCED	R-EVILER	

R

275

Seven letters to eight

R-ADDLING
R-ALLYING
R-AMBLING
R-ANKLING
R-APTNESS
R-AREFIED
R-ECLOSED
R-EDUCING
R-EGALITY
R-EJECTED
R-ELAPSED

R-ELATING
R-ELATION
R-ELATIVE
R-EMAILED
R-EMERGED
R-EMITTED
R-EMITTER
R-EMOTION
R-EMOVING
R-ENEWING
R-ENFORCE

R-ENOUNCE
R-ESTATED
R-ETCHING
R-EVERTED
R-EVOKING
R-EVOLVED
R-EVOLVER
R-EVULSED
R-UNROUND
R-URALITE

R

Handy Hint

JAR (10 points) is an obvious word to spot on the rack. If it won't play then remember that JAR backwards makes the word RAJ which might fit in. RAJ is an Indian word for government and it also takes a useful A hook for RAJA, which then can take an H for RAJAH. Other short reversible words beginning with R are RAW/WAR (6 points) RAP/PAR (5 points) RIM/MIR (5 points).

Some end-hooks
Two letters to three

AI-R	JA-R	OO-R
BA-R	JO-R	OU-R
BO-R	KI-R	PA-R
DO-R	KO-R	PE-R
EA-R	LA-R	PI-R
ER-R	LO-R	SI-R
FA-R	MA-R	TA-R
FE-R	MI-R	TO-R
GO-R	MO-R	YA-R
GU-R	NO-R	
HE-R	NU-R	

Three letters to four

ACE-R	EWE-R	OWE-R
AGA-R	EYE-R	PEA-R
AGE-R	FEE-R	PIE-R
APE-R	FIE-R	PUR-R
AVE-R	FOU-R	SEA-R
BEE-R	GOE-R	SEE-R
BOA-R	HOA-R	SOU-R
BOO-R	HOE-R	SPA-R
BRR-R	HUE-R	SUE-R
BUR-R	ICE-R	TEA-R
CHA-R	JEE-R	TEE-R
CHE-R	LEA-R	TIE-R
DEE-R	LEE-R	USE-R
DOE-R	LIE-R	VEE-R
DOO-R	MEE-R	VIE-R
DYE-R	MOO-R	YEA-R
EVE-R	ONE-R	YOU-R

R

Four letters to five

ABLE-R	DINE-R	HOME-R
BAKE-R	DIVE-R	HOPE-R
BARE-R	DONE-R	HOVE-R
BASE-R	DOPE-R	HUGE-R
BIDE-R	DOSE-R	HYPE-R
BIKE-R	DOVE-R	IDLE-R
BITE-R	DOZE-R	JIVE-R
BLUE-R	EASE-R	JOKE-R
BORE-R	EDGE-R	LACE-R
CAGE-R	FACE-R	LAKE-R
CANE-R	FADE-R	LAME-R
CAPE-R	FAKE-R	LASE-R
CARE-R	FILE-R	LATE-R
CATE-R	FINE-R	LEVE-R
CAVE-R	FIRE-R	LIFE-R
CHAI-R	FIVE-R	LIKE-R
CIDE-R	FREE-R	LINE-R
CITE-R	FUME-R	LIVE-R
CODE-R	GAME-R	LONE-R
COME-R	GATE-R	LOSE-R
COPE-R	GAZE-R	LOVE-R
COVE-R	GIVE-R	LUGE-R
CUBE-R	GONE-R	LUNA-R
CURE-R	HATE-R	LURE-R
CUTE-R	HAVE-R	LUTE-R
DARE-R	HAZE-R	MACE-R
DATE-R	HIDE-R	MAKE-R
DECO-R	HIKE-R	MANO-R
DICE-R	HIRE-R	MATE-R

MAYO-R	RARE-R	SUPE-R
METE-R	RATE-R	SURE-R
MINE-R	RAVE-R	TAKE-R
MITE-R	RAZE-R	TAME-R
MOVE-R	RICE-R	TAPE-R
MUSE-R	RIDE-R	TIGE-R
NAME-R	RIPE-R	TIME-R
NICE-R	RISE-R	TONE-R
NOSE-R	ROPE-R	TRUE-R
NOTE-R	ROTO-R	TUBE-R
OCHE-R	ROVE-R	TUNE-R
ONCE-R	RUDE-R	UNDE-R
PACE-R	RULE-R	VILE-R
PAGE-R	SABE-R	VINE-R
PALE-R	SAFE-R	VOTE-R
PATE-R	SAGE-R	WADE-R
PIKE-R	SANE-R	WAGE-R
PIPE-R	SAVE-R	WAKE-R
POKE-R	SHOE-R	WAVE-R
POSE-R	SIDE-R	WIDE-R
PUKE-R	SIZE-R	WIPE-R
PURE-R	SOLA-R	WISE-R
RACE-R	SORE-R	ZONE-R

R

Five letters to six

ABIDE-R	CRUDE-R	HEAVE-R
ACUTE-R	CURSE-R	HOUSE-R
ADORE-R	CYCLE-R	IRATE-R
AGILE-R	DANCE-R	ISSUE-R
AMPLE-R	DENSE-R	JUDGE-R
AMUSE-R	DODGE-R	JUICE-R
ANGLE-R	DOUSE-R	KNIFE-R
ARGUE-R	DRIVE-R	LANCE-R
BADGE-R	DRONE-R	LARGE-R
BARBE-R	DROVE-R	LATHE-R
BATHE-R	EERIE-R	LATTE-R
BINGE-R	ELATE-R	LEASE-R
BLAME-R	ERASE-R	LEAVE-R
BLAZE-R	EVADE-R	LODGE-R
BOMBE-R	EXILE-R	LUNGE-R
BOOZE-R	FALSE-R	MERGE-R
BRAVE-R	FENCE-R	MINCE-R
BRIBE-R	FLAKE-R	NOOSE-R
BULGE-R	FLAME-R	PARSE-R
CARVE-R	FORCE-R	PASSE-R
CAUSE-R	GLAZE-R	PIECE-R
CHAFE-R	GLIDE-R	PLACE-R
CHASE-R	GLOVE-R	PLANE-R
CLEVE-R	GORGE-R	PRIME-R
CLONE-R	GOUGE-R	PROVE-R
CLOSE-R	GRADE-R	QUAKE-R
CLOVE-R	GRAVE-R	REAVE-R
CONDO-R	GUIDE-R	RECTO-R
CRATE-R	GUISE-R	RIFLE-R

R

280

RINSE-R   SINGE-R   TRACE-R
ROUTE-R   SLATE-R   TRADE-R
SAUCE-R   SLIDE-R   TWICE-R
SCALE-R   SPARE-R   UNITE-R
SCORE-R   SPICE-R   VAGUE-R
SERVE-R   STATE-R   VALUE-R
SHAKE-R   STONE-R   VERGE-R
SHAPE-R   SWIPE-R   WAIVE-R
SHARE-R   TASTE-R   WASTE-R
SHAVE-R   TEASE-R   WHITE-R
SHINE-R   TITLE-R

Six letters to seven

ACCUSE-R   CRINGE-R   FLEECE-R
ADMIRE-R   CRUISE-R   FORAGE-R
ADVISE-R   DAMAGE-R   FREEZE-R
AVENGE-R   DANGLE-R   GAMBLE-R
BABBLE-R   DEBASE-R   GENTLE-R
BAFFLE-R   DEBATE-R   GROOVE-R
BOTTLE-R   DECIDE-R   GROUSE-R
BOUNCE-R   DEFINE-R   HANDLE-R
BROWSE-R   DIVIDE-R   HUDDLE-R
BUNDLE-R   DOUBLE-R   HUMBLE-R
CACKLE-R   ENABLE-R   HURDLE-R
CHANGE-R   ENCODE-R   HUSTLE-R
CHARGE-R   ENDURE-R   IGNITE-R
CHEQUE-R   ESCAPE-R   IMPALE-R
CLEAVE-R   EVOLVE-R   IMPOSE-R
COARSE-R   EXPOSE-R   IMPURE-R
CREASE-R   FIERCE-R   INCITE-R

R

INCOME-R	OBTUSE-R	SECURE-R
INHALE-R	OFFICE-R	SEDUCE-R
INSANE-R	OPPOSE-R	SNOOZE-R
INSIDE-R	PEOPLE-R	SPARSE-R
INSURE-R	PERUSE-R	SQUARE-R
INVADE-R	PICKLE-R	STRIKE-R
IONISE-R	PIERCE-R	STRIPE-R
IONIZE-R	PLEASE-R	TODDLE-R
JUGGLE-R	PLEDGE-R	TROUSE-R
KINDLE-R	POLITE-R	TRUDGE-R
LOATHE-R	PRAISE-R	TUMBLE-R
LOCATE-R	QUARTE-R	UNIQUE-R
LOUNGE-R	RAMBLE-R	UNSAFE-R
MANAGE-R	RATTLE-R	UNSURE-R
MARINE-R	REDUCE-R	UPDATE-R
MENACE-R	REFINE-R	VOYAGE-R
MINUTE-R	REMOTE-R	WAFFLE-R
MUZZLE-R	RESCUE-R	WHEEZE-R
NEEDLE-R	REVISE-R	WIGGLE-R
NOTICE-R	RUSTLE-R	WOBBLE-R
NUZZLE-R	SAMPLE-R	
OBLIGE-R	SAVAGE-R	

R

Seven letters to eight

ACHIEVE-R	BELIEVE-R	COMBINE-R
ADVANCE-R	BICYCLE-R	COMMUTE-R
AIRLINE-R	BREATHE-R	COMPUTE-R
ARRANGE-R	CAPTURE-R	CONJURE-R
BALANCE-R	CAROUSE-R	CONSUME-R
BANDAGE-R	CHUCKLE-R	DECEIVE-R

DECLINE-R	MEASURE-R	RESTORE-R
DIFFUSE-R	MISTAKE-R	REVERSE-R
DISABLE-R	NARRATE-R	REVOLVE-R
DISPOSE-R	NEWCOME-R	REWRITE-R
ENDORSE-R	NURTURE-R	SERVICE-R
ENFORCE-R	OBSCURE-R	SHUTTLE-R
ENHANCE-R	OBSERVE-R	SILENCE-R
EXAMINE-R	OUTLINE-R	SINCERE-R
EXECUTE-R	OUTSIDE-R	STICKLE-R
EXPLORE-R	PERJURE-R	STRANGE-R
FORGIVE-R	PILLAGE-R	SURVIVE-R
FRAGILE-R	POLLUTE-R	TEENAGE-R
GESTURE-R	PRECISE-R	TOASTIE-R
GRAPPLE-R	PREFACE-R	TOPLINE-R
GRUMBLE-R	PREPARE-R	TORTURE-R
IMAGINE-R	PRODUCE-R	TROUBLE-R
IMMENSE-R	PROFILE-R	TWINKLE-R
IMPROVE-R	PROMOTE-R	UPGRADE-R
INQUIRE-R	PROPOSE-R	UPSTATE-R
INTRUDE-R	PROVIDE-R	VENTURE-R
JOYRIDE-R	RECEIVE-R	VILLAGE-R
JUSTICE-R	RECLINE-R	WELCOME-R
LECTURE-R	RECYCLE-R	WHISTLE-R
LICENCE-R	REPLACE-R	WHITTLE-R
LICENSE-R	RESERVE-R	

R

Blockers

It is useful to know which words are blockers and can't therefore be extended before or after. You may want to play a blocker that your opponent can't extend, or you may want to avoid playing a blocker because you want to keep the board open.

Some three-letter blockers beginning with R

RAX	RHY

Some four-letter blockers beginning with R

RAZZ	RELY	ROUX
REFT	ROPY	RUBY

Some five-letter blockers beginning with R (except words ending in '-ED', '-J', '-S', '-X', '-Y' or '-Z')

RABID	REDID	RESAT
RADII	RELIT	RIFER
RARER	RENAL	RUNIC
RASTA	RERAN	

R

Some six-letter blockers beginning with R (except words ending in '-ED', '-J', '-S', '-X', '-Y' or '-Z')

RACIAL	REDONE	RESHOD
RACIER	REDREW	RESHOT
RADDER	REFLEW	RETOOK
RADGER	REGAVE	RETORN
RADISH	REGNAL	RETROD
RAKISH	REGREW	RICHER
RANCID	REHASH	RIDDEN
RAREST	REHUNG	RIFEST
RARING	RELAID	RIPEST
RATHER	RELISH	ROPIER
RAVISH	RESAID	RUEFUL
RAWISH	RESEEN	

R

Bonus words

Bonus words on your rack can be hard to spot, especially for the less experienced player. One way to help find them is by using prefixes and suffixes.

Many larger words include a common prefix or suffix – remembering these and using them where you can is a good way to discover any longer words on your rack, including any potential bonus words. The key prefixes to remember beginning with R are RE- and RED-.

Some words beginning with RE-
Seven-letter words

RE-ACTED	RE-CITED	RE-FILLS
RE-ADAPT	RE-CLAIM	RE-FINED
RE-AGENT	RE-COILS	RE-FORMS
RE-ALIGN	RE-CORDS	RE-FRESH
RE-APING	RE-COUNT	RE-FUSED
RE-APPLY	RE-COVER	RE-GALES
RE-BATED	RE-CYCLE	RE-GENTS
RE-BIRTH	RE-DEEMS	RE-GROUP
RE-BOOTS	RE-DOUBT	RE-GROWN
RE-BOUND	RE-DRAFT	RE-HOUSE
RE-BRAND	RE-DRESS	RE-INTER
RE-BUILD	RE-DUCES	RE-ISSUE
RE-CALLS	RE-ELECT	RE-JOINS
RE-CEDED	RE-ENACT	RE-KEYED
RE-CITAL	RE-ENTRY	RE-LAPSE

R

286

RE-LAXER
RE-LEASE
RE-LIVED
RE-LOADS
RE-LYING
RE-MAINS
RE-MARKS
RE-MATCH
RE-MINDS
RE-MIXED
RE-MORSE
RE-MOVED
RE-NEWER
RE-ORDER
RE-PAINT
RE-PASTS
RE-PEALS
RE-PEATS
RE-PLACE
RE-PLAYS

RE-PLIES
RE-PORTS
RE-PRESS
RE-PRINT
RE-QUEST
RE-READS
RE-ROUTE
RE-SEALS
RE-SERVE
RE-SIDED
RE-SIGNS
RE-SISTS
RE-SOLVE
RE-SOUND
RE-SPIRE
RE-SPITE
RE-START
RE-STATE
RE-STING
RE-STORE

RE-TAILS
RE-TAPED
RE-TEACH
RE-THINK
RE-TIRED
RE-TRACT
RE-TREAD
RE-TREAT
RE-TURNS
RE-UNIFY
RE-UNION
RE-UNITE
RE-VENGE
RE-VERSE
RE-VISED
RE-VOLVE
RE-WORKS
RE-WOUND
RE-WRITE

Eight-letter words

RE-ABSORB
RE-ACTION
RE-ADJUST
RE-APPEAR
RE-ASSESS
RE-BOOTED
RE-BUFFED
RE-BUTTED

RE-CALLED
RE-CAPPED
RE-CEDING
RE-CHARGE
RE-CITING
RE-COILED
RE-COMMIT
RE-CONNED

RE-CORDED
RE-COUPED
RE-COURSE
RE-CYCLED
RE-DEEMED
RE-DEFINE
RE-DEPLOY
RE-DESIGN

R

RE-DOUBLE	RE-LAYING	RE-SEARCH
RE-DUBBED	RE-LEASED	RE-SECURE
RE-EMERGE	RE-LIABLE	RE-SIDING
RE-ENGAGE	RE-LOADED	RE-SISTER
RE-ENLIST	RE-LOCATE	RE-SOLVED
RE-FILLED	RE-MAKING	RE-SORTED
RE-FINERY	RE-MARKED	RE-STORED
RE-FITTED	RE-MASTER	RE-STRICT
RE-FLEXED	RE-MEMBER	RE-TAILED
RE-FORMAT	RE-MINDED	RE-TIRING
RE-FORMED	RE-MOVING	RE-TRACED
RE-FUELED	RE-OCCUPY	RE-TURNED
RE-FUNDED	RE-OFFEND	RE-UNITED
RE-GAINED	RE-PAIRED	RE-USABLE
RE-GROWTH	RE-PEALED	RE-VALUED
RE-HEARSE	RE-PHRASE	RE-VERSED
RE-HEATED	RE-PLACED	RE-VIEWER
RE-IGNITE	RE-PORTER	RE-VISING
RE-INVENT	RE-PRISED	RE-VISION
RE-ISSUED	RE-PUBLIC	RE-WARDED
RE-JOINED	RE-QUITED	RE-WINDER
RE-KINDLE	RE-RECORD	RE-WRITER
RE-LAPSED	RE-ROUTED	
RE-LAUNCH	RE-SEALED	

R

288

Some words beginning with RED-

Seven-letter words

RED-BACK	RED-EYES	RED-RAWN
RED-BIRD	RED-FISH	RED-ROOT
RED-CAPS	RED-FOOT	RED-TAIL
RED-COAT	RED-HEAD	RED-TOPS
RED-DENS	RED-LINE	RED-WING
RED-DING	RED-NECK	RED-WOOD
RED-DISH	RED-NESS	

Eight-letter words

RED-BELLY	RED-OLENT	RED-SHIRT
RED-BRICK	RED-SHANK	RED-START
RED-HORSE	RED-SHIFT	RED-WATER
RED-LINED	RED-SHIRE	

Unusual letter combinations

If you have an unusual combination of letters on your rack, or want to impress your opponent with an unusual word, a few words from World English can come in handy.

Australian words

RAZOO	imaginary coin
REGO	registration of a motor vehicle
RESTO	restored antique, vintage car, etc
ROO	kangaroo
ROUGHIE	something unfair, especially a trick

Canadian words

REDEYE	drink incorporating beer and tomato juice

| RUBABOO | soup made by boiling pemmican |
| RUBBY | rubbing alcohol mixed with cheap wine for drinking |

Hindi words

RAGGEE	cereal grass
RAITA	yoghurt-and-vegetable dish served with curry
RAJ	government
RAJAH	ruler or landlord
RAMTIL	African plant grown in India
RANI	queen or princess
RATHA	four-wheeled carriage drawn by horses or bullocks
ROTI	type of unleavened bread
RUPEE	standard monetary unit of India
RUPIAH	standard monetary unit of Indonesia
RYOT	peasant or tenant farmer

New Zealand words

RAHUI	Maori prohibition
RATA	myrtaceous forest tree
RAUPATU	seizure of land
RAURIKI	sow thistle

South African words

| ROOIKAT | lynx |

Urdu words

| RABI | crop harvested at the end of winter |

R

Essential info
Value: 1 point
Number in set: 4

The **S** is such a valuable letter for making longer plays, especially a seven-letter bonus word, that it ought not to be squandered in a short two-letter word play. The four twos that begin with S could assist in hooking your play onto an existing word: SH (a sound people make to request silence or quiet, 5 points) and SI, SO and ST (2 each). Quite a few three-letter words which use no vowels begin with S (although you will need a Y), including: SHY (9 points), SKY (10) and SPY (8). S also forms various three-letter words using X, one for each vowel except for U: SAX, SEX, SIX and SOX (10 points each).

Two-letter words beginning with S

SH	SI	SO	ST

Some three-letter words beginning with S

SAB	SAY	SHH	SNY	SOV
SAE	SAZ	SIB	SOC	SOX
SAI	SED	SIC	SOG	SOY
SAL	SEL	SIF	SOH	SUQ
SAM	SEN	SIK	SOL	SUR
SAN	SER	SIM	SOM	SUS
SAR	SEZ	SKA	SOT	SWY
SAX	SHA	SMA	SOU	SYE

Some front-hooks
Two letters to three

S-AB	S-AW	S-EX	S-MA	S-OW
S-AD	S-AX	S-HA	S-NY	S-OX
S-AE	S-AY	S-HE	S-OB	S-OY
S-AG	S-EA	S-IF	S-OD	S-PA
S-AI	S-ED	S-IN	S-OH	S-UM
S-AL	S-EE	S-IS	S-OM	S-UN
S-AM	S-EL	S-IT	S-ON	S-UP
S-AN	S-EN	S-KA	S-OP	S-UR
S-AR	S-ER	S-KI	S-OS	S-US
S-AT	S-ET	S-KY	S-OU	S-YE

Three letters to four

S-ADO	S-ALE	S-ATE
S-AGA	S-ALT	S-AVE
S-AGE	S-AND	S-AWN
S-AGO	S-ANE	S-CAB
S-AID	S-ARK	S-CAG
S-AIL	S-ARS	S-CAM
S-AIR	S-ASH	S-CAN
S-AKE	S-ASS	S-CAR

292

S

S-CAT	S-KID	S-NOT
S-CRY	S-KIN	S-NOW
S-CUD	S-KIP	S-OAK
S-CUM	S-KIT	S-OAR
S-EAR	S-LAB	S-ODA
S-EAT	S-LAM	S-OFT
S-EEK	S-LAP	S-OIL
S-EEN	S-LAT	S-OLD
S-ELF	S-LAY	S-OLE
S-ELL	S-LED	S-OON
S-END	S-LEW	S-OOT
S-HAH	S-LID	S-ORE
S-HAM	S-LIP	S-ORT
S-HAW	S-LIT	S-OUP
S-HEW	S-LOB	S-OUR
S-HIN	S-LOG	S-OWN
S-HIP	S-LOP	S-PAM
S-HOD	S-LOT	S-PAN
S-HOE	S-LOW	S-PAR
S-HOP	S-LUG	S-PAT
S-HOT	S-LUM	S-PAY
S-HOW	S-LUR	S-PEC
S-HUN	S-MOG	S-PEW
S-HUT	S-MUG	S-PIN
S-ICK	S-MUT	S-PIT
S-IDE	S-NAG	S-POT
S-ILK	S-NAP	S-PRY
S-ILL	S-NIB	S-PUD
S-INK	S-NIP	S-PUN
S-IRE	S-NOB	S-PUR

S

S-TAB	S-TOP	S-WAG
S-TAG	S-TOT	S-WAN
S-TAR	S-TOW	S-WAP
S-TAT	S-TUB	S-WAT
S-TAY	S-TUN	S-WAY
S-TEN	S-UMP	S-WIG
S-TET	S-URE	S-WOP
S-TEW	S-WAB	

Four letters to five

S-ABLE	S-CRAM	S-HARE
S-AGER	S-CRAN	S-HARK
S-ALLY	S-CREW	S-HARP
S-AUNT	S-CROW	S-HAVE
S-AVER	S-CUFF	S-HEAR
S-AWED	S-CULL	S-HELL
S-CAMP	S-EDGE	S-HERE
S-CANT	S-EVEN	S-HILL
S-CAPE	S-EVER	S-HIRE
S-CARE	S-EWER	S-HOCK
S-CART	S-EXED	S-HOED
S-COFF	S-HACK	S-HONE
S-COLD	S-HAFT	S-HOOK
S-CONE	S-HAKE	S-HOOT
S-COOP	S-HALE	S-HORN
S-COOT	S-HALL	S-HOVE
S-COPE	S-HALT	S-HUCK
S-CORE	S-HAME	S-HUNT
S-CORN	S-HANK	S-HUSH
S-COWL	S-HARD	S-IDLE

S

S-IRED	S-MOCK	S-TACK
S-KELP	S-MOKE	S-TAKE
S-KILL	S-NAIL	S-TALE
S-KINK	S-NIFF	S-TALK
S-LACK	S-OILY	S-TALL
S-LAIN	S-OWED	S-TANK
S-LAKE	S-PACE	S-TART
S-LANG	S-PAIN	S-TATE
S-LASH	S-PARE	S-TEAK
S-LATE	S-PARK	S-TEAL
S-LEEK	S-PATE	S-TEAM
S-LEET	S-PAWN	S-TEED
S-LICE	S-PEAK	S-TEEL
S-LICK	S-PEAR	S-TERN
S-LIME	S-PECK	S-TICK
S-LOAN	S-PELT	S-TIFF
S-LOPE	S-PEND	S-TILE
S-LOTH	S-PIKE	S-TILL
S-LUMP	S-PILL	S-TINT
S-LUNG	S-PINE	S-TOCK
S-LUNK	S-PLAY	S-TONE
S-LUSH	S-POKE	S-TOOK
S-MACK	S-POOL	S-TOOL
S-MALL	S-PORE	S-TOUT
S-MART	S-PORT	S-TOWN
S-MASH	S-POUT	S-TRAP
S-MELL	S-PRAY	S-TRAY
S-MELT	S-PROG	S-TRIP
S-MILE	S-QUAD	S-TUCK
S-MITE	S-QUID	S-URGE

S

S-WARM	S-WELT	S-WIPE
S-WEAR	S-WEPT	S-WISH
S-WEEP	S-WILL	S-WORD
S-WEER	S-WINE	S-WORE
S-WELL	S-WING	

Five letters to six

S-ADDER	S-ELECT	S-LEDGE
S-ADDLE	S-ENDER	S-LIGHT
S-AILED	S-ENTRY	S-LIMED
S-ALLOW	S-EXIST	S-LOPED
S-ALTER	S-HANDY	S-LOWER
S-AMPLE	S-HARPY	S-LOWLY
S-AVANT	S-HAVEN	S-MIDGE
S-AWING	S-HAVER	S-MILER
S-CABBY	S-HEATH	S-MITER
S-CARED	S-HIRED	S-MOGGY
S-CATTY	S-HOVED	S-NAKED
S-COPED	S-HOVEL	S-NAPPY
S-CORED	S-HOVER	S-NATCH
S-CRAWL	S-ICKER	S-NIFFY
S-CREAM	S-ICKLE	S-OAKED
S-CREED	S-IDLED	S-OARED
S-CRIED	S-INKER	S-OFTEN
S-CRIMP	S-INNER	S-OILED
S-CURRY	S-KIDDY	S-OLDER
S-CURVY	S-KITED	S-OMBRE
S-EARED	S-LAKED	S-OUGHT
S-EATER	S-LATER	S-OUPED
S-EDUCE	S-LAYER	S-OWING

S-PACED	S-TARRY	S-TUBBY
S-PARED	S-TENCH	S-UNDER
S-PARKY	S-TICKY	S-UNLIT
S-PARSE	S-TILED	S-UPPER
S-PAYED	S-TITCH	S-URGED
S-PIKER	S-TONED	S-WAGER
S-PINED	S-TOWED	S-WAYED
S-POKED	S-TRAIN	S-WEEPY
S-PORED	S-TRIKE	S-WIPED
S-POTTY	S-TRIPE	S-WITCH
S-PRINT	S-TROLL	S-WOOSH
S-QUASH	S-TROVE	
S-TABLE	S-TRUCK	

Six letters to seven

S-ADDLED	S-CORING	S-HARKED
S-AILING	S-CORNED	S-HARPER
S-ALLIED	S-CORNER	S-HATTER
S-AMPLER	S-CRUMMY	S-HAVING
S-CABBED	S-CUDDLE	S-HIPPED
S-CAMPER	S-CUFFED	S-HOOTER
S-CANNED	S-CUPPER	S-HOPPED
S-CANTER	S-CUTTLE	S-HOVING
S-CARING	S-EATING	S-HUNTED
S-CARPER	S-EDUCED	S-HUSHED
S-COFFER	S-ELFISH	S-INKING
S-COLDER	S-ENDING	S-KIDDED
S-COOPER	S-HACKED	S-KILLED
S-COOTER	S-HALLOW	S-KIPPED
S-COPING	S-HARING	S-KIPPER

S

297

S-KITING	S-MELTED	S-TABLED
S-LACKED	S-MITTEN	S-TACKED
S-LAKING	S-MOCKED	S-TAGGER
S-LAMMED	S-MOLDER	S-TAKING
S-LANDER	S-MOTHER	S-TALKED
S-LAPPED	S-MUGGER	S-TALKER
S-LASHED	S-NAGGED	S-TAMPER
S-LASHER	S-NAILED	S-TEAMED
S-LAYING	S-NAPPED	S-TICKER
S-LEDGED	S-NIPPED	S-TICKLE
S-LEDGER	S-OILING	S-TILTED
S-LENDER	S-PACING	S-TINGED
S-LICKED	S-PANNER	S-TINKER
S-LIMIER	S-PARING	S-TONING
S-LINGER	S-PARKED	S-TOPPED
S-LINKED	S-PARSER	S-TUMBLE
S-LITHER	S-PATTER	S-UNLESS
S-LOGGED	S-PAWNED	S-UNLIKE
S-LOPING	S-PAYING	S-URGING
S-LOWEST	S-PLAYED	S-WAGGER
S-LUGGED	S-PONGED	S-WALLOW
S-LUMBER	S-POOLED	S-WARMED
S-LUMPED	S-PORTED	S-WAYING
S-LUSHED	S-POTTED	S-WEEPER
S-MASHED	S-PRAYED	S-WIPING
S-MATTER	S-PURRED	S-WITHER
S-MELLED	S-TABBED	S-WORDED

Seven letters to eight

S-ADDLING	S-KINLESS	S-PRAYING
S-ALLOWED	S-KIPPING	S-PRINTED
S-ALLYING	S-LACKING	S-QUASHED
S-CANNING	S-LAPPING	S-TABBING
S-CARLESS	S-LASHING	S-TABLING
S-CRAMMED	S-LIGHTLY	S-TACKING
S-CRAWLED	S-LOWDOWN	S-TAKEOUT
S-CREAMED	S-LOWNESS	S-TALKING
S-CRUMPLE	S-LUGGING	S-TEAMING
S-CRUNCHY	S-MASHING	S-TICKING
S-CUFFING	S-MELTING	S-TICKLED
S-CURRIED	S-MOOCHED	S-TILTING
S-EDITION	S-MOULDER	S-TOPPING
S-ELECTED	S-NAPPING	S-TOWAWAY
S-HACKING	S-NIPPING	S-TRAINED
S-HACKLED	S-OFTENER	S-TRAPPED
S-HARKING	S-PANNING	S-TRESSED
S-HEARING	S-PARKING	S-TRIDENT
S-HEATHER	S-PAWNING	S-TRIPPED
S-HILLING	S-PEAKING	S-TRUMPET
S-HIPPING	S-PILLAGE	S-TUMBLED
S-HOCKING	S-PILLING	S-UNBAKED
S-HOOTING	S-PINNING	S-UNBLOCK
S-HOPPING	S-PITTING	S-WADDLED
S-HUNTING	S-PLATTER	S-WARMING
S-HUSHING	S-PLAYING	S-WEEPING
S-HUTTING	S-POOLING	S-WILLING
S-KIDDING	S-PORTING	S-WINGING
S-KILLING	S-POTTING	S-WORDING

S

Some end-hooks
Two letters to three

AA-S	EM-S	LO-S	PE-S
AB-S	EN-S	MA-S	PI-S
AD-S	ER-S	MI-S	PO-S
AG-S	ES-S	ME-S	QI-S
AH-S	FA-S	MI-S	RE-S
AI-S	FE-S	MO-S	SI-S
AL-S	GI-S	MU-S	SO-S
AR-S	GO-S	NA-S	TA-S
AS-S	GU-S	NO-S	TE-S
AY-S	HA-S	NU-S	TI-S
BA-S	HE-S	NY-S	UG-S
BE-S	HI-S	OB-S	UN-S
BI-S	HO-S	OD-S	UP-S
BO-S	ID-S	OE-S	UT-S
BY-S	IF-S	OH-S	WO-S
DA-S	IN-S	OM-S	XI-S
DI-S	IO-S	ON-S	YE-S
DPO-S	IT-S	OO-S	YO-S
EA-S	KA-S	OP-S	YU-S
ED-S	KI-S	OR-S	ZA-S
EF-S	KO-S	OU-S	ZO-S
EH-S	LA-S	OY-S	
EL-S	LI-S	PA-S	

S

Blockers

It is useful to know which words are blockers and can't therefore be extended before or after. You may want to play a blocker that your opponent can't extend, or you may want to avoid playing a blocker because you want to keep the board open.

Some three-letter blockers beginning with S

SAE	SHH	SMA
SAZ	SIX	SOX
SEZ	SLY	SWY

Some four-letter blockers beginning with S

SAGY	SEWN	SOON
SASH	SEXY	SPED
SAWN	SHMO	SPRY
SCRY	SHOD	SUCH
SECO	SIZY	SUNG
SEEN	SOHO	SUSS
SESH	SOME	SWUM

Some five-letter blockers beginning with S (except words ending in '-ED', '-J', '-S', '-X', '-Y' or '-Z')

SAFER	SHERE	SHOWN
SANER	SHEWN	SHUSH
SHALT	SHONE	SINCE
SHAWN	SHORN	SITKA

SKINT	SNUCK	STUNK
SLAIN	SOCKO	SUPRA
SLASH	SORBO	SWANG
SLEPT	SORER	SWAPT
SLIPT	SPAKE	SWEPT
SLUNG	SPENT	SWOPT
SLUNK	STAID	SWORE
SLYER	STASH	SWORN
SMASH	STEPT	SWUNG
SMOTE	STOOD	
SMUSH	STUNG	

Some six-letter blockers ending with S (except words ending in '-ED', '-J', '-S', '-X', '-Y' or '-Z')

SADDER	SCORCH	SHOULD
SAFEST	SCOTCH	SHRANK
SAFING	SEAMAN	SHREWD
SAGEST	SEAMEN	SHRUNK
SAGIER	SEARCH	SHYEST
SAIRER	SEARER	SHYING
SAMIER	SEDENT	SHYISH
SANCTA	SELDOM	SICKER
SANEST	SEMPER	SINFUL
SANING	SEXIER	SIRING
SAPFUL	SHAKEN	SITING
SATING	SHAPEN	SKOOSH
SAYEST	SHAVEN	SKYING
SCOOCH	SHAZAM	SKYLIT
SCOOSH	SHEESH	SLEAZO

SLIEST   SOUGHT   STRODE
SLOWER   SOURER   STRONG
SLYEST   SPEECH   STRUCK
SLYISH   SPLOSH   STRUNG
SMOOSH   SPOILT   SUABLE
SNIDER   SPOKEN   SUAVER
SOAKEN   SPRUNG   SUBSEA
SOBFUL   SPRYER   SUNKEN
SOFTER   STALER   SUNLIT
SOLEMN   STINKO   SUPERB
SOLING   STITCH   SUREST
SORDID   STOLEN   SWOOSH
SOREST   STREWN

Handy Hint: saving the S for last

If you can earn 10 points more by playing the S
then do so, otherwise consider holding it back as an
investment for better scores later in the game.
More experienced players tend to save S tiles
instead of playing them immediately. This is
because S is easy to play at the end of a six-letter
word, thus making it much easier to score a 50-point
bonus word by using all your tiles in one go.

S

Bonus words

Bonus words on your rack can be hard to spot, especially for the less experienced player. One way to help find them is by using prefixes and suffixes.

Many larger words include a common prefix or suffix – remembering these and using them where you can is a good way to discover any longer words on your rack, including any potential bonus words. The key prefixes to remember beginning with S are SEA-, SUB- and SUN- and the key suffixes are -SET, -SHIP, -SKIN, -SMAN and -SOME.

Some words beginning with SEA-
Seven-letter words

SEA-BANK	SEA-LANT	SEA-SICK
SEA-BEDS	SEA-LIFT	SEA-SIDE
SEA-BIRD	SEA-LINE	SEA-SING
SEA-DOGS	SEA-LING	SEA-SONS
SEA-FOLK	SEA-MAID	SEA-TING
SEA-FOOD	SEA-MING	SEA-WALL
SEA-FOWL	SEA-PORT	SEA-WARD
SEA-GULL	SEA-REST	SEA-WEED
SEA-HAWK	SEA-RING	SEA-ZING

S

Eight-letter words

SEA-BEACH	SEA-FRONT	SEA-SCAPE
SEA-BOARD	SEA-GOING	SEA-SCOUT
SEA-BORNE	SEA-HORSE	SEA-SHELL
SEA-COAST	SEA-HOUND	SEA-SHORE
SEA-CRAFT	SEA-MANLY	SEA-SPEAK
SEA-DROME	SEA-MOUNT	SEA-TRAIN
SEA-FARER	SEA-PLANE	SEA-TROUT
SEA-FLOOR	SEA-QUAKE	SEA-WATER

Some words beginning with SUB-
Seven-letter words

SUB-AQUA	SUB-FILE	SUB-SIST
SUB-ARID	SUB-ITEM	SUB-SOIL
SUB-ATOM	SUB-JOIN	SUB-TASK
SUB-BASS	SUB-LETS	SUB-TEND
SUB-BING	SUB-LIME	SUB-TEXT
SUB-CELL	SUB-MISS	SUB-TONE
SUB-CODE	SUB-PLOT	SUB-TYPE
SUB-CULT	SUB-RENT	SUB-UNIT
SUB-DUCE	SUB-RULE	SUB-URBS
SUB-DUED	SUB-SECT	SUB-VERT
SUB-DUES	SUB-SETS	SUB-WAYS
SUB-EDIT	SUB-SIDE	SUB-ZERO

S

Eight-letter words

SUB-ADULT
SUB-AGENT
SUB-BASIN
SUB-CHORD
SUB-CLAIM
SUB-CLASS
SUB-DUING
SUB-DURAL
SUB-ENTRY
SUB-EQUAL
SUB-FLOOR
SUB-GENRE
SUB-GRADE
SUB-GROUP

SUB-HUMAN
SUB-INDEX
SUB-LEASE
SUB-LEVEL
SUB-LIMED
SUB-MERGE
SUB-POLAR
SUB-SCALE
SUB-SENSE
SUB-SERVE
SUB-SIDED
SUB-SIDER
SUB-SKILL
SUB-SONIC

SUB-SPACE
SUB-STAGE
SUB-STATE
SUB-TITLE
SUB-TOPIC
SUB-TOTAL
SUB-TRACT
SUB-URBAN
SUB-URBIA
SUB-VERSE
SUB-WAYED
SUB-WORLD

Some words beginning with SUN-
Seven-letter words

SUN-BACK
SUN-BAKE
SUN-BEAM
SUN-BEDS
SUN-BELT
SUN-BURN
SUN-DIAL
SUN-DOWN

SUN-FISH
SUN-HATS
SUN-LAMP
SUN-LESS
SUN-NIES
SUN-RAYS
SUN-RISE
SUN-ROOF

SUN-SETS
SUN-SPOT
SUN-TANS
SUN-TRAP
SUN-WARD
SUN-WISE

S

Eight-letter words

SUN-BAKED	SUN-BURST	SUN-LIGHT
SUN-BATHE	SUN-DERED	SUN-PROOF
SUN-BERRY	SUN-DRESS	SUN-SHADE
SUN-BLOCK	SUN-DRILY	SUN-SHINE
SUN-BURNT	SUN-GLASS	SUN-SHINY

Some words ending with -SET
Seven-letter words

BACK-SET	HAND-SET	MOON-SET
BONE-SET	HARD-SET	OVER-SET
BRAS-SET	HEAD-SET	TOOL-SET
CHIP-SET	LOCK-SET	TWIN-SET
FILM-SET	MIND-SET	TYPE-SET

Eight-letter words

EARTH-SET	PHOTO-SET	THICK-SET
HEAVY-SET	QUICK-SET	THORN-SET
MARMO-SET	SOMER-SET	UNDER-SET

Some words ending with -SHIP
Seven-letter words

AIR-SHIP	KIN-SHIP	SON-SHIP
END-SHIP	MID-SHIP	WAR-SHIP
GOD-SHIP	PAL-SHIP	WOR-SHIP
GUN-SHIP	PRE-SHIP	

S

Eight-letter words

AMID-SHIP	HARD-SHIP	POET-SHIP
BARD-SHIP	HEAD-SHIP	POPE-SHIP
CLAN-SHIP	HEIR-SHIP	SERF-SHIP
DEAN-SHIP	HERO-SHIP	STAR-SHIP
DUKE-SHIP	KING-SHIP	TANK-SHIP
EARL-SHIP	LADY-SHIP	TOWN-SHIP
FIRE-SHIP	LONG-SHIP	TWIN-SHIP
FLAG-SHIP	LORD-SHIP	WARD-SHIP
FORE-SHIP	MATE-SHIP	

Some words ending with -SKIN
Seven-letter words

CAT-SKIN	DOG-SKIN	OIL-SKIN
COW-SKIN	FOX-SKIN	PIG-SKIN
DOE-SKIN	KID-SKIN	

Eight-letter words

BEAR-SKIN	FISH-SKIN	WINE-SKIN
BUCK-SKIN	GOAT-SKIN	WOLF-SKIN
CALF-SKIN	LAMB-SKIN	WOOL-SKIN
CAPE-SKIN	MOLE-SKIN	
DEER-SKIN	SEAL-SKIN	

S

Some words ending with -SMAN

Seven-letter words

ART-SMAN	MAG-SMAN	ODD-SMAN
BAT-SMAN	MES-SMAN	PAS-SMAN
DAY-SMAN	MOB-SMAN	ROD-SMAN
KIN-SMAN	NEW-SMAN	TAP-SMAN
LEN-SMAN	OAR-SMAN	TOP-SMAN

Eight-letter words

BAIL-SMAN	GANG-SMAN	MARK-SMAN
BAND-SMAN	GILD-SMAN	PRES-SMAN
BANK-SMAN	GLAS-SMAN	PUNT-SMAN
BLUE-SMAN	GOWN-SMAN	RAFT-SMAN
BOAT-SMAN	HEAD-SMAN	RAMP-SMAN
BOND-SMAN	HELM-SMAN	ROAD-SMAN
CHES-SMAN	HERD-SMAN	SALE-SMAN
CLAN-SMAN	HUNT-SMAN	SIDE-SMAN
CLAS-SMAN	ISLE-SMAN	SWAG-SMAN
CORP-SMAN	LAND-SMAN	TALI-SMAN
DOOM-SMAN	LINE-SMAN	TIDE-SMAN
DOOR-SMAN	LINK-SMAN	TOWN-SMAN
GAME-SMAN	LOCK-SMAN	WOOD-SMAN

S

Some words ending with -SOME

Seven-letter words

AWE-SOME	NOI-SOME	WAG-SOME
FUL-SOME	TOY-SOME	WIN-SOME
IRK-SOME	TRI-SOME	WOE-SOME
LIS-SOME	TWO-SOME	

Eight-letter words

BORE-SOME	GRUE-SOME	PLAY-SOME
DARK-SOME	HAND-SOME	PYRO-SOME
DOLE-SOME	JOKE-SOME	RIBO-SOME
DUEL-SOME	LARK-SOME	ROOM-SOME
FEAR-SOME	LONE-SOME	TEDI-SOME
FOUR-SOME	LONG-SOME	TIRE-SOME
FRET-SOME	LOTH-SOME	TOIL-SOME
GLAD-SOME	LOVE-SOME	WORK-SOME
GLEE-SOME	MURK-SOME	

S

Unusual letter combinations

If you have an unusual combination of letters on your rack, or want to impress your opponent with an unusual word, a few words from World English can come in handy.

Australian words

SANGER	sandwich
SCOZZA	rowdy person
SCUNGY	miserable, sordid or dirty person
SHARPIE	a member of a teenage group with short hair and distinctive clothes
SHERANG	boss
SHYPOO	liquor of poor quality
SITELLA	small black-and-white bird
SKEG	rear fin on the underside of a surfboard
SKITE	boast
SMOKO	cigarette break
SPRUIK	speak in public
SWAGMAN	vagrant worker
SWY	a gambling game

Canadian words

SKOOKUM	strong or brave
SNYE	side channel of a river
SPLAKE	hybrid trout bred by Canadian zoologists
SWILER	seal hunter

S

Hindi words

SAMBAR	deer with three-tined antlers
SAMITI	political association
SAMOSA	triangular pastry containing spiced vegetables or meat
SARANGI	stringed instrument played with a bow
SARDAR	Sikh title
SARI	traditional dress of Indian women
SAROD	Indian stringed instrument
SWAMI	title for a Hindu saint or religious teacher

New Zealand words

| SHEEPO | person who brings sheep to the catching pen for shearing |

South African words

SCAMTO	argot of South African Blacks
SKOLLY	hooligan
SNOEK	edible marine fish
SPEK	bacon, fat or fatty pork
STEEN	variety of white grape
STOKVEL	savings pool or syndicate

Urdu words

SAHIB	title placed after a man's name
SARPANCH	head of a village council
SHALWAR	loose-fitting trousers
SHIKAR	hunting
SICE	servant who looks after horses

S

T 1

Essential info
Value: 1 point
Number in set: 6

T is one of the most common consonants in
Scrabble. Four two-letter words begin with T (all
scoring 2 points), but they are easy to remember
as there is one for every vowel except U. Various
useful three-letter words begin with T. Some that
you may not know include TAI (Chinese system of
callisthenics, 3 points), TAO (in Confucian philosophy,
the correct course of action, 3 points) and TEF
(African grass grown for its grain, 6 points). T is one
of the letters of the RETAIN set and is therefore a
good letter to keep if trying to get a bonus word.

Two-letter words beginning with T

TA	TE	TI	TO

Some three-letter words beginning with T

TAD	TAU	TEG	TIG	TUM
TAE	TAV	TEL	TIL	TUN
TAI	TAW	TET	TIX	TUP
TAJ	TAY	TEW	TOC	TUT
TAK	TEC	TEX	TOD	TUX
TAM	TED	THO	TOG	TWP
TAO	TEE	TIC	TOM	TYE
TAT	TEF	TID	TOR	

Hooks

Hooking requires a subtle change in a player's thought process, in that they must look at words already on the board without becoming distracted by their pronunciation. Simple hooking solutions may be overlooked by a player, but things become easier with T as it is one of the most versatile letters when it comes to combining words.

When it comes to end-hooking, players often concentrate on S, as it can be easy to convert a singular word to a plural. However, T can also be highly effective and by learning a few of the hooks below, many more options present themselves to the player.

Handy Hint: Consonantitis

If you are stuck with very few vowels in your rack but you also have a letter T, it is useful to remember that T can form several words using only consonants. These are TSK (a sound uttered in disapproval, 7 points), TWP (a Welsh word meaning stupid, 8 points), TYG (a cup with more than one handle, 7 points), NTH (of an unspecified number), 6 points, and PHT (expression of irritation), 8 points.

Some front-hooks
Two letters to three

T-AB	T-AS	T-EL	T-IS	T-OW
T-AD	T-AT	T-EN	T-IT	T-OY
T-AE	T-AW	T-ES	T-OD	T-UG
T-AG	T-AX	T-ET	T-OE	T-UM
T-AI	T-AY	T-EX	T-OM	T-UN
T AM	T-EA	T-HE	T-ON	T-UP
T-AN	T-ED	T-HO	T OO	T-UT
T-AP	T-EE	T-ID	T-OP	T-WO
T-AR	T-EF	T-IN	T-OR	T-YE

Three letters to four

T-ABS	T-HAT	T-OUR
T-ACT	T-HAW	T-OUT
T-AIL	T-HEM	T-OWN
T-AKE	T HEN	T-RAD
T-ALE	T-HEY	T-RAM
T-ALL	T-HIN	T-RAP
T-APE	T-HIS	T-RAY
T-ARE	T-HUG	T-RIM
T-ART	T-ICK	T-RIP
T-ASK	T-IDE	T-ROD
T-ATE	T-ILL	T-ROT
T-EAR	T-IRE	T-RUE
T-EAT	T-OFF	T-URN
T-ELL	T-OIL	I-WEE
T-END	T-OLD	T-WIG
T-EST	T-ONE	T-WIN
T-HAN	T-OOT	T-WIT

Four letters to five

T-ABLE	T-HORN	T-REND
T-ACHE	T-HOSE	T-RIAL
T-ALKY	T-HUMP	T-RICK
T-ALLY	T-IMID	T-RIPS
T-APED	T-IRED	T-ROLL
T-APER	T-IRES	T-ROOP
T-AUNT	T-ITCH	T-ROUT
T-AWNY	T-OAST	T-RUCK
T-AXED	T-ONER	T-RUER
T-AXES	T-OUCH	T-RULY
T-EACH	T-OWED	T-RUST
T-EASE	T-OWER	T-RUTH
T-EDDY	T-RACE	T-WANG
T-EMPT	T-RACK	T-WEAK
T-EPEE	T-RADE	T-WEED
T-HANK	T-RAIL	T-WEET
T-HEFT	T-RAIN	T-WICE
T-HEIR	T-RAIT	T-WINE
T-HERE	T-RAMP	T-WINY
T-HICK	T-RASH	T-WIST
T-HIGH	T-READ	
T-HING	T-REES	

T

Five letters to six

T-ABBED	T-ERROR	T-OUTER
T-ABLED	T-ESTER	T-OWING
T-ABLET	T-ETHER	T-RACED
T-AILED	T-HANKS	T-RACER
T-ANGLE	T-HATCH	T-RACES
T-ANNOY	T-HAWED	T-RANCE
T-APING	T-HENCE	T-RANCE
T-ASKED	T-HORNY	T-RAVEL
T-ASTER	T-HOUGH	T-RIFLE
T-AUGHT	T-ICKLE	T-ROUGH
T-AXING	T-INGLE	T-ROWEL
T-AXMAN	T-INNER	T-RUSTY
T-EARED	T-IRADE	T-UMBLE
T-EASED	T-IRING	T-URBAN
T-EASER	T-ISSUE	T-URNED
T-EASES	T-OASTS	T-WEEDY
T-ENDED	T-OILED	T-WIGGY
T-ENDER	T-OTTER	T-WINGE
T-ENURE	T-OUTED	T-WIRED
		T-WITCH

T

Six letters to seven

T-ABLING	T-HAWING	T-RIGGER
T-AILING	T-HEREBY	T-RILLED
T-ALLIED	T-HEREIN	T-RIMMED
T-ANGLER	T-HUMPED	T-RIPPED
T-ASKING	T-INNING	T-ROTTER
T-EARFUL	T-OUTING	T-ROUBLE
T-EASING	T-RACING	T-RUCKED
T-EDDIES	T-RACKED	T-RUFFLE
T-ENABLE	T-RAILER	T-RUSTED
T-ENDING	T-RAINED	T-UNABLE
T-ENFOLD	T-RAMPED	T-WEAKER
T-ENURED	T-RAPPER	T-WIGGED
T-ISSUED	T-RASHES	T-WINGED
T-OILING	T-RAVELS	T-WINKLE
T-ESTATE	T-REASON	T-WITCHY
T-HANKER	T-RIFLES	T-WITTER

Seven letters to eight

T-ALLOWED	T-ISSUING	T-RIMMING
T-ALLYING	T-RACKING	T-RIPPING
T-ANGLING	T-RAILING	T-ROTTING
T-ANNOYED	T-RAINING	T-RUCKING
T-APELIKE	T-RAMMING	T-RUSTING
T-EARDROP	T-RAMPING	T-WEEDIER
T-ENFOLDS	T-RAPPING	T-WIGLESS
T-ENTERED	T-RASHING	T-WINGING
T-HATCHED	T-RAVELER	T-WINKLED
T-HICKIES	T-READING	T-WINNING
T-HUMPING	T-RIFLING	T-WITCHES

Some end-hooks
Two letters to three

AI-T	DO-T	HA-T	MA-T	OP-T	SO-T
AL-T	EA-T	HE-T	ME-T	OR-T	TA-T
AN-T	EF-T	HI-T	MO-T	OU-T	TE-T
AR-T	EL-T	HO-T	MU-T	OW-T	TI-T
AT-T	ES-T	JO-T	NA-T	PA-T	TO-T
BA-T	FA-T	KA-T	NE-T	PE-T	WE-T
BE-T	FE-T	KI-T	NO-T	PI-T	WO-T
BI-T	GI-T	LA-T	NU-T	PO-T	YE-T
BO-T	GO-T	LI-T	OF-T	RE-T	
DI-T	GU-T	LO-T	OO-T	SI-T	

Three letters to four

BEE-T	DOL-T	KEP-T	PAS-T	TAR-T
BEN-T	DUE-T	LAS-T	PES-T	TAU-T
BOA-T	EAS-T	LIN-T	PIN-T	TEN-T
BOO-T	FAS-T	LIS-T	POS-T	TES-T
CAN-T	FEE-T	LOS-T	RAN-T	TIN-T
CAR-T	FON-T	LOU-T	RAP-T	TOO-T
CEL-T	FOR-T	MAL-T	REN-T	UNI-T
CHA-T	GEN-T	MAS-T	RES-T	VAS-T
CHI-T	GIF-T	MEL-T	RIF-T	VOL-T
COL-T	GIS-T	MIS-T	ROO-T	WAI-T
COO-T	GOA-T	MOA-T	RUN-T	WAN-T
COS-T	GUS-T	MOO-T	SAL-T	WAT-T
CUR-T	HIN-T	MOS-T	SEA-T	WEN-T
DEB-T	HOO-T	MUS-T	SEN-T	WHA-T
DEF-T	HUN-T	NEW-T	SKI-T	WIS-T
DEN-T	JOL-T	PAC-T	SPA-T	ZOO-T
DIE-T	JUS-T	PAR-T	SUI-T	

Four letters to five

AVER-T	FACE-T	OVER-T
BEAU-T	FILE-T	PLAN-T
BLUR-T	FIRS-T	PLEA-T
BOAS-T	FLEE-T	ROOS-T
BOOS-T	GRAN-T	SHIR-T
BURN-T	GUES-T	SHOO-T
CADE-T	HEAR-T	SIGH-T
CHAR-T	ISLE-T	SPUR-T
CLEF-T	JOIN-T	STAR-T
COME-T	LEAN-T	STUN-T
COVE-T	LEAP-T	TEMP-T
DEAL-T	MEAN-T	TWEE-T
EVEN-T	NIGH-T	VALE-T

Five letters to six

BARES-T	FORES-T	PALES-T
BASAL-T	FORGE-T	PLANE-T
BASES-T	FORGO-T	PURES-T
BLUES-T	GADGE-T	RABBI-T
BONNE-T	GAMES-T	RARES-T
BOUGH-T	HONES-T	RIPES-T
BUDGE-T	IDLES-T	SAFES-T
CACHE-T	LANCE-T	SAGES-T
CLOSE-T	LAXES-T	SHIES-T
COVER-T	LEARN-T	SONNE-T
DIVER-T	LOCUS-T	SORES-T
DRIES-T	MIDGE-T	SPOIL-T
FILLE-T	MODES-T	TURBO-T
FINES-T	MUTES-T	WEIGH-T

T

320

Six letters to seven

ARCHES-T	DEARES-T	RICHES-T
ARTIES-T	EASIES-T	ROSIES-T
BRAVES-T	FALSES-T	SINGLE-T
BROUGH-T	GRAVES-T	STALES-T
BUSIES-T	HOLIES-T	TENSES-T
CLOSES-T	INANES-T	THOUGH-T
CONSUL-T	LAZIES-T	TIDIES-T
COSIES-T	LUSHES-T	TINIES-T
COUPLE-T	NAIVES-T	TRITES-T
COZIES-T	NOBLES-T	UGLIES-T
CRUDES-T	PERCEN-T	WARRAN-T
CURRAN-T	POSIES-T	WAVIES-T

Seven letters to eight

ANGRIES-T	FRESHES-T	ROOMIES-T
BAGGIES-T	FUNNIES-T	ROWDIES-T
BLONDES-T	GENTLES-T	SAVAGES-T
BULLIES-T	HARDIES-T	SECURES-T
CHOICES-T	HEAVIES-T	SHIPMEN-T
CONTRAS-T	INTERNE-T	SILLIES-T
CRAZIES-T	JOLLIES-T	SIMPLES-T
CROSSES-T	LITTLES-T	SQUARES-T
DIPLOMA-T	LUCKIES-T	STABLES-T
DIVINES-T	MATURES-T	SUNBURN-T
DIZZIES-T	MUDDIES-T	SUNNIES-T
EARLIES-T	NASTIES-T	TALKIES-T
EMPTIES-T	READIES-T	TELETEX-T
FEEBLES-T	REDREAM-T	TINNIES-T
FLAKIES-T	REGIMEN-T	UNLEARN-T
FLASHES-T	REMOTES-T	WEARIES-T

T

Blockers

It is useful to know which words are blockers and can't therefore be extended before or after. You may want to play a blocker that your opponent can't extend, or you may want to avoid playing a blocker because you want to keep the board open.

Some three-letter blockers beginning with T

TAJ	THY	TIX	TUX	TWP

Some four-letter blockers beginning with T

THAT	THIS	TIDY	TOED	TORN
THEY	THUS	TINY	TOLD	

Some five-letter blockers beginning with T (except words ending in '-ED', '-J', '-S', '-X', '-Y' or '-Z')

TACIT	THIEF	TIDAL
TAKEN	THINE	TIMID
TEACH	THOSE	TRUER

Some six-letter blockers beginning with T (except words ending in '-ED', '-J', '-S', '-X', '-Y' or '-Z')

TALLER	TAXMEN	THRICE	TRENCH
TAMEST	TENSER	THROWN	TRUEST
TAPING	TERGAL	TINIER	
TAUGHT	THRASH	TINMAN	
TAXMAN	THRESH	TOMATO	

T

Some words beginning with TRI-

Seven-letter words

TRI-ABLE	TRI-COTS	TRI-LOBE	TRI-SECT
TRI-ACID	TRI-DARN	TRI-LOGY	TRI-SEME
TRI-AGED	TRI-DENT	TRI-NARY	TRI-SHAW
TRI-AGES	TRI-DUAN	TRI-ODES	TRI-SOME
TRI-ARCH	TRI-ENES	TRI-ONES	TRI-SOMY
TRI-AXON	TRI-FLED	TRI-OSES	TRI-TEST
TRI-BADE	TRI-FOLD	TRI-OXID	TRI-TIDE
TRI-BLET	TRI-FORM	TRI-PACK	TRI-TONE
TRI-BUTE	TRI-GAMY	TRI-PART	TRI-TONS
TRI-CARS	TRI-GONS	TRI-PIER	TRI-UMPH
TRI-CEPS	TRI-GRAM	TRI-PLED	TRI-VETS
TRI-CLAD	TRI-JETS	TRI-PODS	TRI-VIAL
TRI-CORN	TRI-LITH	TRI-PSIS	TRI-ZONE

T

Eight-letter words

TRI-ACIDS
TRI-AGING
TRI-ALIST
TRI-ANGLE
TRI-AXIAL
TRI-AXONS
TRI-AZINE
TRI-AZOLE
TRI-BALLY
TRI-BASIC
TRI-BLETS
TRI-BRACH
TRI-BUTES
TRI-CHINA
TRI-CHORD
TRI-CLADS
TRI-COLOR
TRI-CORNS
TRI-CYCLE
TRI-DARNS
TRI-DENTS

TRI-ETHYL
TRI-FLING
TRI-FOCAL
TRI-GLYPH
TRI-GRAMS
TRI-GRAPH
TRI-LEMMA
TRI-LITHS
TRI-LOBED
TRI-LOBES
TRI-METER
TRI-MORPH
TRI-MOTOR
TRI-NODAL
TRI-OLEIN
TRI-OXIDE
TRI-OXIDS
TRI-PACKS
TRI-PEDAL
TRI-PHASE
TRI-PHONE

TRI-PLANE
TRI-PLIED
TRI-PLIES
TRI-PLING
TRI-PODAL
TRI-POLIS
TRI-POSES
TRI-SECTS
TRI-SEMES
TRI-SHAWS
TRI-STATE
TRI-STICH
TRI-THING
TRI-TICAL
TRI-TIDES
TRI-TONES
TRI-UNITY
TRI-VALVE
TRI-ZONAL
TRI-ZONES

Some words ending with -TIME
Seven-letter words

AIR-TIME	CEN-TIME	ONE-TIME	TEA-TIME
ANY-TIME	DAY-TIME	PAS-TIME	WAR-TIME
BED-TIME	LAY-TIME	RAG-TIME	
BIG-TIME	MIS-TIME	SEP-TIME	

Eight-letter words

CHOW-TIME	LONG-TIME	REAL-TIME
DOWN-TIME	MARI-TIME	SEED-TIME
FLEX-TIME	MEAL-TIME	SHOW-TIME
FORE-TIME	MEAN-TIME	SOME-TIME
GOOD-TIME	NOON-TIME	TERM-TIME
HALF-TIME	OVER-TIME	XENO-TIME
LIFE-TIME	PLAY-TIME	ZONE-TIME

Some words ending with -TION
Seven-letter words

ALA-TION	DIC-TION	MEN-TION	STA-TION
AMA-TION	EDI-TION	MIC-TION	SUC-TION
AMO-TION	ELA-TION	MIX-TION	TAC-TION
AUC-TION	ELU-TION	ORA-TION	TUI-TION
BAS-TION	EMO-TION	OVA-TION	UNC-TION
CAN-TION	EMP-TION	PAC-TION	UNI-TION
CAP-TION	ENA-TION	POR-TION	
CAU-TION	FAC-TION	REC-TION	
COC-TION	FIC-TION	RUC-TION	
COI-TION	LEC-TION	SEC-TION	

Eight-letter words

ABLA-TION	EDUC-TION	IODA-TION
ABLU-TION	EGES-TION	JOBA-TION
ABOR-TION	EJEC-TION	JUNC-TION
ADAP-TION	ELEC-TION	LAVA-TION
ADDI-TION	EMIC-TION	LEGA-TION
ADNA-TION	ENAC-TION	LENI-TION
ADOP-TION	EQUA-TION	LIBA-TION
AERA-TION	EREC-TION	LIGA-TION
AGNA-TION	ERUP-TION	LIMA-TION
AMBI-TION	EVEC-TION	LOBA-TION
AUDI-TION	EVIC-TION	LOCA-TION
AVIA-TION	EXAC-TION	LOCU-TION
BIBA-TION	EXER-TION	LUNA-TION
CIBA-TION	FETA-TION	LUXA-TION
CITA-TION	FIXA-TION	MONI-TION
COAC-TION	FLEC-TION	MUNI-TION
CONA-TION	FRAC-TION	MUTA-TION
COOP-TION	FRIC-TION	NATA-TION
CREA-TION	FRUI-TION	NEGA-TION
DELA-TION	FUNC-TION	NIDA-TION
DELE-TION	GELA-TION	NIVA-TION
DEMO-TION	GUMP-TION	NODA-TION
DERA-TION	HALA-TION	NOLI-TION
DEVO-TION	HIMA-TION	NOTA-TION
DILA-TION	IDEA-TION	NOVA-TION
DILU-TION	IGNI-TION	NUTA-TION
DONA-TION	ILLA-TION	OBLA-TION
DOTA-TION	INAC-TION	PACA-TION
DURA-TION	INUS-TION	PETI-TION

326

POSI-TION	SANC-TION	TAXA-TION
POTA-TION	SCON-TION	TRAC-TION
PUNI-TION	SEDA-TION	VACA-TION
PUPA-TION	SEDI-TION	VENA-TION
QUES-TION	SOLA-TION	VEXA-TION
REAC-TION	SOLU-TION	VOCA-TION
RELA-TION	SORP-TION	VOLI-TION
REMO-TION	STIC-TION	VOLU-TION
ROGA-TION	SUDA-TION	ZONA-TION
ROTA-TION	SWAP-TION	

Unusual letter combinations

If you have an unusual combination of letters on your rack, or want to impress your opponent with an unusual word, a few words from World English can come in handy.

Australian words

TOOSHIE	angry or upset
TRIELLA	three horse races nominated for a bet
TROPPO	mentally affected by a tropical climate
TRUCKIE	truck driver
TRUGO	game similar to croquet
TUAN	flying phalanger
TUART	type of eucalyptus tree

Canadian words

TILLICUM	friend
TOONIE	Canadian two-dollar coin

| TULLIBEE | whitefish found in the Great Lakes |
| TUPEK | Inuit tent of animal skins |

Hindi words

TABLA	pair of drums whose pitches can be varied
THALI	meal consisting of several small dishes
TIL	sesame
TOLA	unit of weight
TONGA	light two-wheeled vehicle
TOPEE	pith helmet

New Zealand words

TAIAHA	ceremonial fighting staff
TAIHOA	hold on!
TAKAHE	rare flightless bird
TANGI	Maori funeral ceremony
TANIWHA	legendary monster
TAONGA	treasure
TAPU	sacred or forbidden
TARSEAL	bitumen surface of a road
TAUIWI	non-Maori people of New Zealand
TIKANGA	Maori customs
TOETOE	type of tall grass
TOITOI	type of tall grass
TWINK	white correction fluid

T

Urdu words

TAHSIL   administrative division
TALOOKA   subdivision of a district
TAMASHA   show or entertainment
TANDOORI   method of cooking on a spit in
                      a clay oven

T

Essential info
Value: 1 point
Number in set: 4

U can be a difficult tile to play effectively. In fact, there are no particularly high-scoring short words which start with U. In order to make the best of your tiles, some handy words to remember are UH (5 points), UM (4 points), UP (4 points) and UG (3 points). Also, when aiming for short words, you can save yourself some time by remembering that there are no valid three-letter words beginning with U which use Q, X or Z.

Two-letter words beginning with U

UG	UM	UP	US
UH	UN	UR	UT

Some three-letter words beginning with U

UDO	UNI	URP
UGH	UPO	UTA
UMM	URB	UTE
UMP	URD	UTU
UMU	URE	

Hooks

Hooking requires a subtle change in a player's thought process, in that they must look at words already on the board without becoming distracted by their pronunciation.

Some front-hooks
Two letters to three

U-DO	U-PO	U-TE
U-MM	U-RE	
U-MU	U-TA	

Three letters to four

U-DAL	U-NIS	U-SER
U-DON	U-NIT	U-TIS
U-LES	U-PAS	U-VAE
U-LEX	U-SED	U-VAS

Four letters to five

U-LAMA	U-RASE	U-RITE
U-NARY	U-RATE	U-SAGE
U-NITE	U-REAL	U-SING
U-PEND	U-REDO	U-SURE
U-PLAY	U-RENT	U-TILE
U-PLED	U-RIAL	U-VEAL
U-RARE	U-RINE	

U

Five letters to six

U-LEXES	U-PLEAD	U-REDIA
U-LOSES	U-PLINK	U-SABLE
U-NEATH	U-PLOOK	U-SAGER
U-NITER	U-PRATE	U-SAGES
U-NOWED	U-PREST	U-SURED
U-PASES	U-PRISE	U-SURER
U-PHANG	U-PROLL	U-SWARD
U-PLAID	U-PROSE	

Six letters to seven

U-NEARED	U-PLINKS	U-PREACH
U-NEATEN	U-PLYING	U-PRISER
U-PENDED	U-PRAISE	U-REDIAL
U-PLIGHT	U-PRATED	U-SURING

Seven letters to eight

U-PENDING	U-PRAISED	U-PRISING
U-PLAYING	U-PRAISER	U-PROLLED
U-PLINKED	U-PRATING	

Some end-hooks
Two letters to three

AM-U	KY-U	SO-U
AY-U	LO-U	TA-U
EA-U	ME-U	UM-U
EM-U	MO-U	UT-U
FE-U	PI-U	YO-U

Three letters to four

AIT-U	LAT-U	RAT-U
BAL-U	LEK-U	RIM-U
BAP-U	LIE-U	SUS-U
BED-U	LIT-U	TAB-U
BUB-U	MAS-U	TAP-U
EME-U	MEN-U	TAT-U
FRA-U	MOT-U	TEG-U
FUG-U	MUM-U	THO-U
GEN-U	NAM-U	TUI-U
GUR-U	PAT-U	VAT-U
HAP-U	PUD-U	WUD-U
HUH-U	PUL-U	
KOR-U	PUP-U	

U

Four letters to five

BANT-U	CORN-U	PARE-U
BATT-U	FOND-U	PEND-U
BITO-U	HAIK-U	PIKA-U
BUCK-U	JAMB-U	PILA-U
BUND-U	KAWA-U	QUIP-U
BUSS-U	LASS-U	TEND-U
CENT-U	MUNT-U	VERT-U

Five letters to six

CONGO-U	HALER-U	MANAT-U

Six letters to seven

MANITO-U	TAMARA-U
SUBMEN-U	TURACO-U

U

Handy Hint

UKE (7 points) is a short form of UKULELE (11 points). There are not many short high-scoring words beginning with U: UKE and UGH (a sound people make when they dislike or are disgusted by something) are the highest-scoring three-letter words at 7 points each. UMM and UMP also score 7.

Blockers

It is useful to know which words are blockers and can't therefore be extended before or after. You may want to play a blocker that your opponent can't extend, or you may want to avoid playing a blocker because you want to keep the board open.

Some four-letter blockers beginning with U

UNDO   UPGO   UPSY

Some five-letter blockers beginning with U (except words ending in '-ED', '-J', '-S', '-X', '-Y' or '-Z')

UNAPT	UNHIP	UPTER
UNBID	UNMET	UREAL
UNDID	UNRID	URNAL
UNDUE	UNWET	UTERI
UNDUG	UPBYE	
UNGOT	UPLIT	

Some six-letter blockers beginning with U (except words ending in '-ED', '-J', '-S', '-X', '-Y' or '-Z')

ULTIMO	UNLASH	UNWISH
UMBRAL	UNLOST	UNWORN
UNBENT	UNMADE	UPBLEW
UNBORE	UNMEEK	UPDREW
UNCAST	UNMEET	UPGONE
UNCHIC	UNMESH	UPGREW
UNCLAD	UNMIXT	UPGUSH
UNCOOL	UNMOWN	UPHAND
UNCUTE	UNOPEN	UPHELD
UNDEAD	UNPAID	UPHILD
UNDEAR	UNPENT	UPHOVE
UNDONE	UNPURE	UPHUNG
UNDREW	UNREAL	UPLAID
UNEVEN	UNRENT	UPMOST
UNFELT	UNSAID	UPPISH
UNFIRM	UNSAWN	UPROSE
UNFOND	UNSENT	UPRUSH
UNGAIN	UNSEWN	UPSENT
UNHEWN	UNSHOD	UPTOOK
UNHUNG	UNSOLD	UPTORE
UNHURT	UNSPUN	UPTORN
UNIFIC	UNSUNG	UPWENT
UNITAL	UNSUNK	URETIC
UNJUST	UNTOLD	URSINE
UNKEPT	UNTORN	USABLE
UNKIND	UNTROD	
UNLAID	UNWELL	

U

Bonus words

Bonus words on your rack can be hard to spot, especially for the less experienced player. One way to help find them is by using prefixes and suffixes.

Many larger words include a common prefix or suffix – remembering these and using them where you can is a good way to discover any longer words on your rack, including any potential bonus words. The key prefixes to remember beginning with U are UN- and UP- and the key suffix is -URE.

Some words beginning with UN-
Seven-letter words

UN-ACTED	UN-BOLTS	UN-CLEAN
UN-ADDED	UN-BONED	UN-CLEAR
UN-AGING	UN-BOUND	UN-CLING
UN-AIDED	UN-BOWED	UN-CLIPS
UN-AIMED	UN-BOXED	UN-CLOAK
UN-AIRED	UN-BURNT	UN-CLOGS
UN-ARMED	UN-CAGED	UN-CODED
UN-AWARE	UN-CANNY	UN-COILS
UN-BAKED	UN-CASED	UN-CORKS
UN-BEGUN	UN-CHAIN	UN-COUTH
UN-BENDS	UN-CHECK	UN-COVER
UN-BINDS	UN-CITED	UN-CUFFS
UN-BLOCK	UN-CIVIL	UN-CURED
UN-BLOWN	UN-CLASP	UN-CURLS

U

UN-DATED	UN-GROWN	UN-MIXED
UN-DEALT	UN-GUARD	UN-MORAL
UN-DOERS	UN-GULAR	UN-MOUNT
UN-DOING	UN-HANDS	UN-MOVED
UN-DRAWN	UN-HAPPY	UN-NAMED
UN-DRESS	UN-HASTY	UN-NERVE
UN-DRUNK	UN-HEALS	UN-OILED
UN-DYING	UN-HEARD	UN-PACKS
UN-EAGER	UN-HELMS	UN-PAVED
UN-EARTH	UN-HINGE	UN-PICKS
UN-EATEN	UN-HITCH	UN-PLACE
UN-ENDED	UN-HOOKS	UN-PLUGS
UN-EQUAL	UN-HORSE	UN-POSED
UN-FAIRS	UN-HUMAN	UN-QUIET
UN-FAKED	UN-KEMPT	UN-QUOTE
UN-FAZED	UN-KNOWN	UN-RATED
UN-FENCE	UN-LACED	UN-RAVEL
UN-FILED	UN-LADED	UN-READY
UN-FIRED	UN-LATCH	UN-RESTS
UN-FLUSH	UN-LEARN	UN-ROBED
UN-FOLDS	UN-LEASH	UN-ROLLS
UN-FORMS	UN-LINED	UN-SAFER
UN-FOUND	UN-LIVED	UN-SATED
UN-FROCK	UN-LOADS	UN-SAVED
UN-FROZE	UN-LOCKS	UN-SCARY
UN-FUNNY	UN-LOVED	UN-SCREW
UN-FUSSY	UN-LUCKY	UN-SEATS
UN-GLUED	UN-MAKER	UN-SEWED
UN-GODLY	UN-MANLY	UN-SHELL
UN-GORED	UN-MASKS	UN-SHOED

UN-SHORN	UN-STICK	UN-TRIED
UN-SHOWN	UN-STRAP	UN-TRUER
UN-SIGHT	UN-STUCK	UN-TRUST
UN-SIZED	UN-STUNG	UN-TRUTH
UN-SLAIN	UN-SURER	UN-TWIST
UN-SLUNG	UN-TAKEN	UN-TYING
UN-SNAGS	UN-TAMED	UN-USUAL
UN-SOLID	UN-TAXED	UN-VEILS
UN-SOUND	UN-THAWS	UN-WAGED
UN-SPENT	UN-TILED	UN-WINDS
UN-SPILT	UN-TIMED	UN-WIRED
UN-SPLIT	UN-TIRED	UN-WISER
UN-SPOOL	UN-TONED	UN-WOUND
UN-STACK	UN-TRACE	UN-WRAPS

Eight-letter words

UN-ABATED	UN-BIDDEN	UN-CANNED
UN-ACTIVE	UN-BILLED	UN-CAPPED
UN-AFRAID	UN-BITTEN	UN-CARING
UN-AGEING	UN-BOLTED	UN-CAUGHT
UN-AMUSED	UN-BONDED	UN-CHOSEN
UN-ARGUED	UN-BOOKED	UN-CLENCH
UN-ARMING	UN-BOUGHT	UN-CLOTHE
UN-AVOWED	UN-BOWING	UN-CLUTCH
UN-BAITED	UN-BRIDLE	UN-COATED
UN-BEARED	UN-BROKEN	UN-COCKED
UN-BEATEN	UN-BURDEN	UN-COILED
UN-BEGGED	UN-BURIED	UN-COMMON
UN-BELIEF	UN-BUTTON	UN-COOKED
UN-BIASED	UN-CALLED	UN-CORKED

UN-COUPLE	UN-GAINLY	UN-NERVED
UN-CUFFED	UN-GENTLE	UN-OPENED
UN-CURLED	UN-GIVING	UN-PACKED
UN-DARING	UN-GUIDED	UN-PAIRED
UN-DECENT	UN-HANDED	UN-PLAYED
UN-DENIED	UN-HARMED	UN-PRICED
UN-DERATE	UN-HEEDED	UN-PROVED
UN-DINTED	UN-HELPED	UN-QUOTED
UN-DOCILE	UN-HINGED	UN-REALLY
UN-DRIVEN	UN-HOLIER	UN-REASON
UN-EARNED	UN-HOOKED	UN-RESTED
UN-EASIER	UN-HORSED	UN-RINSED
UN-EASILY	UN-IRONED	UN-ROLLED
UN-EDIBLE	UN-ISSUED	UN-SAFELY
UN-EDITED	UN-JAMMED	UN-SALTED
UN-ENDING	UN-JOINED	UN-SAVORY
UN-ENVIED	UN-KINDER	UN-SEATED
UN-ERRING	UN-LAWFUL	UN-SEEING
UN-EVENLY	UN-LEADED	UN-SEEMLY
UN-FALLEN	UN-LEARNT	UN-SETTLE
UN-FAMOUS	UN-LIKELY	UN-SHAKEN
UN-FASTEN	UN-LISTED	UN-SHAVEN
UN-FENCED	UN-LOADED	UN-SIGNED
UN-FILLED	UN-LOCKED	UN-SOILED
UN-FILMED	UN-LOVING	UN-SOLVED
UN-FOLDED	UN-MANNED	UN-SPOILT
UN-FORCED	UN-MARKED	UN-SUBTLE
UN-FORMED	UN-MASKED	UN-SURELY
UN-FROZEN	UN-MENDED	UN-TAPPED
UN-FURLED	UN-MOVING	UN-THRONE

U

UN-TIDILY	UN-VERSED	UN-WIELDY
UN-TIEING	UN-VIABLE	UN-WISELY
UN-TITLED	UN-WANTED	UN-WORTHY
UN-TOWARD	UN-WARILY	
UN-USABLE	UN-WASHED	

Some words beginning with UP-
Seven-letter words

UP-BEATS	UP-HEAVE	UP-STAGE
UP-BRAID	UP-HOLDS	UP-STAIR
UP-BRING	UP-LIFTS	UP-STAND
UP-CHUCK	UP-LOADS	UP-START
UP-CLOSE	UP-LYING	UP-STATE
UP-COMES	UP-PINGS	UP-SURGE
UP-CURVE	UP-RAISE	UP-SWELL
UP-DATED	UP-RATED	UP-SWING
UP-DRAFT	UP-REACH	UP-TAKEN
UP-ENDED	UP-RIGHT	UP-TEMPO
UP-FIELD	UP-RISEN	UP-TIGHT
UP-FLUNG	UP-RIVER	UP-TOWNS
UP-FRONT	UP-ROOTS	UP-TURNS
UP-GOING	UP-SCALE	UP-WARDS
UP-GROWN	UP-SLOPE	

U

Eight-letter words

UP-COMING	UP-LANDER	UP-SETTER
UP-DATING	UP-LIFTED	UP-SIZING
UP-DIVING	UP-LINKED	UP-SPOKEN
UP-ENDING	UP-LOADED	UP-SPRUNG
UP-FLOWED	UP-LOOKED	UP-STAGED
UP-FURLED	UP-MARKET	UP-STREAM
UP-GAZING	UP-RATING	UP-STROKE
UP-GRADED	UP-RISING	UP-SURGED
UP-GROWTH	UP-ROARED	UP-TAKING
UP-HEAPED	UP-ROOTED	UP-THROWN
UP-HEAVED	UP-SCALED	UP-TURNED

Some words ending with -URE
Seven-letter words

BRAV-URE	FISS-URE	PREC-URE
CAPT-URE	FIXT-URE	PROC-URE
CENS-URE	FLEX-URE	RAPT-URE
CLOS-URE	GEST-URE	RUPT-URE
CONJ-URE	LEAS-URE	SEIS-URE
COUT-URE	LECT-URE	SEIZ-URE
CULT-URE	LEIS-URE	STAT-URE
DENT-URE	MEAS-URE	TEXT-URE
DISC-URE	MIXT-URE	TONS-URE
EPIC-URE	NURT-URE	TORT-URE
ERAS-URE	OBSC-URE	VENT-URE
FACT-URE	PAST-URE	VERD-URE
FAIL-URE	PERJ-URE	VULT-URE
FEAT-URE	PICT-URE	

U

Eight-letter words

ANNEX-URE
APERT-URE
ARMAT-URE
AVENT-URE
BROCH-URE
COIFF-URE
CREAT-URE
DENAT-URE
DOUBL-URE
EXPOS-URE
FIXAT-URE
FRACT-URE

IMMAT-URE
INSEC-URE
JUNCT-URE
LIGAT-URE
MANIC-URE
MOIST-URE
OVERC-URE
OVERS-URE
OVERT-URE
PEDIC-URE
PLEAS-URE
PRESS-URE

PUNCT-URE
REASS-URE
REFIG-URE
REINJ-URE
REINS-URE
RENAT-URE
REPOS-URE
RESEC-URE
SINEC-URE
TAINT-URE
TINCT-URE
TREAS-URE

Unusual letter combinations

If you have an unusual combination of letters on
your rack, or want to impress your opponent with
an unusual word, a few words from World English
can come in handy. Some beginning with U include:

Australian words

UMPIE   umpire
UNCO   awkward or clumsy
UPTA   of poor quality
UTE   utility

Hindi word

URD   bean plant

U

Essential info
Value: 4 points
Number in set: 2

It is important to note that there are no two-letter words with the **V** which can make it a natural blocker, preventing parallel plays. Generally it is easier to play the V with vowels but watch out for some good-scoring in combination with other high-scoring consonants such as VEX (13 points), VLY (9 points), VOW (9 points), VUM (8 points).

Three-letter words beginning with V

VAC	VAW	VLY
VAE	VEE	VOE
VAG	VID	VOR
VAR	VIM	VOX
VAS	VIN	VUG
VAV	VIS	VUM

Hooks

Hooking requires a subtle change in a player's thought process, in that they must look at words already on the board without becoming distracted by their pronunciation.

Some front-hooks
Two letters to three

V-AE	V-EE	V-OR
V-AG	V-ET	V-OW
V-AN	V-EX	V-OX
V-AR	V-ID	V-UG
V-AS	V-IN	V-UM
V-AT	V-IS	
V-AW	V-OE	

Three letters to four

V-AIL	V-EGO	V-ILL
V-AIN	V-ELD	V-IRE
V-AIR	V-ELL	V-ITA
V-ALE	V-END	V-LEI
V-AMP	V-ERA	V-OAR
V-ANE	V-ERS	V-OLE
V-ANT	V-EST	V-ROT
V-ARE	V-ICE	V-ROW
V-ARY	V-IDE	V-UGH

V

Four letters to five

V-AGUE	V-ETCH	V-OARS
V-AIRY	V-EXED	V-OLES
V-ALES	V-EXES	V-OMER
V-ARIA	V-IBEX	V-OMIT
V-ARNA	V-ICED	V-OUCH
V-AUNT	V-IRED	V-OWED
V-EALE	V-IRID	V-OWER
V-EERY	V-ISIT	V-ROOM
V-ERST	V-LIES	

Five letters to six

V-AGILE	V-AWARD	V-EXING
V-AGUED	V-EALES	V-ICING
V-AILED	V-EGGED	V-IRING
V-ALINE	V-ELATE	V-IZARD
V-ALLEY	V-ENDED	V-ORANT
V-AMPED	V-ENDER	V-OTARY
V-ASTER	V-ENDUE	V-OWING
V-ATMAN	V-ENTER	
V-AUNTY	V-ERVEN	

V

Six letters to seven

V-ACUATE	V-ASSAIL	V-ENDING
V-ACUITY	V-AUNTER	V-ENTAIL
V-AILING	V-AUNTIE	V-ESTRAL
V-AIRIER	V-EGGING	V-OCULAR
V-ALGOID	V-ELATED	V-OUCHED
V-AMPING	V-ENATIC	V-ROOMED

Seven letters to eight

V-AGILITY	V-ENTAYLE	V-IRIDIAN
V-AIRIEST	V-ERISTIC	V-OTARIES
V-ALLEYED	V-ERMINED	V-OUCHING
V-ENATION	V-ICELESS	V-ROOMING
V-ENOLOGY	V-ICELIKE	

Some end-hooks
Two letters to three

DE-V	GU-V	RE-V
DI-V	LA-V	SO-V
GO-V	PA-V	TA-V

Three letters to four

CHA-V	DEE-V	MIR-V
CHI-V	ERE-V	PER-V

Four letters to five

GANE-V	OLLA-V	PARE-V

Blockers

It is useful to know which words are blockers and can't therefore be extended before or after. You may want to play a blocker that your opponent can't extend, or you may want to avoid playing a blocker because you want to keep the board open.

Some three-letter blockers beginning with V

VLY   VOX

Some four-letter blockers beginning with V

VAGI	VERD	VIAE	VIZY
VAIN	VETO	VIBS	VROT
VERA	VEXT	VIVO	

Handy Hint

If you have a V and the board is quite blocked then it is more likely that vowels on your rack, or on the board, will help you out. Look out for plays involving AVA, AVE, OVA, UVA, VAE, VAU (all 6 points). Even if you have two Vs the vowels could rescue you with VIVA VIVE VIVO (all 10 points). There is also VAV (A Hebrew letter, 9 points).

V

Some five-letter blockers beginning with V (except words ending in '-ED', '-J', '-S', '-X', '-Y' or '-Z')

VACUA	VENAE	VIRID
VAGAL	VENAL	VITAE
VAIRE	VERRA	VIVID
VALID	VILDE	VOILA
VAPID	VILLI	VOLTA
VASAL	VINIC	VOLTI
VATIC	VIOLD	VULGO
VELUM	VIRAL	

Some six-letter blockers beginning with V (except words ending in '-ED', '-J', '-S', '-X', '-Y' or '-Z')

VACANT	VENIAL	VIRENT
VAGILE	VERIER	VIRILE
VAGROM	VERMAL	VIRING
VAGUER	VERNAL	VISCID
VAINER	VIABLE	VISIVE
VALVAL	VIBIER	VISTAL
VALVAR	VICING	VOLAGE
VANMAN	VIDUAL	VOLING
VANMEN	VILLAE	VORAGO
VARSAL	VILLAR	VORANT
VASTER	VINFAL	VORPAL
VATMAN	VINIER	VOSTRU
VATMEN	VINING	

V

349

Unusual letter combinations

If you have an unusual combination of letters on your rack, or want to impress your opponent with an unusual word, a few words from World English can come in handy. Here are a few examples beginning with V.

Australian words

VAG	vagrant
VEGO	vegetarian
VIGORO	women's game similar to cricket

Hindi words

VAHANA	vehicle in Indian myth
VANDA	type of orchid
VINA	stringed musical instrument

South African words

VLEI	area of marshy ground
VOEMA	vigour or energy
VROU	woman or wife

V

W 4

There are only two two-letter words beginning with **W**: WE (5 points) and WO (an old-fashioned spelling of woe, also 5). There are, however, many short, common-usage words which can return good scores such as WAX (13 points), WHO (9 points) and WOK (10 points). The highest-scoring three-letter word beginning with W is WIZ (short form of wizard, 15 points).

Two-letter words beginning with W

WE   WO

Some three-letter words beginning with W

WAB	WEN	WOK
WAE	WEX	WOP
WAI	WEY	WOT
WAN	WHA	WOW
WAP	WIS	WOX
WAT	WIZ	WUS
WAW	WOF	WYE
WEM	WOG	WYN

W

Some front-hooks
Two letters to three

W-AB	W-AY	W-IT
W-AD	W-ED	W-OE
W-AE	W-EE	W-OF
W-AG	W-EM	W-ON
W-AI	W-EN	W-OO
W-AN	W-ET	W-OP
W-AR	W-EX	W-OS
W-AS	W-HA	W-OW
W-AT	W-HO	W-OX
W-AW	W-IN	W-US
W-AX	W-IS	W-YE

W

Three letters to four

W-ADD	W-AWA	W-HIT
W-AFF	W-AWE	W-HOA
W-AFT	W-AWL	W-HOM
W-AGE	W-EAN	W-HOP
W-AID	W-EAR	W-HOT
W-AIL	W-EEK	W-HOW
W-AIN	W-EFL	W-HUP
W-AIR	W-EEN	W-ICE
W-AIT	W-EFT	W-ICH
W-AKE	W-ELD	W-ICK
W-ALE	W-ELK	W-IDE
W-ALL	W-ELL	W-ILL
W-AND	W-ELT	W-IMP
W-ANE	W-END	W-INK
W-ANT	W-ERE	W-INN
W-ANY	W-EST	W-IRE
W-ARB	W-ETA	W-ISH
W-ARD	W-HAE	W-OKE
W-ARE	W-HAM	W-OLD
W-ARK	W-HAP	W-OOF
W-ARM	W-HAT	W-OON
W-ART	W-HEN	W-OOT
W-ARY	W-HET	W-ORD
W-ASH	W-HEW	W-ORE
W-ASP	W-HEY	W-ORT
W-ATE	W-HID	W-RAP
W-ATT	W-HIM	W-REN
W-AUK	W-HIN	W-RIT
W-AVE	W-HIP	

W

Four letters to five

W-ADDY	W-HEAT	W-OMEN
W-AGED	W-HEEL	W-OOFY
W-AGER	W-HEFT	W-OOSE
W-AGON	W-HELM	W-OOZY
W-AIDE	W-HELP	W-OULD
W-AKED	W-HERE	W-OVEN
W-ALLY	W-HIPT	W-OWED
W-ANNA	W-HISH	W-OXEN
W-ARED	W-HISS	W-RACK
W-ARTY	W-HIST	W-RANG
W-ASHY	W-HIZZ	W-RAPT
W-ATAP	W-HOLE	W-RAST
W-AVER	W-HOOF	W-RATE
W-AXED	W-HOOP	W-RATH
W-EAVE	W-HOOT	W-REAK
W-ECHT	W-HOPS	W-RECK
W-EDGE	W-HORE	W-REST
W-EDGY	W-HOSE	W-RICK
W-EXED	W-HUMP	W-RING
W-EXES	W-HUPS	W-RITE
W-HACK	W-ICKY	W-ROKE
W-HALE	W-IDES	W-RONG
W-HANG	W-ILLY	W-ROOT
W-HARE	W-INCH	W-ROTE
W-HEAL	W-IRED	W-RUNG
W-HEAR	W-ITCH	

W

354

Five letters to six

W-ACKER	W-AXING	W-HOLLY
W-ADDED	W-EANED	W-HOOSH
W-ADDER	W-EARED	W-ICHES
W-ADDLE	W-EASEL	W-ICKER
W-AFTER	W-EAVED	W-IGGED
W-AGGER	W-EAVES	W-ILLER
W-AGING	W-EBBED	W-IMPED
W-AILED	W-EDGED	W-INDOW
W-AIRED	W-EIGHT	W-INKED
W-AIVER	W-ELDER	W-INKER
W-AKING	W-ENDED	W-INKLE
W-ALLOW	W-ESTER	W-INNED
W-AMBLE	W-ETHER	W-INNER
W-ANGLE	W-EXING	W-INTER
W-ANION	W-HALED	W-IRING
W-ANKER	W-HALER	W-ISHES
W-ANKLE	W-HAMMY	W-ITCHY
W-ANTED	W-HEELS	W-ITHER
W-ARKED	W-HEEZE	W-IZARD
W-ARMED	W-HENCE	W-ONNED
W-ARMER	W-HERRY	W-ORMER
W-ARRAY	W-HEUGH	W-OUBIT
W-ASHED	W-HEWED	W-OUNDY
W-ASHEN	W-HILLY	W-OWING
W-ASHES	W-HINGE	W-RASSE
W-ASTER	W-HINNY	W-RETCH
W-AUGHT	W-HIPPY	W-RIGHT

W

Six letters to seven

W-ADDING	W-ENDING	W-HITTER
W-ADDLED	W-HACKED	W-HIZZED
W-AILING	W-HACKER	W-HOLISM
W-AIRING	W-HALING	W-HOLIST
W-AMBLED	W-HAMMED	W-HOOFED
W-ANGLED	W-HANGED	W-HOOPED
W-ANGLER	W-HAPPED	W-HOOPER
W-ANTING	W-HEELED	W-HOOPLA
W-APPEND	W-HEELER	W-HOOTED
W-ARKING	W-HEEZED	W-HOPPED
W-ARLING	W-HELMED	W-HOPPER
W-ARMING	W-HELPED	W-HUMPED
W-ARRANT	W-HEREAT	W-HUPPED
W-ARTIER	W-HEREBY	W-IGGING
W-ASHERY	W-HEREIN	W-ILLEST
W-ASHIER	W-HEREOF	W-IMPING
W-ASHING	W-HEREON	W-IMPISH
W-ASPISH	W-HERETO	W-IMPLED
W-ASSAIL	W-HETHER	W-INCHED
W-ATTEST	W-HEWING	W-INCHER
W-AXLIKE	W-HIDDER	W-INCHES
W-EANING	W-HINGED	W-INDIGO
W-EARING	W-HINGER	W-INKING
W-EAVING	W-HIPPED	W-INKLED
W-EBBING	W-HIPPER	W-INNING
W-EDGIER	W-HISHED	W-ITCHED
W-EDGING	W-HISSED	W-ITCHES
W-EIGHTY	W-HISTED	W-ONNING
W-ELDING	W-HITHER	W-OOZIER

W-OOZILY	W-RASSLE	W-RINGED
W-RACKED	W-REAKED	W-RINGER
W-RANGED	W-RECKED	W-ROOTED
W-RAPPED	W-RESTED	W-ROUGHT
W-RAPPER	W-RESTER	
W-RASSES	W-RICKED	

Seven letters to eight

W-ADDLING	W-HELPING	W-INCHING
W-AGELESS	W-HERRIED	W-INDOWED
W-ALLEYED	W-HINGING	W-INKLING
W-ALLOWED	W-HINNIED	W-IRELESS
W-AMBLING	W-HINNIES	W-ITCHIER
W-ANGLING	W-HIPLIKE	W-ITCHING
W-ANTHILL	W-HIPPIER	W-OOFIEST
W-ARRAYED	W-HIPPING	W-OOZIEST
W-ARTIEST	W-HIPSTER	W-OULDEST
W-ARTLESS	W-HIRLING	W-RACKFUL
W-ASHIEST	W-HISHING	W-RACKING
W-ASTABLE	W-HISSING	W-RANGING
W-EANLING	W-HISTING	W-RAPPING
W-EASELED	W-HIZZING	W-RASSLED
W-EDGIEST	W-HOOFING	W-REAKING
W-HACKING	W-HOOPING	W-RECKING
W-HAMMING	W-HOOSHED	W-RESTING
W-HANGING	W-HOOSHES	W-RETCHED
W-HAPPING	W-HOOTING	W-RICKING
W-HEELING	W-HOPPING	W-RINGING
W-HEEZING	W-HUMPING	W-ROOTING
W-HELMING	W-HUPPING	

357

W

Some end-hooks
Two letters to three

BO-W	KA-W	PE-W
DA-W	KO-W	PO-W
DE-W	LA-W	RE-W
DO-W	LO-W	SO-W
FA-W	MA-W	TA-W
FE-W	ME-W	TE-W
HA-W	MO-W	TO-W
HE-W	NA-W	WO-W
HO-W	NE-W	YA-W
JA-W	NO-W	YE-W
JO-W	PA-W	YO-W

Three letters to four

ALE-W	CHA-W	SHE-W
ANE-W	CHE-W	SKA-W
ARE-W	ENE-W	SPA-W
AVO-W	FRO-W	THE-W
BRA-W	PRO-W	VIE-W
BRO-W	SHA-W	WHO-W

Four letters to five

BEDE-W	PAWA-W	THRO-W
KOTO-W	PILA-W	VINE-W
NAVE-W	SINE-W	VROU-W
PAPA-W	SYBO-W	

W

Five letters to six

BARRO-W

BURRO-W

HALLO-W

HOLLO-W

MATLO-W

MISSA-W

MORRO-W

OUTRO-W

PURSE-W

REVIE-W

UNCLE-W

Six letters to seven

DAYGLO-W

Seven letters to eight

BUDGERO-W

RICKSHA-W

Handy Hint

Some of the more unusual words beginning with
W are WAKIKI (Melanesian shell currency, 12 points),
WAMBLE (move unsteadily, 13 points), WUXIA
(genre of Chinese fiction and film, concerning the
adventures of sword-wielding chivalrous heroes,
15 points) and WYVERN (heraldic beast having
a serpent's tail, a dragon's head and a body with
wings and two legs, 15 points).

W

Blockers

It is useful to know which words are blockers and can't therefore be extended before or after. You may want to play a blocker that your opponent can't extend, or you may want to avoid playing a blocker because you want to keep the board open.

Three-letter blocker beginning with W
WOX

Some four-letter blockers beginning with W

WADY	WERT	WILY
WARY	WHAE	WIRY
WAVY	WHIO	WOST
WAXY	WHOA	WOWF
WENA	WHOT	WYCH
WERE	WICH	

W

360

Some five-letter blockers beginning with W (except words ending in '-ED', '-J', '-S', '-X', '-Y' or '-Z')

WANNA	WHOSE	WOWEE
WAXEN	WHOSO	WOXEN
WELCH	WIDER	WRAPT
WELSH	WILCO	WROTE
WENCH	WINCH	WROTH
WHAMO	WISER	WRUNG
WHICH	WISHT	WRYER
WHIPT	WOMEN	

Some six-letter blockers beginning with W (except words ending in '-ED', '-J', '-S', '-X', '-Y' or '-Z')

WANIER	WHILST	WISEST
WANKLE	WHITER	WISING
WANNER	WHOMSO	WITHAL
WARIER	WHOOSH	WITING
WARING	WIDEST	WOEFUL
WARMAN	WIDISH	WORSER
WARMEN	WIFING	WOWING
WASHEN	WILFUL	WRENCH
WASSUP	WILIER	WRETCH
WAVIER	WILING	WROKEN
WAXIER	WIMMIN	WRYEST
WHATSO	WIRIER	WRYING

W

Bonus words

Bonus words on your rack can be hard to spot, especially for the less experienced player. One way to help find them is by using prefixes and suffixes.

Many larger words include a common prefix or suffix – remembering these and using them where you can is a good way to discover any longer words on your rack, including any potential bonus words. The key prefix to remember is WAR- and the key suffixes are -WARD, -WARDS, -WAY, -WISE, -WOOD, -WORK, -WORM and -WORT.

Some words beginning with WAR-
Seven-letter words

WAR-BLED	WAR-LOCK	WAR-SAWS
WAR-DENS	WAR-LORD	WAR-SHIP
WAR-DING	WAR-MING	WAR-SLED
WAR-DOGS	WAR-PATH	WAR-TIER
WAR-FARE	WAR-PING	WAR-TIME
WAR-HEAD	WAR-RAND	WAR-WOLF
WAR-KING	WAR-RANT	WAR-WORK
WAR-LESS	WAR-RAYS	WAR-WORN
WAR-LIKE	WAR-RENS	WAR-ZONE
WAR-LING	WAR-RING	

Eight-letter words

WAR-BLING	WAR-FARER	WAR-POWER
WAR-CRAFT	WAR-HORSE	WAR-RAYED
WAR-DERED	WAR-MAKER	WAR-SLING
WAR-DRESS	WAR-MOUTH	
WAR-FARED	WAR-PLANE	

Some words ending with -WARD
Seven-letter words

AIR-WARD	NAY-WARD	SUN-WARD
AWK-WARD	NOR-WARD	VAN-WARD
BED-WARD	OUT-WARD	WAY-WARD
FOR-WARD	SEA-WARD	WEY-WARD
HAY-WARD	SKY-WARD	
LEE-WARD	STE-WARD	

Eight-letter words

BACK-WARD	HELL-WARD	REAR-WARD
BECO-WARD	HIND-WARD	SELF-WARD
CITY-WARD	HIVE-WARD	SIDE-WARD
DOWN-WARD	HOME-WARD	UNTO-WARD
EAST-WARD	KIRK-WARD	WEST-WARD
FORE-WARD	LAND-WARD	WIND-WARD
GOAL-WARD	LEFT-WARD	WOOD-WARD
HEAD-WARD	MOON-WARD	WOOL-WARD

W

Some words ending with -WAY
Seven-letter words

ARCH-WAY	HADA-WAY	ROLL-WAY
AREA-WAY	HALF-WAY	ROPE-WAY
BELT-WAY	HALL-WAY	RUNA-WAY
BIKE-WAY	HEAD-WAY	SHIP-WAY
CART-WAY	HIGH-WAY	SIDE-WAY
CUTA-WAY	LANE-WAY	SKID-WAY
DOOR-WAY	LAYA-WAY	SLIP-WAY
FAIR-WAY	LIFE-WAY	SOME-WAY
FARA-WAY	PACK-WAY	TAXI-WAY
FISH-WAY	PARK-WAY	THRU-WAY
FLYA-WAY	PART-WAY	TIDE-WAY
FOLK-WAY	PATH-WAY	TOLL-WAY
FOOT-WAY	RACE-WAY	TOWA-WAY
FREE-WAY	RAIL-WAY	TRAM-WAY
GANG-WAY	RING-WAY	WALK-WAY
GATE-WAY	ROAD-WAY	WIND-WAY
GETA-WAY	RODE-WAY	WIRE-WAY

W

Eight-letter words

AISLE-WAY	GIVEA-WAY	STAIR-WAY
ALLEY-WAY	GREEN-WAY	STAYA-WAY
BROAD-WAY	GUIDE-WAY	STOWA-WAY
CABLE-WAY	HIDEA-WAY	TAKEA-WAY
CASTA-WAY	HORSE-WAY	TEARA-WAY
CAUSE-WAY	MOTOR-WAY	THATA-WAY
CLEAR-WAY	OVERS-WAY	THISA-WAY
CRAWL-WAY	RIDGE-WAY	TRACK-WAY
CROSS-WAY	RIVER-WAY	TRAIN-WAY
CYCLE-WAY	ROCKA-WAY	UNDER-WAY
DRIVE-WAY	ROLLA-WAY	WALKA-WAY
ENTRY-WAY	ROUTE-WAY	WASHA-WAY
EVERY-WAY	SLIDE-WAY	WASTE-WAY
FADEA-WAY	SOARA-WAY	WATER-WAY
FLOOD-WAY	SPEED-WAY	
FOLDA-WAY	SPILL-WAY	

Some words ending with -WISE
Seven-letter words

AIR-WISE	FAN-WISE	SUN-WISE
ANY-WISE	MAN-WISE	TAX-WISE
END-WISE	MAP-WISE	

W

Eight-letter words

ARCH-WISE	LIKE-WISE	SOME-WISE
BEND-WISE	LONG-WISE	STEP-WISE
CRAB-WISE	OVER-WISE	SUCH-WISE
DROP-WISE	PAIR-WISE	TEAM-WISE
EDGE-WISE	RING-WISE	TENT-WISE
FLAT-WISE	SIDE-WISE	

Some words ending with -WOOD
Seven-letter words

BAR-WOOD	DOG-WOOD	NUT-WOOD
BAY-WOOD	ELM-WOOD	PLY-WOOD
BOG-WOOD	INK-WOOD	RED-WOOD
BOX-WOOD	LOG-WOOD	SAP-WOOD

Eight-letter words

BACK-WOOD	DEAD-WOOD	PINE-WOOD
BASS-WOOD	FIRE-WOOD	ROSE-WOOD
BEAR-WOOD	FUEL-WOOD	SOFT-WOOD
BENT-WOOD	HARD-WOOD	SOUR-WOOD
BLUE-WOOD	IRON-WOOD	TEAK-WOOD
COLT-WOOD	KING-WOOD	WILD-WOOD
CORD-WOOD	MILK-WOOD	WORM-WOOD
CORK-WOOD	PEAR-WOOD	

W

Some words ending with -WORK

Seven-letter words

ART-WORK	OUT-WORK	TOP-WORK
CUT-WORK	PIN-WORK	TUT-WORK
DAY-WORK	PRE-WORK	WAR-WORK
LEG-WORK	RAG-WORK	WAX-WORK
NET-WORK	RIB-WORK	WEB-WORK
NON-WORK	TIN-WORK	

Eight-letter words

BACK-WORK	HAND-WORK	RACK-WORK
BEAD-WORK	HEAD-WORK	ROAD-WORK
BODY-WORK	HOME-WORK	ROPE-WORK
BOOK-WORK	IRON-WORK	SEAT-WORK
BUSY-WORK	LACE-WORK	STUD-WORK
CAGE-WORK	LEAD-WORK	TASK-WORK
CASE-WORK	LIFE-WORK	TEAM-WORK
FARM-WORK	MESH-WORK	TIME-WORK
FIRE-WORK	OPEN-WORK	WIRE-WORK
FOOT-WORK	OVER-WORK	WOOD-WORK
FRET-WORK	PART-WORK	YARD-WORK
HACK-WORK	PILE-WORK	
HAIR-WORK	PIPE-WORK	

W

367

Some words ending with -WORM
Seven-letter words

BAG-WORM	EEL-WORM	SEA-WORM
BUD-WORM	LOB-WORM	WAX-WORM
CAT-WORM	LUG-WORM	WEB-WORM
CUT-WORM	PIN-WORM	
EAR-WORM	RAG-WORM	

Eight-letter words

ARMY-WORM	HAIR-WORM	SHIP-WORM
BOLL-WORM	HOOK-WORM	SILK-WORM
BOOK-WORM	HORN-WORM	SLOW-WORM
CASE-WORM	INCH-WORM	TAPE-WORM
CORN-WORM	LEAF-WORM	TUBE-WORM
FIRE-WORM	LUNG-WORM	WHIP-WORM
FISH-WORM	MEAL-WORM	WIRE-WORM
FLAT-WORM	PILL-WORM	WOOD-WORM
GLOW-WORM	RING-WORM	
GRUB-WORM	SAND-WORM	

Some words ending with -WORT
Seven-letter words

AWL-WORT	FEL-WORT	MUG-WORT
BLA-WORT	FIG-WORT	RAG-WORT
BUG-WORT	MAD-WORT	RIB-WORT
FAN-WORT	MUD-WORT	

Eight-letter words

BELL-WORT	HORN-WORT	PILL-WORT
COLE-WORT	LEAD-WORT	PIPE-WORT
DAME-WORT	LUNG-WORT	SALT-WORT
DANE-WORT	MILK-WORT	SAND-WORT
DROP-WORT	MODI-WORT	SOAP-WORT
FLEA-WORT	MOON-WORT	STAR-WORT
GOUT-WORT	MOOR-WORT	WALL-WORT
HONE-WORT	PILE-WORT	WART-WORT

Unusual letter combinations

If you have an unusual combination of letters on your rack, or want to impress your opponent with an unusual word, a few words from World English can come in handy.

Australian words

WADDY	heavy wooden club used by native Australians
WAGGA	blanket made of sacks stitched together
WALLABY	marsupial resembling a small kangaroo
WANDOO	eucalyptus tree with white bark
WARATAH	shrub with dark green leaves and crimson flowers
WARB	dirty or insignificant person
WHARFIE	wharf labourer
WILGA	small drought-resistant tree
WIRILDA	acacia tree with edible seeds

W

369

WIRRAH	saltwater fish with bright blue spots
WOMBAT	burrowing marsupial
WOOMERA	spear-throwing stick
WURLEY	Aboriginal hut

Canadian words

| WAWA | speech or language |
| WENDIGO | evil spirit or cannibal |

Hindi words

| WALLAH | person in charge of a specific thing |

New Zealand words

WAI	water
WAKA	Maori canoe
WEKA	flightless bird
WERO	warrior's challenge
WETA	long-legged wingless insect
WHANAU	family
WHENAU	native land

X

Essential info
Value: 8 points
Number in set: 1
Power Tile

X may be the most versatile of the power tiles. It is extremely useful when it comes to tagging as it forms a two-letter word with every vowel. The only two valid two-letter words starting with X are XI (14th letter in the Greek alphabet, 9 points) and XU (the Vietnamese unit of currency, also 9 points) and the only three-letter word is XIS (plural of XI). Therefore, if you have an X on your rack and are thinking of playing short words, it probably makes more sense to think of words which contain or end with X (such as AX, 9 points, or EX, also 9) rather than those which begin with it.

Two-letter words beginning with X

XI   XU

Some three-letter words using X

AXE	FAX	KEX	MIX
BOX	FIX	LAX	MUX
COX	FOX	LEX	NIX
DEX	GOX	LOX	NOX
DUX	HEX	LUX	OXO
EXO	HOX	MAX	OXY

X

PAX	SAX	TIX	WOX
PIX	SEX	TUX	YEX
POX	SIX	VEX	ZAX
PYX	SOX	VOX	ZEX
RAX	TAX	WAX	
REX	TEX	WEX	

Some four-letter words using X

Some useful four-letter words you may not know include BRUX (to grind one's teeth, 13 points), NIXY (a female water sprite, 14 points) and WEXE (obsolete form of wax, 14 points).

APEX	FAUX	NEXT
AXED	FIXT	NIXY
AXIS	FLAX	ONYX
AXLE	FLEX	ORYX
BOXY	FLUX	OXEN
BRUX	FOXY	OXER
COAX	GREX	OXID
CRUX	HOAX	PIXY
DEXY	IBEX	PLEX
DIXY	JAXY	POXY
DOUX	JEUX	ROUX
EAUX	JINX	SEXY
EXAM	JYNX	TAXI
EXEC	LYNX	TEXT
EXED	MAXI	VEXT
EXIT	MINX	WAXY
EXON	MIXT	WEXE
EXPO	MYXO	XYST

X

Hooks
Hooking requires a subtle change in a player's thought process, in that they must look at words already on the board without becoming distracted by their pronunciation.

Some front-hooks
Two letters to three
X-IS

Four letters to five
X-ERIC   X-YLEM

Five letters to six
X-YLEMS

Six letters to seven
X-EROSES   X-EROTIC

Some end-hooks
Two letters to three

BO-X	MI-X	TA-X
DE-X	MU-X	TE-X
FA-X	NO-X	TI-X
GO-X	PA-X	WE-X
HE-X	PI-X	WO-X
HO-X	PO-X	YE-X
LA-X	RE-X	ZA-X
LO-X	SI-X	
MA-X	SO-X	

X

Three letters to four

APE-X	EAU-X	JEU-X	PRE-X
BRU-X	FLU-X	JIN-X	ULE-X
CRU-X	HOA-X	ONY-X	

Four letters to five

BEAU-X	LATE-X	REDO-X
BORA-X	LIMA-X	SILE-X
CARE-X	LURE-X	SORE-X
CHOU-X	MALA-X	TELE-X
CODE-X	MIRE-X	VIBE-X
FORE-X	MURE-X	VITE-X
GALA-X	PYRE-X	

Five letters to six

ADIEU-X	BIJOU-X	BOYAU-X	DUPLE-X

Six letters to seven

BATEAU-X	GATEAU-X	SIMPLE-X
BUREAU-X	MILIEU-X	TRIPLE-X
CADEAU-X	MINIMA-X	
COTEAU-X	RESEAU-X	

Seven letters to eight

BANDEAU-X	FABLIAU-X	PONCEAU-X
BATTEAU-X	JAMBEAU-X	RONDEAU-X
BERCEAU-X	MANTEAU-X	ROULEAU-X
CAMAIEU-X	MORCEAU-X	TABLEAU-X
CHAPEAU-X	NOUVEAU-X	TONNEAU-X
CHATEAU-X	OCTUPLE-X	TRUMEAU-X
COUTEAU-X	PLATEAU-X	

X

374

Blockers

It is useful to know which words are blockers and can't therefore be extended before or after. You may want to play a blocker that your opponent can't extend, or you may want to avoid playing a blocker because you want to keep the board open.

Two-letter blocker beginning with X

XU

Some five-letter blockers beginning with X (except words ending in '-ED', '-J', '-S', '-X', '-Y' or '-Z')

XERIC   XOANA   XYLIC   XYSTI

Some six-letter blockers beginning with X (except words ending in '-ED', '-J', '-S', '-X', '-Y' or '-Z')

XENIAL   XENIUM   XOANON   XYLOID   XYSTOI

Handy Hint

Power tile letters may be less common than others in the set but there are many simple and easy-to-remember words that use them. Some examples for X include: BOX (12 points), FOX (13), WAX (13), EXAM (13), NEXT (11) and TEXT (11). You could even impress your opponent with words beginning with X such as XENIA (12 points) and XERIC (14 points).

X

375

Bonus words
Seven-letter words

XANTHAM
XANTHAN
XANTHIC
XANTHIN
XENOPUS
XERAFIN
XERARCH
XERASIA
XEROMAS

XEROSES
XEROSIS
XEROTES
XEROTIC
XEROXED
XEROXES
XERUSES
XIPHOID
XYLENES

XYLENOL
XYLIDIN
XYLITOL
XYLOGEN
XYLOMAS
XYLONIC
XYLOSES
XYSTERS

Eight-letter words

XANTHAMS
XANTHANS
XANTHATE
XANTHEIN
XANTHENE
XANTHINE
XANTHINS
XANTHISM
XANTHOMA
XANTHONE
XANTHOUS

XENOGAMY
XENOGENY
XENOLITH
XENOPHYA
XENOTIME
XENURINE
XERANSES
XERANSIS
XERANTIC
XERAPHIM
XEROMATA

XEROSERE
XEROXING
XYLIDINE
XYLITOLS
XYLOCARP
XYLOIDIN
XYLOLOGY
XYLOMATA
XYLONITE
XYLOTOMY

X

Essential info
Value: 4 points
Number in set: 2

Y is worth 4 points on its own, making it a tile with good scoring potential. There are four two-letter words beginning with Y but they use all the vowels except for I: YA, YE, YO and YU (5 points each). High-scoring three-letter words beginning with Y include YEW (9 points) and YOB (8 points). Y is also excellent for end hooking onto nouns for use as adjectives.

Two-letter words beginning with Y

YA	YE	YO	YU

Some three-letter words beginning with Y

YAD	YAW	YGO	YON
YAE	YAY	YID	YOW
YAG	YEA	YIN	YUG
YAH	YEH	YOD	YUK
YAM	YEP	YOK	YUM
YAR	YEX	YOM	YUP

Hooks

Hooking requires a subtle change in a player's thought process, in that they must look at words already on the board without becoming distracted by their pronunciation.

Some front-hooks
Two letters to three

Y-AD	Y-AY	Y-GO	Y-OS
Y-AE	Y-EA	Y-ID	Y-OU
Y-AG	Y-EH	Y-IN	Y-OW
Y-AH	Y-EN	Y-OB	Y-UG
Y-AM	Y-ES	Y-OD	Y-UM
Y-AR	Y-ET	Y-OM	Y-UP
Y-AW	Y-EX	Y-ON	Y-US

Three letters to four

Y-AFF	Y-EGG	Y-OOF
Y-ALE	Y-ELK	Y-OOP
Y-APP	Y-ELL	Y-ORE
Y-ARD	Y-ELM	Y-OUK
Y-ARE	Y-EST	Y-OUR
Y-ARK	Y-EVE	Y-OWE
Y-ATE	Y-ILL	Y-OWL
Y-AWL	Y-IRK	Y-UKE
Y-AWN	Y-ODE	Y-ULE
Y-EAN	Y-OKE	Y-UMP
Y-EAR	Y-OLD	

Y

Four letters to five

Y-ABBA	Y-CLAD	Y-LIKE
Y-ACCA	Y-COND	Y-MOLT
Y-AGER	Y-DRAD	Y-OGEE
Y-AMEN	Y-EARD	Y-OURN
Y-ARCO	Y-EARN	Y-OWED
Y-AULD	Y-EAST	Y-ULAN
Y-AWED	Y-EVEN	Y-UPON
Y-AWNY	Y-EXED	
Y-BORE	Y-FERE	

Five letters to six

Y-ACKER	Y-BRENT	Y-IRKED
Y-AGGER	Y-CLEPT	Y-OWING
Y-ANKER	Y-EANED	Y-OWLED
Y-ANTRA	Y-EARDS	Y-OWLER
Y-ARKED	Y-EARLY	Y-PIGHT
Y-ARROW	Y-EMMER	Y-PLAST
Y-AWING	Y-ESSES	Y-SHEND
Y-AWNED	Y-ESTER	Y-SHENT
Y-AWNER	Y-EUKED	Y-UMPED
Y-BLENT	Y-EXING	Y-UMPIE
Y-BOUND	Y-ICKER	Y-WROKE

Six letters to seven

Y-ARKING	Y-EARDED	Y-MOLTEN
Y-AWNERS	Y-EARNED	Y-OWLING
Y-AWNIER	Y-EARNER	Y-PLIGHT
Y-AWNING	Y-EASTED	Y-SLAKED
Y-CLEPED	Y-EUKING	Y-UMPIES
Y-EANING	Y-IRKING	Y-UMPING

Seven letters to eight

Y-ATAGHAN	Y-EANLING	Y-EASTING
Y-AWNIEST	Y-EARDING	Y-OURSELF
Y-BOUNDEN	Y-EARLIES	
Y-CLEEPED	Y-EARNING	

Y

Handy Hint

Some useful short high-scoring words beginning with Y are YEX (Scots word for hiccup or cough, 13 points), YOK (a noisy laugh, 10 points) and YUK (a noise used to express disgust or dislike, also 10 points).

Some end-hooks
Two letters to three

AB-Y	GU-Y	NO-Y
AN-Y	HA-Y	ON-Y
AR-Y	HE-Y	OX-Y
BA-Y	HO-Y	PA-Y
BE-Y	JA-Y	SH-Y
BO-Y	JO-Y	SO-Y
DA-Y	KA-Y	ST-Y
DE-Y	LA-Y	TA-Y
DO-Y	LO-Y	TO-Y
FA-Y	MA-Y	WE-Y
FE-Y	MO-Y	YA-Y
GO-Y	NA-Y	

Three letters to four

ACH-Y	BON-Y	COW-Y
ADD-Y	BOX-Y	COX-Y
AFF-Y	BRA-Y	COZ-Y
AIR-Y	BUR-Y	DEF-Y
ALA-Y	BUS-Y	DEN-Y
ALL-Y	CAG-Y	DEW-Y
ARM-Y	CAN-Y	DEX-Y
ARS-Y	CHA-Y	DID-Y
ART-Y	CIT-Y	DOG-Y
ASH-Y	COL-Y	DOM-Y
AWA-Y	CON-Y	DOP-Y
AWN-Y	COP-Y	DOR-Y
BOD-Y	COR-Y	DOT-Y
BOG-Y	COS-Y	EAS-Y

EEL-Y	MAN-Y	PUL-Y
EGG-Y	MAR-Y	PUN-Y
ELM-Y	MAT-Y	QUA-Y
FAD-Y	MIX-Y	RIM-Y
FOG-Y	MOB-Y	RUB-Y
FOX-Y	MOL-Y	SAG-Y
FRA-Y	MON-Y	SHA-Y
FUM-Y	MOP-Y	SPA-Y
FUR-Y	NIX-Y	SUM-Y
GAB-Y	NOS-Y	TAK-Y
GAM-Y	NOW-Y	TED-Y
GAP-Y	OAK-Y	THE-Y
GOB-Y	OAR-Y	TID-Y
GOE-Y	OBE-Y	TIN-Y
GOR-Y	OIL-Y	TOD-Y
GUL-Y	OKA-Y	TOE-Y
HER-Y	OLD-Y	TON-Y
HOM-Y	ORB-Y	TOR-Y
HUG-Y	OWL-Y	TOW-Y
ICK-Y	PAC-Y	TUN-Y
IFF-Y	PAL-Y	TWA-Y
ILL-Y	PAT-Y	UPS-Y
INK-Y	PIN-Y	VAR-Y
JOE-Y	PIP-Y	VIN-Y
JUD-Y	PIT-Y	WAD-Y
LAC-Y	PIX-Y	WAN-Y
LAD-Y	POL-Y	WAR-Y
LEV-Y	POS-Y	WAX-Y
LIN-Y	POX-Y	WIN-Y
LOG-Y	PRE-Y	YUK-Y

Y

Four letters to five

ACID-Y	BONE-Y	CHEW-Y
AGON-Y	BOOK-Y	COAL-Y
ANNO-Y	BOOM-Y	COCK-Y
ANTS-Y	BOOT-Y	CONE-Y
ARTS-Y	BOSS-Y	CONK-Y
AUNT-Y	BOTH-Y	COOK-Y
BALD-Y	BRIN-Y	COPS-Y
BALM-Y	BUFF-Y	CORE-Y
BAND-Y	BULK-Y	CORK-Y
BARB-Y	BULL-Y	CORN-Y
BARK-Y	BUMP-Y	COSE-Y
BARM-Y	BUNG-Y	COVE-Y
BARN-Y	BUNN-Y	COZE-Y
BASS-Y	BUNT-Y	CULT-Y
BATT-Y	BURL-Y	CURL-Y
BAWD-Y	BURR-Y	CURR-Y
BEAD-Y	BUSH-Y	CUSH-Y
BEAK-Y	BUSK-Y	CUTE-Y
BEAN-Y	BUST-Y	DAFF-Y
BEEF-Y	BUTT-Y	DAIS-Y
BEER-Y	BUZZ-Y	DAMP-Y
BELL-Y	CAGE-Y	DEAR-Y
BEND-Y	CAKE-Y	DECO-Y
BIFF-Y	CALM-Y	DEED-Y
BILL-Y	CAMP-Y	DEIF-Y
BING-Y	CARB-Y	DEII-Y
BITS-Y	CARN-Y	DICE-Y
BLOW-Y	CARR-Y	DICK-Y
BLUE-Y	CASK-Y	DILL-Y

DING-Y	FLAK-Y	GOOS-Y
DINK-Y	FLAM-Y	GOUT-Y
DIRT-Y	FLAX-Y	GRAV-Y
DISH-Y	FLUE-Y	GRIM-Y
DITT-Y	FOAM-Y	GRIP-Y
DITZ-Y	FOLK-Y	GULL-Y
DOLL-Y	FOOD-Y	GUNG-Y
DOOM-Y	FOOT-Y	GUNK-Y
DOPE-Y	FORA-Y	GUSH-Y
DORK-Y	FORK-Y	GUST-Y
DOWD-Y	FORT-Y	GUTS-Y
DOWN-Y	FULL-Y	GYPS-Y
DUCK-Y	FUNK-Y	HAIL-Y
DUMP-Y	FUSS-Y	HAIR-Y
DUNG-Y	FUZZ-Y	HAND-Y
DUSK-Y	GAME-Y	HANK-Y
DUST-Y	GASP-Y	HARD-Y
EARL-Y	GAUD-Y	HARP-Y
EBON-Y	GAWK-Y	HAST-Y
EMPT-Y	GEEK-Y	HEAD-Y
EVER-Y	GERM-Y	HEFT-Y
FAIR-Y	GILL-Y	HERB-Y
FAWN-Y	GIMP-Y	HILL-Y
FELT-Y	GINN-Y	HISS-Y
FIER-Y	GIPS-Y	HOAR-Y
FILL-Y	GIRL-Y	HOKE-Y
FILM-Y	GLUE-Y	HOLE-Y
FISH-Y	GOLD-Y	HOME-Y
FIST-Y	GOOD-Y	HONE-Y
FIZZ-Y	GOOF-Y	HONK-Y

Y

HOOD-Y	LEER-Y	MOOD Y
HOOK-Y	LEFT-Y	MORA-Y
HORN-Y	LIME-Y	MOSS-Y
HUFF-Y	LOAM-Y	MUCK-Y
HULK-Y	LOFT-Y	MUMM-Y
HUNK-Y	LOLL-Y	MUMS-Y
HUSK-Y	LOON-Y	MURK-Y
HUSS-Y	LOOP-Y	MUSH-Y
RON-Y	LORD-Y	MUSK-Y
TCH Y	LOUS-Y	NARK-Y
AKE-Y	LOVE-Y	NEED-Y
AZZ-Y	LUCK-Y	NERD-Y
ELL-Y	LUMP-Y	NIFF-Y
ERK-Y	LUST-Y	NOSE-Y
IFF-Y	MALT-Y	PACE-Y
IVE-Y	MANG-Y	PALL-Y
OKE-Y	MASH-Y	PALM-Y
OLL-Y	MATE-Y	PANS-Y
OWL-Y	MEAL-Y	PARK-Y
UMP-Y	MEAN-Y	PART-Y
UNK-Y	MEAT-Y	PAST-Y
KELP-Y	MELT-Y	PATS-Y
KICK-Y	MERC-Y	PEAK-Y
KISS-Y	MESS-Y	PEAT-Y
KOOK-Y	MIFF-Y	PERK-Y
LACE-Y	MILK-Y	PHON-Y
LAIR-Y	MINT-Y	PICK-Y
LARD-Y	MISS-Y	PINE-Y
LEAF-Y	MIST-Y	PINK-Y
LEAK-Y	MOLD-Y	PITH-Y

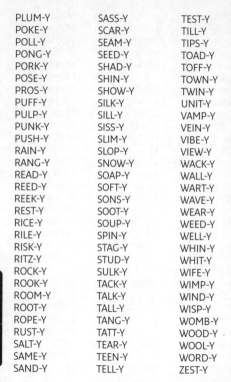

PLUM-Y	SASS-Y	TEST-Y
POKE-Y	SCAR-Y	TILL-Y
POLL-Y	SEAM-Y	TIPS-Y
PONG-Y	SEED-Y	TOAD-Y
PORK-Y	SHAD-Y	TOFF-Y
POSE-Y	SHIN-Y	TOWN-Y
PROS-Y	SHOW-Y	TWIN-Y
PUFF-Y	SILK-Y	UNIT-Y
PULP-Y	SILL-Y	VAMP-Y
PUNK-Y	SISS-Y	VEIN-Y
PUSH-Y	SLIM-Y	VIBE-Y
RAIN-Y	SLOP-Y	VIEW-Y
RANG-Y	SNOW-Y	WACK-Y
READ-Y	SOAP-Y	WALL-Y
REED-Y	SOFT-Y	WART-Y
REEK-Y	SONS-Y	WAVE-Y
REST-Y	SOOT-Y	WEAR-Y
RICE-Y	SOUP-Y	WEED-Y
RILE-Y	SPIN-Y	WELL-Y
RISK-Y	STAG-Y	WHIN-Y
RITZ-Y	STUD-Y	WHIT-Y
ROCK-Y	SULK-Y	WIFE-Y
ROOK-Y	TACK-Y	WIMP-Y
ROOM-Y	TALK-Y	WIND-Y
ROOT-Y	TALL-Y	WISP-Y
ROPE-Y	TANG-Y	WOMB-Y
RUST-Y	TATT-Y	WOOD-Y
SALT-Y	TEAR-Y	WOOL-Y
SAME-Y	TEEN-Y	WORD-Y
SAND-Y	TELL-Y	ZEST-Y

Y

Five letters to six

ANGST-Y	CHEER-Y	DROPS-Y
ARMOR-Y	CHILL-Y	EARTH-Y
AUGUR-Y	CHIRP-Y	EATER-Y
BAKER-Y	CHOKE-Y	EIGHT-Y
BARON-Y	CHUFF-Y	FAULT-Y
BEACH-Y	CHUNK-Y	FEIST-Y
BEARD-Y	CLASS-Y	FELON-Y
BEAUT-Y	CLOUD-Y	FILTH-Y
BEECH-Y	CLUCK-Y	FINER-Y
BLEAR-Y	CLUNK-Y	FLAKE-Y
BLOCK-Y	COLON-Y	FLESH-Y
BLOKE-Y	COUNT-Y	FLINT-Y
BLOOD-Y	CRAFT-Y	FLOAT-Y
BLOWS-Y	CRANK-Y	FLOSS-Y
BLUES-Y	CRAWL-Y	FLOUR-Y
BOOZE-Y	CREAK-Y	FLUFF-Y
BOWER-Y	CREAM-Y	FLUNK-Y
BRAIN-Y	CREEP-Y	FOLKS-Y
BRAND-Y	CRISP-Y	FOOTS-Y
BRASS-Y	CROAK-Y	FREAK-Y
BRAWN-Y	CRUST-Y	FRIAR-Y
BRICK-Y	CURVE-Y	FRILL-Y
BROOD-Y	CUTES-Y	FRISK-Y
BROTH-Y	DRAFT-Y	FRIZZ-Y
BROWN-Y	DRAWL-Y	FROST-Y
BRUSH-Y	DREAM-Y	FROTH-Y
CHALK-Y	DREAR-Y	FRUIT-Y
CHEAP-Y	DRESS-Y	FRUMP-Y
CHEEK-Y	DROOP-Y	GLASS-Y

Y

387

GLITZ-Y	PEACH-Y	SLINK-Y
GLOOM-Y	PEARL-Y	SLUSH-Y
GLOSS-Y	PHONE-Y	SMART-Y
GNARL-Y	PLUCK-Y	SMELL-Y
GRAIN-Y	POINT-Y	SMILE-Y
GRASS-Y	PRICE-Y	SMITH-Y
GREED-Y	PRIOR-Y	SMOKE-Y
GROWL-Y	PUNCH-Y	SNAKE-Y
GRUMP-Y	QUACK-Y	SNEAK-Y
GUILT-Y	QUIRK-Y	SNIFF-Y
HEART-Y	RIGHT-Y	SNOOP-Y
HERES-Y	ROOTS-Y	SPACE-Y
HORSE-Y	ROUGH-Y	SPARK-Y
HOUSE-Y	RUDER-Y	SPEED-Y
HURRA-Y	SAVOR-Y	SPICE-Y
JAPER-Y	SCARE-Y	SPIKE-Y
LEMON-Y	SCREW-Y	SPOOK-Y
LIVER-Y	SCUZZ-Y	SPORT-Y
MARSH-Y	SHAND-Y	STEAD-Y
MEDLE-Y	SHARP-Y	STEAM-Y
MEREL-Y	SHELL-Y	STEEL-Y
MIGHT-Y	SHIFT-Y	STICK-Y
MISER-Y	SHIRT-Y	STING-Y
MOULD-Y	SHORT-Y	STINK-Y
MOUTH-Y	SHOUT-Y	STOCK-Y
NIGHT-Y	SINEW-Y	STONE-Y
ONION-Y	SKANK-Y	STORE-Y
PAPER-Y	SKIMP-Y	STORM-Y
PARLE-Y	SLANG-Y	STRIP-Y
PATCH-Y	SLEEP-Y	STUFF-Y

STUMP-Y	TOOTH-Y	VINER-Y
SUGAR-Y	TOOTS-Y	WAFER-Y
SWAMP-Y	TOUCH-Y	WATER-Y
SWEAT-Y	TRASH-Y	WEIRD-Y
SWEET-Y	TREAT-Y	WHIFF-Y
SWIRL-Y	TREND-Y	WHIMS-Y
SYRUP-Y	TRICK-Y	WHINE-Y
TEENS-Y	TRUST-Y	WHIRL-Y
THICK-Y	TWANG-Y	WHIRR-Y
THING-Y	TWEED-Y	WHISK-Y
THORN-Y	TWEEN-Y	WHITE-Y
TITCH-Y	TWIRL-Y	WIELD-Y
TOAST-Y	TWIST-Y	WORTH-Y

Six letters to seven

ALMOND-Y	BURSAR-Y	DRAPER-Y
ANALOG-Y	BUTTER-Y	DROUTH-Y
ANARCH-Y	CARVER-Y	DYNAST-Y
ARCHER-Y	CHINTZ-Y	EPONYM-Y
ARMOUR-Y	CHOOSE-Y	FACTOR-Y
AUTUMN-Y	CITRUS-Y	FARMER-Y
BALSAM-Y	CLIQUE-Y	FIBBER-Y
BATTER-Y	CLOVER-Y	FIDDLE-Y
BILLOW-Y	COOKER-Y	FIDGET-Y
BLIGHT-Y	COPPER-Y	FISHER-Y
BLOTCH-Y	COTTON-Y	FLAVOR-Y
BRAVER-Y	CRUNCH-Y	FLIGHT-Y
BREATH-Y	CURSOR-Y	FLOWER-Y
BREWER-Y	CUTLER-Y	FORGER-Y
BRIBER-Y	DODDER-Y	GADGET-Y

GINGER-Y	NURSER-Y	SHRILL-Y
GLITCH-Y	ORANGE-Y	SILVER-Y
GOSSIP-Y	ORATOR-Y	SKETCH-Y
GRAVEL-Y	PANICK-Y	SLAVER-Y
GROCER-Y	PAUNCH-Y	SMOOTH-Y
GROUCH-Y	PEDLAR-Y	SPIDER-Y
GUNNER-Y	PEPPER-Y	SPLASH-Y
HACKER-Y	PHLEGM-Y	SPRING-Y
HAUGHT-Y	PILFER-Y	SQUASH-Y
HEALTH-Y	PILLOW-Y	SQUEAK-Y
HICCUP-Y	POTTER-Y	STARCH-Y
HONEST-Y	POWDER-Y	STREAK-Y
HOSIER-Y	PREACH-Y	STRING-Y
IMAGER-Y	QUIVER-Y	STRIPE-Y
JARGON-Y	RAGGED-Y	SURGER-Y
JITTER-Y	RAISIN-Y	TANNER-Y
JOINER-Y	RAUNCH-Y	THIRST-Y
KITSCH-Y	RECTOR-Y	THRIFT-Y
LATHER-Y	RIFLER-Y	TIMBER-Y
LECHER-Y	ROBBER-Y	TRICKS-Y
LENGTH-Y	ROCKER-Y	TWITCH-Y
LOTTER-Y	RUBBER-Y	UNREAD-Y
MARTYR-Y	SAVOUR-Y	VELVET-Y
MASTER-Y	SCRUFF-Y	VICTOR-Y
MISTER-Y	SENSOR-Y	WASHER-Y
MOCKER-Y	SERVER-Y	WEALTH-Y
MODEST-Y	SHADOW-Y	WEASEL-Y
MONGER-Y	SHIVER-Y	WEIGHT-Y
MUMMER-Y	SHLOCK-Y	WILLOW-Y
NAUGHT-Y	SHOWER-Y	WINTER-Y

Y

Seven letters to eight

ADVISOR-Y
AUDITOR-Y
BISCUIT-Y
BLADDER-Y
BLOSSOM-Y
BLUSTER-Y
BOULDER-Y
BURGLAR-Y
BUTCHER-Y
CABBAGE-Y
CAJOLER-Y
CALAMAR-Y
CARTOON-Y
CHANCER-Y
CHEATER-Y
CHIFFON-Y
CHIRRUP-Y
CITATOR-Y
CLATTER-Y
COBBLER-Y
COLLIER-Y
CREAMER-Y
CRYOGEN-Y
CURATOR-Y
CUSTARD-Y
DASTARD-Y
DELIVER-Y
DRAUGHT-Y
DRUDGER-Y

ENTREAT-Y
FEATHER-Y
FLATTER-Y
FLICKER-Y
FLUSTER-Y
FRIPPER-Y
FRUITER-Y
GIMMICK-Y
GLITTER-Y
GLUTTON-Y
GREENER-Y
GRINDER-Y
GYRATOR-Y
HATCHER-Y
HEATHER-Y
HOMONYM-Y
INCISOR-Y
JEALOUS-Y
JEOPARD-Y
KNACKER-Y
LAMINAR-Y
LEATHER-Y
MILITAR-Y
MONARCH-Y
MONITOR-Y
MUSTARD-Y
NEGATOR-Y
NITPICK-Y
ORDINAR-Y

PARADOX-Y
PEDAGOG-Y
PLASTER-Y
POLYGAM-Y
POLYMER-Y
PUDDING-Y
QUIZZER-Y
RECOVER-Y
REFINER-Y
RUBBISH-Y
SADDLER-Y
SAVAGER-Y
SCHLOCK-Y
SCRATCH-Y
SCREECH-Y
SCRUNCH-Y
SEMINAR-Y
SHIMMER-Y
SHMALTZ-Y
SLIPPER-Y
SLOBBER-Y
SLUMBER-Y
SMOTHER-Y
SOLDIER-Y
SPINNER-Y
SPUTTER-Y
SQUELCH-Y
STEALTH-Y
STUDENT-Y

SYNONYM-Y	TOURIST-Y	UNWORTH-Y
TABLOID-Y	TRICKER-Y	VILLAIN-Y
THUNDER-Y	TWITTER-Y	WARRANT-Y
TITULAR-Y	UNTRUST-Y	WHISKER-Y

Blockers

It is useful to know which words are blockers and can't therefore be extended before or after. You may want to play a blocker that your opponent can't extend, or you may want to avoid playing a blocker because you want to keep the board open.

Some three-letter blockers beginning with Y

| YAE | YEH | YEX |

Four-letter blocker beginning with Y

YUTZ

Some five-letter blockers beginning with Y (except words ending in '-ED', '-J', '-S', '-X', '-Y' or '-Z')

| YAULD | YOKUL | YOUSE | YUCKO |
| YOGIC | YOURN | YUCCH | YUMMO |

Some six-letter blockers beginning with Y (except words ending in '-ED', '-J', '-S', '-X', '-Y' or '-Z')

| YAKUZA | YEOMAN | YIKING |
| YAWING | YEOMEN | YIPPEE |

Some words ending with -YARD
Seven-letter words

BEE-YARD	INN-YARD	TAN-YARD
HAL-YARD	LAN-YARD	

Eight-letter words

BACK-YARD	FEED-YARD	SALE-YARD
BALL-YARD	FORE-YARD	SAVO-YARD
BARN-YARD	HAUL-YARD	SHIP-YARD
BOAT-YARD	JUNK-YARD	SHOW-YARD
BONE-YARD	KAIL-YARD	TILT-YARD
COAL-YARD	KALE-YARD	VINE-YARD
DEER-YARD	KIRK-YARD	WHIN-YARD
DOCK-YARD	MAIN-YARD	WILL-YARD
DOOR-YARD	METE-YARD	WOOD-YARD
FARM-YARD	RICK-YARD	

Y

Unusual letter combinations

If you have an unusual combination of letters on your rack, or want to impress your opponent with an unusual word, a few words from World English can come in handy.

Australian words

YABBER	talk or jabber
YABBY	small freshwater crayfish
YACCA	grass tree
YARRAN	small hardy tree
YATE	small eucalyptus tree
YIKE	argument, squabble or fight
YUCKO	disgusting
YUMMO	delicious

South African word

YEBO	yes

Z₁₀

Essential info
Value: 10 points
Number in set: 1
Power tile

Z is one of the most valuable tiles in the Scrabble set. It is easier to use than, for example, Q, as it is not so heavily reliant on another letter (as is Q on U). Various three-letter words using Z can be remembered easily as sets of two, with another fixed consonant and alternating vowels, for example ZIG, ZAG and especially ZAX, ZEX (using two power tiles and thus potentially achieving huge scores). Sets of three are also useful to keep in mind, such as CAZ, COZ, CUZ.

Two-letter words beginning with Z

ZA	ZO

Some three-letter words beginning with Z

ZAG	ZED	ZEL	ZHO	ZIT
ZAX	ZEE	ZEP	ZIG	ZOA
ZEA	ZEK	ZEX	ZIN	ZOL

Some three-letter words using Z

ADZ	COZ	FIZ	POZ	SEZ
AZO	CUZ	LUZ	REZ	WIZ
BEZ	DZO	MIZ	RIZ	
CAZ	FEZ	MOZ	SAZ	

Some four-letter words using Z

Some interesting four-letter words using the letter Z are AZYM (unleavened bread, 18 points) and NAZE (marshy headland, 13 points). Words beginning with Z which may be unfamiliar include ZATI (a type of macaque, 13 points) and ZOEA (larva of a crab or crustacean, 13 points). Don't forget words such as JAZY (wig, 23 points) and QUIZ (22 points) as they use more than one power tile and can return relatively high scores considering their length.

ADZE	HAZE	OYEZ	YUZU	ZITE
AZAN	HAZY	PHIZ	ZACK	ZITI
AZON	IZAR	PIZE	ZANY	ZOEA
AZYM	JAZZ	PREZ	ZARF	ZOIC
BIZE	KUZU	QUIZ	ZATI	ZONA
BOZO	LAZO	RAZE	ZEAL	ZONE
BUZZ	LAZY	RAZZ	ZEBU	ZONK
CHEZ	LUTZ	RITZ	ZEIN	ZOOM
CHIZ	MAZE	RIZA	ZERK	ZORI
COZE	MAZY	SITZ	ZEST	ZOUK
COZY	MEZE	SWIZ	ZETA	ZOOM
CZAR	MOZE	TIZZ	ZIFF	ZOOT
FOZY	MOZO	TOZE	ZILA	ZULU
FAZE	MZEE	TREZ	ZILL	ZUPA
FIZZ	NAZE	TZAR	ZIMB	ZURF
FUTZ	NAZI	VIZY	ZINC	ZYGA
FUZZ	OOZE	WHIZ	ZING	ZYME
GAZE	ORZO	YUTZ	ZIPS	

Some front-hooks
Two letters to three

Z-AG	Z-ED	Z-HO	Z-OS
Z-AS	Z-EE	Z-IN	
Z-AX	Z-EL	Z-IT	
Z-EA	Z-EX	Z-OO	

Three letters to four

Z-ARF	Z-IFF	Z-OON
Z-ERK	Z-ILL	Z-OOT
Z-ETA	Z-OBO	Z-OUK

Four letters to five

Z-AMIA	Z-HOMO	Z-OPPO
Z-ANTE	Z-INKY	Z-UPAS
Z-AYIN	Z-LOTE	

Z

Five letters to six

Z-ANANA	Z-INKED	Z-ONERS
Z-ESTER	Z-ITHER	

Six letters to seven

Z-INCITE	Z-OOGENY	Z-OOLITH
Z-INKIER	Z-OOIDAL	Z-ORBING
Z-OOGAMY	Z-OOLITE	

Seven letters to eight

Z-OOLITIC	Z-OOPHYTE	Z-OOSPORE
Z-OOLOGIC	Z-OOSPERM	

Handy Hint

Power tile letters may be less common than others in the set but there are many simple and easy-to-remember words that use them. Some examples for Z include: LAZY (16 points), QUIZ (22), ZERO (13), ZAP (14), ZOOM (15) and ZONE (13).

Z

Some end-hooks

Two letters to three

AD-Z	FE-Z	PO-Z
BE-Z	MI-Z	RE-Z
BI-Z	MO-Z	

Three letters to four

CHI-Z	MOZ-Z	SIT-Z
GEE-Z	PHI-Z	
MIZ-Z	POZ-Z	

Four letters to five

BORT-Z	GREN-Z	SPIT-Z
CAPI-Z	MILT-Z	WARE-Z
CHIZ-Z	PLOT-Z	WOOT-Z

Five letters to six

QUART-Z	SPELT-Z	SPRIT-Z

Six letters to seven

SCHNOZ-Z

Blockers

It is useful to know which words are blockers and can't therefore be extended before or after. You may want to play a blocker that your opponent can't extend, or you may want to avoid playing a blocker because you want to keep the board open.

Some three-letter blockers using Z

BEZ	SAZ	ZOA
CAZ	SEZ	ZUZ
FEZ	ZAX	
LUZ	ZEX	

Some four-letter blockers using Z

FOZY	MOZZ	TUZZ
FUTZ	PHIZ	VIZY
GAZY	PUTZ	YUTZ
JAZY	SITZ	ZITE
MAZY	SIZY	ZIZZ

Bonus words

Bear in mind that the UK suffix -ISE may be substituted for the American -IZE in Scrabble. Both are acceptable and this will make the Z much easier to play when forming verb examples.

The lists are separated by prefix, and many feature the prefix ZOO- (involving animals) such as the

well-known ZOOLOGY (the study of animals,
o points) and the less-well-known ZOOLATRY (the
worship of animals as divine beings, also 20 points).

Seven-letter words

ABTIEH	ZEALANT	ZEOLITE
ACATON	ZEALFUL	ZIFFIUS
ADDICK	ZEALOUS	ZIGANKA
AITECH	ZESTFUL	ZIKURAT
AKUSKA	ZESTIER	ZITHERN
AKUSKI	ZESTING	ZLOTYCH
AMARRA	ZETETIC	ZILLION
AMARRO	ZEUXITE	ZIMOCCA
AMBUCK	ZEBRAIC	ZINCATE
AMOUSE	ZEBRINA	ZINCIER
AMPONE	ZEBRINE	ZINCIFY
AMPONI	ZEBROID	ZINCING
ANELLA	ZEBRULA	ZINCITE
ANIEST	ZEBRULE	ZINCKED
ANJERO	ZECCHIN	ZINCODE
APATEO	ZEDOARY	ZINCOID
APPIER	ZELATOR	ZINCOUS
APPING	ZELKOVA	ZINGANI
APTIAH	ZEMSTVA	ZINGANO
APTIEH	ZEMSTVO	ZINGARA
AREEBA	ZENAIDA	ZINGARE
ARNICH		ZINGARI

Z

401

ZINGARO ZONULES ZORBING
ZINKIER ZONULET ZORGITE
ZINKIFY ZORILLA
ZINKING ZOOECIA ZORILLE
ZOARIAL ZOOGAMY ZORILLO
ZOARIUM ZOOGENY
ZOOGLEA ZOYSIAS
ZOCCOLO ZOOGONY
ZOOIDAL ZUFFOLI
ZOECIUM ZOOLITE ZUFFOLO
ZOEFORM ZOOLITH
ZOISITE ZOOLOGY ZYGOSIS
ZOONITE ZYGOTIC
ZOMBIFY ZOONOMY
ZONALLY ZOOPERY ZYMOGEN
ZONATED ZOOTAXY ZYMOSAN
ZONKING ZOOTOMY ZYMOSIS
ZONULAE ZOOTYPE ZYMOTIC
ZONULAR ZYMURGY

Eight-letter words

ZABAIONE ZAMZAWED ZEBRINNY
ZABAJONE ZECCHINE
ZADDIKIM ZAPPIEST ZECCHINI
ZAIBATSU ZARATITE ZECCHINO
ZARZUELA ZELATRIX
ZAKOUSKA
ZAKOUSKI ZASTRUGA ZEMINDAR
ZASTRUGI ZEMSTVOS
ZAMBOMBA
ZAMINDAR ZEALLESS ZENITHAL
ZAMPOGNA ZEALOTRY ZEOLITIC

Z

402

ZEPPELIN
ZERUMBET
ZESTIEST
ZESTLESS
ZIBELINE
ZIGGURAT
ZIGZAGGY
ZIKKURAT
ZIMOCCAS
ZINCIEST
ZINCKIER
ZINCKIFY
ZINCKING
ZINCODES
ZINDABAD
ZINGIBER
ZINGIEST
ZINKIEST
ZIRCALOY
ZIRCONIA
ZIRCONIC
ZODIACAL
ZOETROPE
ZOIATRIA
ZOMBIISM
ZOMBORUK

ZONATION
ZONELESS
ZONETIME
ZOOBLAST
ZOOCHORE
ZOOCHORY
ZOOCYTIA
ZOOECIUM
ZOOGENIC
ZOOGLEAE
ZOOGLEAL
ZOOGLOEA
ZOOGRAFT
ZOOLATER
ZOOLATRY
ZOOLITIC
ZOOLOGIC
ZOOMANCY
ZOOMANIA
ZOOMETRY
ZOOMORPH
ZOONITIC
ZOONOMIA
ZOONOMIC
ZOONOSIS
ZOONOTIC
ZOOPATHY
ZOOPERAL
ZOOPHOBE
ZOOPHORI

ZOOPHYTE
ZOOSCOPY
ZOOSPERM
ZOOSPORE
ZOOTHOME
ZOOTIEST
ZOOTOMIC
ZOOTOXIC
ZOOTOXIN
ZOOTROPE
ZOOTYPIC
ZOPILOTE
ZUCCHINI
ZUCHETTA
ZUCHETTO
ZWIEBACK
ZYGAENID
ZYGANTRA
ZYGODONT
ZYGOMATA
ZYGOSITY
ZYGOTENE
ZYLONITE
ZYMOGENE
ZYMOGENS
ZYMOGRAM
ZYMOLOGY
ZYMOTICS

Z

Unusual letter combinations

If you have an unusual combination of letters on your rack, or want to impress your opponent with an unusual word, a few words from World English can come in handy.

Australian words

ZAMBUCK	St John ambulance attendant
ZIFF	beard

Hindi words

ZENANA	part of a house reserved for women
ZILA	administrative district in India

Zho and Tell

There are various alternative spellings for ZHO (a Tibetan breed of cattle, developed by crossing the yak with common cattle). These are DSO, DZO, DZHO and ZO, all of which it is worth remembering in order to form short, high-scoring words (ZHO scores 15 points and DZO is worth 13).

Z

Two- and three-letter words

Two-letter words

AA volcanic rock
AB abdominal muscle
AD short form of advertisement
AE Scots word meaning one or a single
AG agriculture
AH expression of pleasure, pain, or sympathy
AI the three-toed sloth
AL Asian shrub or tree
AM part of the verb to be
AN the indefinite article used before an initial vowel sound
AR the letter R
AS while, because, since
AT used to indicate location or position
AW expression of disapproval, commiseration, or appeal
AX US spelling of axe
AY yes
BA the soul represented as a bird with a human head
BE exist, live
BI short for bisexual
BO exclamation used to startle or surprise

BY near to, at the side of, via; a bye
CH obsolete form of I
DA Burmese knife
DE of or from
DI plural form of deus
DO perform, complete; a party
EA dialect word for river
ED education
EE Scots word for eye
EF the letter F
EH exclamation of surprise or inquiry
EL elevated railway
EM printing meaurement
EN printing measurement
ER expression of hesitation
ES the letter S
ET past tense of eat
EX former spouse or partner
FA variant spelling of fah
FE charge, fee
FY variant spelling of fie
GI martial arts suit
GO to move or proceed; a turn or attempt
GU musical instrument
HA exclamation of derision, triumph, or surprise
HE male person or animal
HI hello

405

HM	expression of thoughtful consideration	NO	expression of denial, refusal, etc
HO	exclamation used to attract attention	NU	13th Greek letter
		NY	nigh; to approach
ID	unconscious primitive instincts	OB	objection
		OD	hypothetical force
IF	in case that; an uncertainty or condition	OE	grandchild
		OF	belonging to
IN	inside, within; a way of approaching a person	OH	exclamation of surprise, pain, etc
		OI	exclamation used to attract attention
IO	cry of joy or grief		
IS	part of the verb to be	OM	intonation chanted as a mantra
IT	nonhuman thing		
JA	yes	ON	not off; the side of the field on which the batsman stands
JO	Scots word for a sweetheart		
		OO	Scots word for wool
KA	ancient Egyptian spirit	OP	short for operation
KI	Japanese martial art	OR	conjunction used to join alternatives; gold
KO	Maori digging-stick		
KY	Scots word for cows	OS	bone
LA	variant spelling of lah	OU	South African slang for a man
LI	Chinese unit of length		
LO	look!	OW	exclamation of pain
MA	word for mother	OX	adult castrated bull
ME	refers to the speaker or writer	OY	grandchild
		PA	word for father
MI	musical term	PE	17th Hebrew letter
MM	expression of satisfaction	PI	16th Greek letter
MO	short for moment	PO	chamberpot
MU	12th Greek letter	QI	vital energy believed to circulate in the body
MY	of or belonging to the speaker or writer		
		RE	musical term
NA	Scots word for no		
NE	not, nor		

H	exclamation to request silence
I	musical term
O	variant spelling of soh
T	exclamation to request silence
A	thank you
E	musical term
I	variant spelling of te
O	towards, in the direction of
JG	cause loathing in, hate
JH	expression of uncertainty
JM	sound of hesitation
JN	dialect variant of one
JP	in a higher place; a rise or success
JR	sound of hesitation
JS	refers to the speaker or writer and another
JT	syllable used for the note C
VE	refers to the speaker or writer and another
WO	archaic spelling of woe
KI	14th Greek letter
KU	monetary unit
YA	you
YE	archaic word for you
YO	expression of greeting
YU	jade
ZA	pizza
ZO	Tibetan breed of cattle

Three-letter words

AAH	exclamation of pleasure, satisfaction, etc
AAL	Asian shrub or tree
AAS	plural form of aa
ABA	type of cloth from Syria
ABB	yarn used in weaving
ABO	offensive word for Aborigine
ABS	plural form of ab
ABY	pay the penalty for
ACE	playing card
ACH	Scots expression of surprise
ACT	something done, deed
ADD	combine
ADO	fuss, trouble
ADS	plural form of ad
ADZ	heavy hand tool
AFF	Scots word for off
AFT	at or towards the rear
AGA	Ottoman military commander
AGE	length of time
AGO	in the past
AGS	plural form of ag
AHA	exclamation of triumph, surprise, etc
AHI	the yellowfin tuna
AHS	plural form of ah
AIA	nursemaid in East
AID	assistance or support
AIL	trouble, afflict
AIM	point or direct at target

AIN	Scots word for own	APP	short for application program
AIR	the mixture of gases forming the earth's atmosphere	APT	suitable, appropriate
AIS	plural form of ai	ARB	short form of arbitrageur
AIT	islet, esp in a river	ARC	part of a circle or curve
AKA	New Zealand vine	ARD	primitive plough
AKE	old spelling of ache	ARE	100 square metres
ALA	wing	ARF	barking sound
ALB	Christian priest's robe	ARK	the boat built by Noah
ALE	kind of beer	ARM	upper limb
ALF	uncultivated Australian	ARS	plural form of ar
ALL	the whole quantity of something	ART	creation of works of beauty
ALP	high mountain	ARY	dialect form of any
ALS	plural form of al	ASH	substance left after burning
ALT	musical term	ASK	request an answer from
AMA	wet nurse	ASP	small poisonous snake
AMI	male friend	ASS	donkey
AMP	ampere	ATE	part of the verb to eat
AMU	atomic mass unit	ATT	old Siamese coin
ANA	in equal quantities	AUA	the yellow-eye mullet
AND	conjunction used to express addition	AUE	Maori exclamation of pain, distress, etc
ANE	Scots word for one	AUF	old word for oaf
ANI	type of tropical American bird	AUK	northern sea bird
ANN	payment to a parish minister's widow	AVA	Scots word for at all
		AVE	welcome or farewell
ANT	small insect	AVO	Macao currency unit
ANY	one or some	AWA	Scots word for away
APE	primate	AWE	wonder and respect mixed with dread
APO	type of protein	AWL	pointed tool

408

AWN	bristles growing from certain grasses	BEZ	part of deer's horn
AXE	tool with a sharp blade	BIB	cloth worn by babies
AYE	yes	BID	offer to buy something, esp in competition
AYS	plural form of ay		
AYU	small Japanese fish	BIG	of considerable size, number, etc
AZO	chemistry term		
BAA	sound of a sheep	BIN	container for rubbish
BAC	baccalaureate	BIO	short for biography
BAD	not good	BIS	twice
BAG	flexible container	BIT	small piece or portion
BAH	expression of contempt or disgust	BIZ	short for business
		BOA	large snake
BAL	balmoral, an ankle-high shoe	BOB	move up and down repeatedly
BAM	cheat, hoax	BOD	person
BAN	prohibit or forbid	BOG	wet spongy ground
BAP	large soft bread roll	BOH	exclamation used to startle or surprise
BAR	length of metal, etc		
BAS	plural form of ba	BOI	lesbian who dresses like a boy
BAT	club used to hit the ball in sports		
		BOK	S African antelope
BAY	semicircular indentation of a shoreline	BON	good
		BOO	shout of disapproval
BED	piece of furniture	BOP	dance to pop music
BEE	insect that makes honey	BOR	neighbour
BEG	solicit (money, etc)	BOS	plural form of bo
BEL	unit for comparing two power levels	BOT	larva of a botfly
		BOW	lower head as sign of respect
BEN	mountain peak		
BES	variant of beth, 2nd Hebrew letter	BOX	container
		BOY	male child
BET	wager	BRA	brassiere
BEY	Ottoman official	BRO	family member

409

BRR	used to suggest shivering	CHE	dialectal form of I
BRU	South African word for friend	CHI	22nd Greek letter
		CID	leader
BUB	youngster	CIG	short for cigarette
BUD	swelling on a plant	CIS	chemistry term
BUG	insect	CIT	town dweller
BUM	buttocks	CLY	to steal or seize
BUN	sweet bread roll or cake	COB	male swan
BUR	washer fitting around the end of a rivet	COD	large food fish
		COG	tooth on the rim of a gearwheel
BUS	large motor vehicle	COL	high mountain pass
BUT	except, only	CON	deceive, swindle
BUY	acquire by paying money	COO	make a soft murmuring sound
BYE	goodbye	
BYS	plural form of by	COP	copper
CAA	Scots word for call	COR	exclamation of surprise or admiration
CAB	taxi	
CAD	dishonourable man	COS	cosine
CAG	short for cagoule	COT	baby's cot with high sides
CAM	device that converts a circular motion	
CAN	be able to	COW	mature female bovine animal
CAP	covering for the head	
CAR	motor vehicle	COX	coxswain
CAT	furry mammal	COY	affectedly shy or modest
CAW	cry of a crow or raven	COZ	archaic word for cousin
CAY	small low island	CRU	vineyard
CAZ	short for casual	CRY	shed tears
CEE	3rd letter of the alphabet	CUB	the young of some animals
CEL	short for celluloid	
CEP	another name for porcino	CUD	partially digested food
		CUE	signal to an actor or musician to begin
CHA	tea	
		CUM	with

410

UP	drinking vessel	DIB	fish with a bobbing bait
UR	mongrel dog	DID	part of the verb to do
UT	divide with a sharp instrument	DIE	cease living
		DIF	short for difference
UZ	cousin	DIG	cut into earth, esp with a spade
WM	geology term		
AB	pat lightly	DIM	badly lit
AD	word for father	DIN	loud unpleasant noise
AE	Scots word for do	DIP	plunge briefly into liquid
AG	cut daglocks from sheep	DIS	treat someone with contempt
AH	term used in Morse code		
AK	system of mail delivery	DIT	term used in Morse code
AL	decalitre	DIV	stupid or foolish person
AM	barrier built across a river to create a lake	DOB	(as in dob in) inform against
AN	judo term	DOC	doctor
AP	flyfishing with a floss silk line	DOD	cut the hair of
		DOE	female deer
AS	plural form of da	DOF	South African word for stupid
AW	jackdaw		
AY	period of 24 hours	DOG	domesticated four-legged mammal
EB	debutante		
EE	Scots word for die	DOH	musical term
EF	very good	DOL	unit of pain intensity
EG	water (a plant, etc)	DOM	title given to monks
EI	plural form of deus	DON	put on (clothing)
EL	differential operator	DOO	Scots word for dove
EN	home of a wild animal	DOP	tot of alcoholic drink
EV	Hindu god	DOR	European dung beetle
EW	drops of water that form on the ground	DOS	plural form of do
		DOT	small round mark
EX	dextroamphetamine	DOW	Arab vessel
EY	commanders of the Janissaries of Algiers	DOY	beloved person
		DRY	lacking moisture

411

DSO	Tibetan breed of cattle	EFS	plural form of ef
DUB	give (a person or place) a name	EFT	newt
		EGG	oval or round object laid by female birds
DUD	ineffectual person		
DUE	something owed	EGO	conscious mind of an individual
DUG	part of the verb to dig		
DUH	response implying that the speaker is stupid	EHS	plural form of eh
		EIK	Scots form of eke
DUI	plural form of duo	EKE	increase, enlarge, or lengthen
DUN	brownish-grey		
DUO	duet	ELD	old age
DUP	open	ELF	small mischievous fairy
DUX	the top pupil in a class or school	ELK	large deer of N Europe and Asia
		ELL	unit of length equal to approximately 45 inches
DYE	colouring substance		
DZO	Tibetan breed of cattle		
EAN	give birth	ELM	tree with serrated leaves
EAR	organ of hearing	ELS	plural form of el
EAS	plural form of ea	ELT	young female pig
EAT	chew and swallow food	EME	uncle
EAU	drainage channel	EMO	type of music
EBB	(of tide water) flow back	EMS	plural form of em
ECH	Shakespearean word for eke out	EMU	large flightless bird
		END	come to a finish
ECO	short for ecology	ENE	variant of even
ECU	French coin	ENG	phonetics symbol
EDH	character of the runic alphabet	ENS	existence in the most general abstract sense
EDS	plural form of ed	EON	long period of time
EEK	expression indicating shock	ERA	period of time
		ERE	before
EEL	snakelike fish	ERF	plot of land for building purposes
EEN	Scots form of eye		
EFF	say the word 'fuck'	ERG	unit of work or energy

ERK	aircraftman	FAW	gypsy
ERN	archaic variant of earn	FAX	electronic system for sending documents
ERR	make a mistake		
ERS	bitter vetch	FAY	fairy or sprite
ESS	the letter S	FED	FBI agent
EST	treatment that helps people achieve psychological growth	FEE	charge
		FEG	segment from an orange
ETA	7th Greek letter	FEH	Hebrew coin
ETH	character of the runic alphabet	FEM	feminine
		FEN	flat marshy land
EUK	itch	FER	same as far
EVE	evening or day before an event	FES	plural form of fe
		FET	fetch
EVO	evening	FEU	right of use of land
EWE	female sheep	FEW	not many
EWK	itch	FEY	whimsically strange
EWT	archaic form of newt	FEZ	brimless tasselled cap
EXO	excellent	FIB	trivial lie
EYE	organ of sight	FID	spike for separating strands of rope
FAA	Scots word for fall		
FAB	excellent	FIE	exclamation of disapproval
FAD	short-lived fashion		
FAE	Scots word for from	FIG	soft pear-shaped fruit
FAG	slang word for cigarette	FIL	Shakespearean word for the shaft of a vehicle
FAH	musical term		
FAN	object used to create a current of air	FIN	the organs of locomotion in fish
		FIR	tree
FAP	drunk	FIT	be appropriate for
FAR	at, to, or from a great distance	FIX	make or become firm, stable, or secure
FAS	plural form of fa		
FAT	having excess flesh on the body	FIZ	make a hissing sound
		FLU	viral infection

413

FLY	move through the air on wings	GAN	archaic word for begin
FOB	short watch chain	GAP	break or opening
FOE	enemy, opponent	GAR	pike-like fish
FOG	mass of condensed water vapour in the air	GAS	airlike substance that is not liquid or solid
FOH	expression of disgust	GAT	pistol or revolver
FON	fool	GAU	district set up by the Nazi Party
FOP	man excessively concerned with fashion	GAY	homosexual
FOR	in the place of, in favour of	GED	Scots word for pike
FOU	Scots word for full	GEE	mild exclamation of surprise
FOX	reddish-brown bushy-tailed animal	GEL	jelly-like substance
FOY	loyalty	GEM	precious stone or jewel
FRA	brother: a title given to an Italian monk or friar	GEN	information
FRO	back or from	GEO	small fjord or gully
FRY	cook in fat or oil	GET	obtain or receive
FUB	put off, fob	GEY	intensifier
FUD	rabbit's tail	GHI	clarified butter
FUG	hot stale atmosphere	GIB	metal wedge
FUM	mythological phoenix	GID	disease of sheep
FUN	enjoyment or amusement	GIE	Scots word for give
		GIF	obsolete word for if
FUR	soft hair of a mammal	GIG	single performance by musicians
GAB	talk or chatter	GIN	spirit flavoured with juniper berries
GAD	go about in search of pleasure	GIO	gully, creek
GAE	Scots word for go	GIP	pain, torture
GAG	choke or retch	GIS	plural form of gi
GA	girl	GIT	contemptible person
GAM	school of whales	GJU	musical instrument
		GNU	ox-like antelope
		GOA	Tibetan gazelle

414

GOB	lump of a soft substance	HAO	monetary unit
GOD	worshipped spirit	HAP	luck, chance
GOE	Spenserian word for go	HAS	part of the verb to have
GON	geometrical grade	HAT	covering for the head
GOO	sticky substance	HAW	hawthorn berry
GOR	God!	HAY	grass cut and dried as fodder
GOS	plural form of go		
GOT	part of the verb to get	HEH	exclamation of surprise
GOV	short for governor	HEM	bottom edge of a garment
GOX	gaseous oxygen		
GOY	Jewish word for a non-Jew	HEN	female domestic fowl
		HEP	fruit of the dog rose
GUB	white man	HER	refers to a female person or animal
GUE	musical instrument		
GUL	oriental carpet design	HES	plural form of he
GUM	flesh in which the teeth are set	HET	short for heterosexual
		HEW	cut with an axe
GUN	weapon	HEX	evil spell
GUP	gossip	HEY	expression of surprise or for catching attention
GUR	unrefined cane sugar		
GUS	plural form of gu	HIC	sound of a hiccup
GUT	intestine	HID	part of the verb to hide
GUV	short for governor	HIE	hurry
GUY	man or boy	HIM	refers to a male person or animal
GYM	gymnasium		
GYP	swindle	HIN	Hebrew unit of capacity
		HIP	part of the body between pelvis and thigh
HAD	part of the verb to have		
HAE	Scots form of have	HIS	belonging to him
HAG	ugly old woman	HIT	strike, touch forcefully
HAH	exclamation of derision, triumph, or surprise	HMM	expression of thoughtful consideration
HAJ	Muslim pilgrimage		
HAM	meat from a pig's thigh	HOA	exclamation to attract attention
HAN	archaic form of have		

HOB	flat top part of a cooker	HYE	hurry
HOC	Latin for this	HYP	hypotenuse
HOD	open wooden box attached to a pole	ICE	water in its solid state
HOE	long-handled tool	ICH	dialect form of I
HOG	castrated male pig	ICK	expression of disgust
HOH	exclamation to attract attention	ICY	very cold
HOI	cry used to attract attention	IDE	silver fish
		IDS	plural form of id
HOM	sacred plant	IFF	conjunction used in logic
HON	short for honey	IFS	plural form of if
HOO	expression of boisterous emotion	IGG	ignore, snub
		ILK	type
HOP	jump on one foot	ILL	not in good health
HOS	plural form of ho	IMP	mischievous small creature
HOT	having a high temperature		
		INK	coloured liquid used for writing or printing
HOW	in what way		
HOX	hamstring	INN	pub or small hotel
HOY	cry used to attract attention	INS	plural form of in
		ION	atom
HUB	centre of a wheel	IOS	plural form of io
HUE	colour	IRE	anger
HUG	clasp tightly in the arms	IRK	irritate, annoy
HUH	exclamation of derision	ISH	issue, expiry
HUI	meeting of Maori people	ISM	doctrine, system, or practice
HUM	low continuous vibrating sound		
		ISO	short segment of film
		ITA	type of palm
HUN	member of Asiatic nomadic peoples	ITS	belonging to it
		IVY	evergreen climbing plant
HUP	cry to make a horse turn	IWI	Maori tribe
HUT	small house, shelter, or shed	JAB	poke sharply
		JAG	cut unevenly
		JAI	victory (to)

JAK	South and South East Asian tree	KAF	letter of the Hebrew alphabet
JAM	pack tightly into a place	KAI	New Zealand word for food
JAP	splash, spatter		
JAR	wide-mouthed container	KAK	S African offensive word for faeces
JAW	bone in which the teeth are set	KAM	Shakespearean word for crooked
JAY	bird	KAS	plural form of ka
JEE	move a horse faster	KAT	shrub whose leaves have narcotic properties
JET	aircraft		
JEU	game	KAW	cry of a crow
JEW	obsolete offensive word meaning haggle	KAY	the letter K
		KEA	large parrot
JIB	triangular sail	KEB	Scots word meaning miscarry a lamb
JIG	type of lively dance		
JIN	Chinese unit of weight	KED	(as in sheep ked) sheep tick
JIZ	wig		
JOB	occupation	KEF	marijuana
JOE	Scots word for a sweetheart	KEG	small metal beer barrel
		KEN	know
JOG	run at a gentle pace	KEP	catch
JOL	party	KET	Scots word for carrion
JOR	movement in Indian music	KEX	type of plant
		KEY	device for operating a lock
JOT	write briefly		
JOW	ring (a bell)	KHI	letter of the Greek alphabet
JOY	feeling of great delight		
JUD	large block of coal	KID	child
JUG	container for liquids	KIF	marijuana
JUN	monetary unit	KIN	person's relatives collectively
JUS	right, power, or authority		
JUT	project or stick out	KIP	sleep
KAB	ancient Hebrew measure	KIR	alcoholic drink
KAE	jackdaw		

KIS	plural form of ki	LEE	sheltered side
KIT	outfit or equipment	LEG	limb
KOA	Hawaiian tree	LEI	(in Hawaii) garland of flowers
KOB	antelope		
KOI	type of carp	LEK	monetary unit
KON	Spenserian word for know	LEP	Spenserian word for leap
		LES	offensive short form of lesbian
KOP	African hill		
KOR	ancient Hebrew unit of capacity	LET	allow, permit
		LEU	monetary unit
KOS	Indian unit of distance	LEV	monetary unit
KOW	branch, bunch of twigs	LEW	tepid
KUE	the letter Q	LEX	system or body of laws
KYE	Scots word for cows	LEY	land temporarily under grass
KYU	judo term		
LAB	laboratory	LEZ	offensive short form of lesbian
LAC	(in India and Pakistan) 100,000 rupees		
		LIB	short for liberation
LAD	boy or young man	LID	movable cover
LAG	go too slowly	LIE	make a deliberately false statement
LAH	musical term		
LAM	thrash, beat	LIG	function with free refreshments
LAP	part between the waist and knees		
		LIN	cease
LAR	boy or young man	LIP	fleshy folds at the mouth
LAS	plural form of la	LIS	fleur-de-lis
LAT	former coin of Latvia	LIT	part of the verb to light
LAV	short for lavatory	LOB	ball struck or thrown in a high arc
LAW	rule binding on a community		
		LOD	type of logarithm
LAX	not strict	LOG	portion of a felled tree
LAY	part of the verb to lie	LOO	word for lavatory
LEA	meadow	LOP	cut away (twigs and branches)
LED	part of the verb to lead		

OR	exclamation of surprise or dismay	MAT	piece of fabric
OS	approval, praise	MAW	animal's mouth
OT	great number	MAX	the full extent
OU	Scots word for love	MAY	used to express possibility
OW	not tall or high	MED	doctor
OX	smoked salmon	MEE	Malaysian noodle dish
OY	narrow spade with a single footrest	MEG	short for megabyte
UD	lord	MEL	pure form of honey
UG	carry or drag with great effort	MEM	13th letter in the Hebrew alphabet
UM	chimney	MEN	plural form of man
UR	musical horn	MES	plural form of me
UV	love	MET	part of the verb to meet
UX	unit of illumination	MEU	the plant spignel
UZ	supposedly indestructible bone	MEW	cry of a cat
YE	caustic solution	MHO	former name for siemens
YM	bloodhound	MIB	marble used in games
MAA	bleat	MIC	short for microphone
MAC	short for macintosh	MID	intermediate
MAD	mentally deranged	MIG	marble used in games
MAE	(as in mae west) inflatable life jacket	MIL	unit of length
MAG	short for magazine	MIM	prim
MAK	Scots word for make	MIR	Russian peasant commune
MAL	illness, pain	MIS	plural form of mi
MAM	word for mother	MIX	combine or blend
MAN	adult male	MIZ	shortened form of misery
MAP	representation of the earth's surface	MNA	Greek weight
MAR	spoil or impair	MOA	large extinct flightless bird
MAS	plural form of ma	MOB	disorderly crowd

MOC	short for moccasin
MOD	sixties youth group
MOE	more
MOG	short for moggy
MOI	me
MOL	SI unit mole
MOM	word for mother
MON	dialect variant of man
MOO	cry of a cow
MOP	cleaning device
MOR	layer of acidic humus
MOS	plural form of mo
MOT	girl or young woman
MOU	Scots word for mouth
MOW	to cut grass or crops
MOY	coin
MOZ	hex
MUD	wet soft earth
MUG	large drinking cup
MUM	word for mother
MUN	dialect word for must
MUS	plural form of mu
MUT	printing measurement
MUX	spoil
MYC	oncogene
NAB	arrest (someone)
NAE	Scots word for no
NAG	scold constantly
NAH	no
NAM	distraint
NAN	word for grandmother
NAP	short sleep
NAS	has not or was not
NAT	supporter of nationalism

NAW	no
NAY	no
NEB	beak of a bird
NED	derogatory Scots word for a young working-class male
NEE	born
NEF	church nave
NEG	photographic negative
NEK	mountain pass
NEP	catmint
NET	meshed fabric
NEW	recently made
NIB	writing point of a pen
NID	pheasant's nest
NIE	archaic spelling of nigh
NIL	nothing
NIM	game with matchsticks
NIP	pinch
NIS	friendly goblin
NIT	egg or larva of a louse
NIX	be careful!
NOB	person of social standing
NOD	lower and raise (one's head)
NOG	alcoholic drink
NOH	drama of Japan
NOM	name
NON	not
NOO	a Scots word for now
NOR	and not
NOS	plural form of no
NOT	expressing negation
NOW	at or for the present time

NOX	nitrogen oxide
NOY	harass
NTH	of an unspecified number
NUB	point or gist
NUN	female member of a religious order
NUR	knot of wood
NUS	plural form of nu
NUT	fruit
NYE	flock of pheasants
NYS	plural form of ny
OAF	stupid person
OAK	tree
OAR	pole with a broad blade
OAT	grass grown for its edible seed
OBA	Yoruba chief or ruler
OBE	ancient village
OBI	Japanese sash
OBO	ship carrying oil and ore
OBS	plural form of ob
OCA	South American herbaceous plant
OCH	expression of surprise
ODA	room in a harem
ODD	unusual, peculiar
ODE	lyric poem
ODS	plural form of od
OES	plural form of oe
OFF	not on; away
OFT	often
OHM	unit of electrical resistance

OHO	exclamation of surprise or derision
OHS	plural form of oh
OIK	person regarded as inferior
OIL	viscous liquid
OKA	unit of weight
OKE	unit of weight
OLD	having lived for a long time
OLE	exclamation of approval
OLM	salamander
OMS	plural form of om
ONE	single
ONO	Hawaiian fish
ONS	plural form of on
ONY	Scots word for any
OOF	money
OOH	exclamation of surprise
OOM	title of respect
OON	Scots word for oven
OOP	Scots word meaning to bind
OOR	Scots word for our
OOS	plural form of oo
OOT	Scots word for out
OPE	archaic word for open
OPS	plural form of op
OPT	show a preference
ORA	plural form of os
ORB	decorated sphere
ORC	whale
ORD	point of a weapon
ORE	mineral

ORF	disease of sheep	PAS	dance step
ORS	plural form of or	PAT	tap lightly
ORT	fragment	PAV	short for pavlova
OSE	long winding ridge of gravel, sand, etc	PAW	animal's foot
		PAX	kiss of peace
OUD	musical instrument	PAY	give money for goods
OUK	Scots word for week	PEA	plant, vegetable
OUP	Scots word meaning to bind	PEC	pectoral muscle
		PED	pannier
OUR	belonging to us	PEE	urinate
OUS	plural form of ou	PEG	pin or clip
OUT	outside	PEH	letter in the Hebrew alphabet
OVA	plural of ovum		
OWE	be obliged to pay money	PEN	instrument for writing in ink
OWL	bird of prey		
OWN	used to indicate possession	PEP	high spirits
		PER	for each
OWT	dialect word for anything	PES	technical name for foot
OXO	(as in oxo acid) acid that contains oxygen	PET	animal kept for companionship
		PEW	seat in a church
OXY	oxygen	PHI	21st letter in the Greek alphabet
OYE	grandchild		
OYS	plural form of oy	PHO	noodle soup
PAC	soft shoe	PHT	expression of irritation or reluctance
PAD	material for protection		
PAH	exclamation of disgust, disbelief, etc	PIA	pious
		PIC	photograph, picture
PAL	friend	PIE	pastry dish
PAM	knave of clubs	PIG	animal
PAN	metal container for cooking	PIN	piece of stiff wire for fastening
PAP	soft food, mash	PIP	small seed in a fruit
PAR	usual or average condition	PIR	Sufi master

422

PIS	plural form of pi
PIT	hole in the ground
PIU	musical term meaning more
PIX	photographs
PLU	beaver skin used as a unit of value
PLY	work at (a job or trade)
POA	type of grass
POD	seed case of peas
POH	exclamation expressing contempt
POI	ball of woven flax
POL	short for politician
POM	short for pommy
POO	defecate
POP	make a small explosive sound
POS	plural form of po
POT	round deep container
POW	sound imitative of a collision, explosion, etc
POX	disease
POZ	short for positive
PRE	before
PRO	in favour of
PRY	make an impertinent inquiry
PSI	23rd letter of the Greek alphabet
PST	sound to attract attention
PUB	building with a licensed bar

PUD	short for pudding
PUG	small snub-nosed dog
PUH	exclamation expressing contempt
PUL	Afghan monetary unit
PUN	play on words
PUP	young dog
PUR	obsolete form of purr
PUS	yellowish fluid
PUT	place in a position
PUY	small volcanic cone
PYA	monetary unit of Myanmar
PYE	book for finding Church services
PYX	receptacle for the Eucharistic Host
QAT	shrub whose leaves have narcotic properties
QIS	plural form of qi
QUA	in the capacity of
RAD	former unit of radiation
RAG	fragment of cloth
RAH	US word for cheer
RAI	type of Algerian pop music
RAJ	(in India) government
RAM	male sheep
RAN	part of the verb to run
RAP	hit with a sharp quick blow
RAS	headland
RAT	long-tailed rodent
RAW	uncooked

423

RAX	stretch or extend
RAY	single line of light
REB	soldier in the American Civil War
REC	short for recreation ground
RED	colour
REE	Scots word for walled enclosure
REF	short for referee
REG	short for registration number
REH	(in India) surface crust on the soil
REI	former Portuguese coin
REM	dose of ionizing radiation
REN	archaic variant of run
REO	language
REP	short for representative
RES	residence
RET	moisten or soak flax
REV	revolution (of an engine)
REW	archaic spelling of rue
REX	king
REZ	reservation
RHO	17th letter in the Greek alphabet
RHY	archaic spelling of rye
RIA	long narrow inlet of the seacoast
RIB	bone
RID	clear or relieve (of)
RIF	discharge from military service

RIG	arrange in a dishonest way
RIM	edge or border
RIN	Scots variant of run
RIP	tear violently
RIT	Scots word for cut or slit
RIZ	dialectal past form of rise
ROB	steal from
ROC	mythological bird
ROD	slender straight bar
ROE	mass of eggs in a fish
ROK	mythological bird
ROM	male gypsy
ROO	kangaroo
ROT	decompose or decay
ROW	straight line of people or things
RUB	apply pressure and friction
RUC	mythological bird
RUD	redness, flush
RUE	feel regret for
RUG	small carpet
RUM	alcoholic drink
RUN	move quickly
RUT	furrow made by wheels
RYA	Scandinavian rug
RYE	grain
SAB	short for saboteur
SAC	pouchlike structure in an animal
SAD	sorrowful, unhappy
SAE	Scots word for so
SAG	sink in the middle

AI	capuchin monkey	SHH	sound made to ask for silence
AL	salt	SHY	not at ease in company
AM	collect, gather up	SIB	blood relative
AN	short for sanatorium	SIC	so or thus
AP	fluid that circulates in plants	SIF	South African slang for disgusting
AR	marine fish	SIK	Australian slang for excellent
AT	part of the verb to sit	SIM	simulation game on a computer
AU	archaic past form of see	SIN	offence or transgression
AV	saveloy	SIP	drink in small mouthfuls
AW	hand tool	SIR	polite term of address for a man
AX	saxophone		
AY	speak or utter	SIS	short for sister
AZ	musical instrument	SIT	rest one's body on the buttocks and thighs
EA	mass of salt water		
EC	short for second	SIX	one more than five
ED	old spelling of said	SKA	type of West Indian pop music
EE	perceive with the eyes or mind	SKI	snow sport
EG	metal stud on shoe sole	SKY	upper atmosphere
EI	type of whale	SLY	crafty
EL	Scots word for self	SMA	Scots word for small
EN	monetary unit	SNY	side channel of a river
ER	unit of weight	SOB	weep with convulsive gasps
ET	put in a specified position or state	SOC	feudal right to hold court
EW	join with thread	SOD	(piece of) turf
EX	state of being male or female	SOG	soak
		SOH	musical term
EY	Scots word for part of cow	SOL	liquid colloidal solution
EZ	informal spelling of says	SOM	monetary unit
HA	be quiet		
HE	female person or animal		

425

SON	male offspring
SOP	concession to pacify someone
SOS	plural form of so
SOT	habitual drunkard
SOU	former French coin
SOV	sovereign
SOW	scatter or plant
SOX	informal spelling of socks
SOY	(as in soy sauce) salty dark brown sauce
SPA	resort with a mineral-water spring
SPY	obtain secret information
SRI	title of respect
STY	pigpen
SUB	short for subeditor
SUD	singular form of suds
SUE	start legal proceedings against
SUI	of himself, herself, itself
SUK	open-air marketplace
SUM	result of addition, total
SUN	star around which the earth revolves
SUP	swallow liquid
SUQ	open-air marketplace
SUR	above
SUS	become aware of
SWY	gambling game
SYE	strain something
SYN	Scots word for since

TAB	small flap or projecting label
TAD	small bit or piece
TAE	Scots word for to
TAG	label bearing information
TAI	(as in tai chi chuan) Chinese system of callisthenics
TAJ	tall conical cap
TAK	Scots word for take
TAM	short for tam-o'-shanter
TAN	coloration of the skin
TAO	philosophical term
TAP	knock lightly
TAR	thick black liquid
TAS	cup, goblet, or glass
TAT	tatty or tasteless article(s)
TAU	19th letter in the Greek alphabet
TAV	22nd letter in the Hebrew alphabet
TAW	convert skins into leather
TAX	compulsory payment levied
TAY	Irish dialect word for tea
TEA	drink
TEC	short for detective
TED	dry hay
TEE	small peg for golf
TEF	grass grown for its grain
TEG	two-year-old sheep
TEL	large mound formed from accumulated rubbish

TEN	one more than nine	TOT	small child
TES	plural form of te	TOW	drag, esp by means of a rope
TET	9th letter of the Hebrew alphabet	TOY	something designed to be played with
TEW	toil		
TEX	unit of weight	TRY	make an effort or attempt
THE	definite article		
THO	short for though	TSK	expression of disapproval
THY	of or associated with you (thou)	TUB	open round container
		TUG	pull hard
TIC	spasmodic muscular twitch	TUI	New Zealand bird
		TUM	stomach
TID	girl	TUN	large beer cask
TIE	fasten with string	TUP	male sheep
TIG	children's game	TUT	sound of mild reprimand
TIL	another name for sesame	TUX	short for tuxedo
		TWA	two
TIN	soft metallic element	TWO	one more than one
TIP	narrow or pointed end of anything	TWP	stupid
		TYE	trough used in mining
TIS	plural form of ti	TYG	cup with two handles
TIT	small songbird	UDO	perennial plant
TIX	tickets	UDS	'God's' or 'God save'
TOC	communication code for T	UEY	u-turn
		UFO	flying saucer
TOD	unit of weight	UGH	exclamation of disgust
TOE	digit of the foot	UGS	plural form of ug
TOG	unit of thermal resistance	UKE	short for ukulele
		ULE	rubber tree
TOM	male cat	ULU	type of knife
TON	unit of weight	UMM	sound of hesitation
TOO	also, as well	UMP	short for umpire
TOP	highest point or part	UMU	type of oven
TOR	high rocky hill	UNI	short for university

UNS	plural form of un	VEX	frustrate, annoy
UPO	upon	VIA	by way of
UPS	plural form of up	VID	video
URB	urban area	VIE	compete (with someone)
URD	type of plant with edible seeds	VIG	interest on a loan
		VIM	force, energy
URE	extinct wild ox	VIN	French wine
URN	container for the ashes of the dead	VIS	power, force, or strength
		VLY	low marshy ground
URP	dialect word for vomit	VOE	bay or narrow creek
USE	put into service or action	VOL	short for volume
UTA	type of lizard	VOR	(in dialect) warn
UTE	utility vehicle	VOW	solemn and binding promise
UTS	plural form of ut		
UTU	reward	VOX	voice or sound
UVA	grape or berry	VUG	small cavity in a rock or vein
VAC	short for vacation		
VAE	bay or narrow creek	VUM	swear, vow
VAG	vagrant	WAB	Scots word for web
VAN	motor vehicle for transporting goods	WAD	small mass of soft material
		WAE	old form of woe
VAR	unit of reactive power	WAG	move rapidly from side to side
VAS	vessel or tube that carries a fluid		
		WAI	in New Zealand, water
VAT	large container for liquids	WAN	pale and sickly-looking
		WAP	strike
VAU	sixth letter of the Hebrew alphabet	WAR	fighting between nations
VAV	sixth letter of the Hebrew alphabet	WAS	part of the verb to be
		WAT	Thai Buddhist monastery or temple
VAW	Hebrew letter		
VEE	the letter V	WAW	sixth letter of the Hebrew alphabet
VEG	short for vegetable		
VET	check the suitability of		

WAX solid shiny fatty or oily substance

WAY manner or method

WEB net spun by a spider

WED marry

WEE small or short

WEM womb or belly

WEN cyst on the scalp

WET covered or soaked with water

WEX wax

WEY measurement of weight

WHA Scots word for who

WHO which person

WHY for what reason

WIG artificial head of hair

WIN come first in a competition

WIS know or suppose

WIT clever humour

WIZ accomplished person, whizz

WOE grief

WOF fool

WOG Australian word meaning influenza

WOK bowl-shaped Chinese cooking pan

WON monetary unit

WOO seek the love or affection of

WOP strike or beat

WOS plural form of wo

WOT wit, to know

WOW exclamation of astonishment

WOX obsolete form of the verb to wax

WRY drily humorous

WUD Scots word for wood

WUS casual term of address

WYE the letter Y

WYN rune equivalent to English W

XIS plural form of xi

YAD pointer used for reading the Torah

YAE Scots word meaning one or a single

YAG artificial crystal

YAH exclamation of derision or disgust

YAK Tibetan ox with long shaggy hair

YAM tropical root vegetable

YAP bark with a high-pitched sound

YAR nimble

YAW turn from side to side while moving

YAY exclamation of approval

YEA yes

YEH yes

YEN monetary unit of Japan

YEP affirmative statement

YES expresses consent

YET up until then or now

YEW evergreen tree

429

YEX	hiccup, belch
YGO	archaic form of the verb to go
YID	offensive word for a Jew
YIN	Scots word for one
YIP	emit a high-pitched bark
YOB	bad-mannered aggressive youth
YOD	10th letter in the Hebrew alphabet
YOK	chuckle
YOM	day
YON	that or those over there
YOS	plural form of yo
YOU	person or people addressed
YOW	variant of ewe
YUG	one of the four ages of mankind
YUK	expression of dislike or disgust
YUM	expression of delight
YUP	informal affirmative statement
YUS	plural form of yu
ZAG	change direction sharply

ZAP	kill (by shooting)
ZAS	plural form of za
ZAX	small axe for cutting slates
ZEA	type of grass
ZED	the letter Z
ZEE	the letter Z
ZEK	Soviet prisoner
ZEL	Turkish cymbal
ZEP	type of long sandwich
ZEX	tool for cutting roofing slate
ZHO	Tibetan breed of cattle
ZIG	change direction sharply
ZIN	short form of zinfandel
ZIP	fastener with two rows of teeth
ZIT	spot or pimple
ZIZ	short sleep
ZOA	plural form of zoon
ZOL	South African slang for a cannabis cigarette
ZOO	place where live animals are kept
ZOS	plural form of zo
ZUZ	silver coin of ancient Palestine
ZZZ	informal word for sleep